INTERPERSONAL AND INTRAPERSONAL EXPECTANCIES

Do our expectancies about ourselves and about others have any effect on our actual experiences? Over fifty years of research studies suggest not only that this is the case, but also that our expectancies can shape other people's experience in different contexts. In some cases they can help, but other times they can do harm instead.

Interpersonal and Intrapersonal Expectancies provides a theory, a research review, and a summary of the current knowledge on intra- and interpersonal expectancy effects and related phenomena. Based on extensive study, and written by eminent experts from some of the world's leading academic institutions, the book presents the most recent knowledge on social and psychological mechanisms of forming both intra- and interpersonal expectancies. It also considers how expectancies are sustained and what their consequences are, as well as discussing the latest theoretical concepts and the most up-to-date research on expectancy effects.

This book represents the first review of the phenomenon of interpersonal expectancies in over twenty years, and the only publication presenting a complementary view of both intra- and interpersonal expectancies. It aims to open up a discussion between researchers and theoreticians from both perspectives, and to promote an integrative approach that incorporates both.

Sławomir Trusz Assistant Professor of Education, Pedagogical University, Institute of Educational Sciences, Kraków, Poland.

Przemysław Bąbel Assistant Professor of Psychology, Jagiellonian University, Institute of Psychology, Pain Research Group, Kraków, Poland.

INTERPERSONAL AND INTRAPERSONAL EXPECTANCIES

Edited by Sławomir Trusz and Przemysław Bąbel

LONDON AND NEW YORK

First published 2016
by Routledge
2 Park Square, Milton Park, Abingdon, Oxon OX14 4RN

and by Routledge
711 Third Avenue, New York, NY 10017

Routledge is an imprint of the Taylor & Francis Group, an informa business

© 2016 selection and editorial matter, Sławomir Trusz and Przemysław Bąbel; individual chapters, the contributors

The right of the editors to be identified as the authors of the editorial material, and of the authors for their individual chapters, has been asserted in accordance with sections 77 and 78 of the Copyright, Designs and Patents Act 1988.

All rights reserved. No part of this book may be reprinted or reproduced or utilized in any form or by any electronic, mechanical, or other means, now known or hereafter invented, including photocopying and recording, or in any information storage or retrieval system, without permission in writing from the publishers.

Trademark notice: Product or corporate names may be trademarks or registered trademarks, and are used only for identification and explanation without intent to infringe.

British Library Cataloguing in Publication Data
A catalogue record for this book is available from the British Library

Library of Congress Cataloging in Publication Data
Names: Trusz, Slawomir, editor. | Babel, Przemyslaw, editor.
Title: Interpersonal and intrapersonal expectancies/edited by Slawomir Trusz and Przemyslaw Babel.
Description: Abingdon, Oxon; New York, NY: Routledge, 2016.
Identifiers: LCCN 2015044170| ISBN 9781138118928 (hardback: alk. paper) | ISBN 9781138118935 (pbk.: alk. paper) | ISBN 9781315652535 (e-book)
Subjects: LCSH: Expectation (Psychology) | Interpersonal relations. | Self-efficacy.
Classification: LCC BF323.E8 I67 2016 | DDC 155.9/2—dc23
LC record available at http://lccn.loc.gov/2015044170

ISBN: 978-1-138-11892-8 (hbk)
ISBN: 978-1-138-11893-5 (pbk)
ISBN: 978-1-315-65253-5 (ebk)

Typeset in Bembo and Stone Sans
by Florence Production Ltd, Stoodleigh, Devon, UK
Printed in Great Britain by Ashford Colour Press Ltd.

Sławomir Trusz dedicates the book to Wojtuś, with wishes for fulfilment of the best and deepest expectations. Przemysław Bąbel dedicates the book to Gustaw and Ignacy, hoping they will read it some day.

CONTENTS

List of contributors	*xi*
Acknowledgements	*xiv*

1 Two perspectives on expectancies: an introduction   1
Sławomir Trusz and Przemysław Bąbel

PART 1
Intrapersonal expectancies

Preface: expectancy about self   23
Irving Kirsch

2 Response expectancy   25
Irving Kirsch

3 The story of motivational concordance   35
Michael E. Hyland

4 Self-efficacy   41
James E. Maddux

5 Hypnosis, memory, and expectations   47
Jessica Baltman and Steven Jay Lynn

6 Generalized expectancies for negative mood regulation: development, assessment, and implications of a construct   52
Salvatore J. Catanzaro and Jack Mearns

viii Contents

7 **Smoking-related expectancies** 62
Peter S. Hendricks and Thomas H. Brandon

8 **Response expectancy and cancer care** 69
Madalina Sucala, Julie Schnur and Guy H. Montgomery

9 **How expectancies shape placebo effects** 76
Zev M. Medoff and Luana Colloca

PART 2
Interpersonal expectancies

Preface: Expectancy about others 87
Lee Jussim

10 **When and why do expectations create reality?
Reflections on behavioral confirmation in social
interaction** 89
Mark Snyder

11 **Identity negotiation in social interaction: past,
present and future** 96
William B. Swann, Jr and Jennifer K. Bosson

12 **Motivation matters: the functional context of
expectation confirmation processes** 102
Steven L. Neuberg

13 **Why accuracy dominates self-fulfilling prophecies
and bias** 110
Lee Jussim and Sean T. Stevens

14 **Understanding the connections between self-fulfilling
prophecies and social problems** 117
Jennifer Willard and Stephanie Madon

15 **Pygmalion and the classroom after 50 years** 125
Elisha Babad

16 **Children's awareness of differential treatment: toward a
contextual understanding of teacher expectancy effects** 134
Rhona S. Weinstein

Contents **ix**

17 Individual differences in response to expectations 141
Charles K. West

**18 High and low expectation teachers: the importance
of the teacher factor** 145
Christine Rubie-Davies

**19 Inaccurate teacher expectations: relationships with
student and class characteristics and its effect on
long-term student performance** 157
*Hester de Boer, Anneke C. Timmermans and Margaretha P. C.
van der Werf*

**20 Expectancy effects: an attempt to integrate intra-
and interpersonal perspectives** 162
Przemysław Bąbel and Sławomir Trusz

Author index 179
Subject index 185

CONTRIBUTORS

Elisha Babad Hebrew University of Jerusalem, School of Education, Jerusalem, Israel. Email: elishababad@gmail.com

Przemysław Bąbel Jagiellonian University, Institute of Psychology, Pain Research Group, Kraków, Poland. Email: przemyslaw.babel@uj.edu.pl

Jessica Baltman Binghamton University, Psychology Department, NY, USA. Email: jbaltma1@binghamton.edu

Jennifer K. Bosson University of South Florida, Department of Psychology, Tampa, FL, USA. Email: jbosson@usf.edu

Thomas H. Brandon Department of Health Outcomes and Behavior, Moffitt Cancer Center, and Department of Psychology, University of South Florida, Tampa, FL, USA. Email: Thomas.Brandon@Mofitt.org

Salvatore J. Catanzaro Illinois State University, Department of Psychology, Normal, IL, USA. Email: catanzar@ilstu.edu

Luana Colloca University of Maryland, Baltimore, School of Nursing, Baltimore, MD. University of Maryland Baltimore, School of Medicine, Department of Anaesthesiology. University of Maryland Baltimore, UM Center to Advance Chronic Pain Research, USA. Email: colloca@son.umaryland.edu

Hester de Boer University of Groningen, Institute for Educational Research (GION), Groningen, the Netherlands. Email: hester.de.boer@rug.nl

xii List of contributors

Peter S. Hendricks University of Alabama at Birmingham, Department of Health Behavior, Birmingham, AL, USA. Email: phendricks@uab.edu

Michael E. Hyland Plymouth University, School of Psychology, Plymouth PL4 8AA, UK. Phone +44 (0)1752 584834. Email: mhyland@Plymouth.ac.uk

Lee Jussim The State University of New Jersey–New Brunswick, Department of Psychology, Rutgers, Piscataway, NJ, USA. Email: jussim@rci.rutgers.edu

Irving Kirsch Program in Placebo Studies, Harvard Medical School, Program in Placebo Studies, 144 Medford Street, Arlington, MA, USA. Email: irvkirsch@gmail.com

Steven Jay Lynn Binghamton University, Psychology Department, Binghampton, NY, USA. Email: stevenlynn100@gmail.com

James E. Maddux George Mason University, Department of Psychology and Center for the Advancement of Well-Being, Washington, DC, USA. Email: jemaddux@aol.com

Stephanie Madon Psychology Department, Iowa State University, Ames, IA, USA. Email: madon@iastate.edu

Jack Mearns California State University, Fullerton, Department of Psychology, Fullerton, CA, USA. Email: jmearns@fullerton.edu

Zev M. Medoff National Institute of Mental Health, National Institutes of Health, Bethesda, MD, USA. Email: zev.medoff@nih.gov

H. Lee Moffitt University of South Florida, Cancer Center and Research Institute, Tampa, FL, USA. Email: Thomas.brandon@moffitt.org

Guy H. Montgomery Icahn School of Medicine at Mount Sinai, Department of Oncological Sciences, New York, NY, USA. Email: guy.montgomery@mssm.edu

Steven L. Neuberg Arizona State University, Department of Psychology, Tempe, AZ, USA 85287–1104. Phone: 480–965–7845. Email: steven.neuberg@asu.edu

Christine Rubie-Davies University of Auckland, Faculty of Education, Auckland, New Zealand. Email: c.rubie@auckland.ac.nzd

Julie Schnur Icahn School of Medicine at Mount Sinai, Department of Oncological Sciences, New York, NY, USA. Email: julie.schnur@mssm.edu

Mark Snyder University of Minnestoa, Department of Psychology, Minneapolis, MN, USA. Email: msnyder@umn.edu

Sean T. Stevens The State University of New Jersey, New Brunswick, Department of Psychology Rutgers, Piscataway, NJ, USA. Email: stevenss@rci.rutgers.edu

Madalina Sucala Icahn School of Medicine at Mount Sinai, Department of Oncological Sciences, New York, NY, USA. Email: madalina.sucala@mssm.edu

William B. Swann, Jr University of Texas at Austin, Department of Psychology, Austin, TX, USA. Email: Swann@utexas.edu

Anneke C. Timmermans University of Groningen, Institute for Educational Research (GION), the Netherlands. Email: a.c.timmermans@rug.nl

Sławomir Trusz Pedagogical University, Institute of Educational Sciences, Kraków, Poland. Email: trusz@up.krakow.pl

Margaretha P. C. van der Werf University of Groningen, Institute for Educational Research (GION), the Netherlands. Email: m.p.c.van.der.werf@rug.nl

Rhona S. Weinstein University of California, Berkeley, Department of Psychology, Berkeley, CA, USA. Email: rhona_weinstein@berkeley.edu

Charles K. West University of Illinois at Champaign-Urbana, Department of Educational Psychology, St Champaign, IL, USA. Email: c-west@uiuc.edu

Jennifer Willard Kennesaw State University, Kennesaw, Psychology Department, GA, USA. Email: jwillar3@kennesaw.edu

ACKNOWLEDGEMENTS

The editors warmly thank all the contributing authors for their fruitful collaboration and the effort put into the preparation of interesting papers. We would like to express our special gratitude to Irving Kirsch and Lee Jussim for writing the Prefaces to the book. Moreover, Sławomir Trusz would like to thank his family for their patience and benevolent support. Przemysław Bąbel would like to thank Luana Colloca for hosting him at the University of Maryland, Baltimore, while he was working on the edition of the book. The edition of this book was supported by the National Science Centre in Poland under grant number 2012/05/D/HS6/ 03350 awarded to Sławomir Trusz and under grant number 2014/14/E/HS6/ 00415 awarded to Przemysław Bąbel.

1

TWO PERSPECTIVES ON EXPECTANCIES[1]

An introduction

Sławomir Trusz and Przemysław Bąbel

From myths, anecdotes and scientific evidence one may learn that expectancy affects experience. Klopfer (1957) describes the case of "Mr. Wright," who had a lymphosarcoma (cancer of the lymph nodes) with tumors the size of oranges. There was no hope of a recovery for him. However, Mr. Wright heard that the hospital in which he was staying was conducting a clinical trial on a new drug for cancer called Krebiozen. He begged to be involved in the trial. Although Mr. Wright met none of the criteria for inclusion in the trial, he got the approval and had an injection. Two days later his physician was in shock to see Mr. Wright joking with the nurses and with tumors half their original size. Unfortunately, some time later, Mr. Wright read medical reports questioning the effectiveness of Krebiozen and relapsed. Mr. Wright's physician then convinced him that he would receive a new, much more powerful version of the drug, but in fact he got a shot of distilled water. Nevertheless, Mr. Wright's response to this second injection was even better than to the first one, and he went home . . . navigating his own airplane. He was "the picture of health" until he read a report definitely stating that Krebiozen was worthless. He died two days later.

Mr. Wright's case shows not only that expectancies may help, but that they may also do harm. Indeed, it is a well-documented fact that expectancies can do harm. Voodoo death seems to be one of the most dramatic examples of this. Benson (1997) relates the story of an 18-year-old Aborigine, whose hex was that he should not eat wild game hen. "One day, when this young man was traveling, he stayed at a friend's home and had breakfast. He asked whether the food contained wild game hen and was assured that it did not, even though it actually did. The man ate this food and went off. When he visited this friend two years later, the friend asked, 'Have you ever eaten wild game hen?' 'No,' replied the young man, whereupon his host said, 'Ha, I tricked you two years ago.' Within 24 hours the hexed man passed away. In other words, it was clearly not the ingestion of the wild game hen that had caused his demise" (Benson, 1997, p. 613).

Not only do our own expectancies shape our experience, but also one's expectancies may shape other people's experience. According to an ancient story, Pygmalion, the king of Cyprus and a skillful sculptor, falls in love with a statue of the perfect woman he had carved himself. Thanks to his own desire and a little help from Aphrodite, the goddess of love, the statue then comes to life. Pygmalion calls the woman Galatea and marries her. This myth was popularized in mass culture by George Bernard Shaw's comedy *Pygmalion*, in which a phonetics professor, Henry Higgins, as a result of a bet, teaches a simple flower seller, Eliza Doolittle, correct English. His teaching, encouragement, and expectations bring about an outcome which surprises everyone. In 1964, Shaw's play was adapted for the screen by George Cukor as a musical, *My Fair Lady*, with Audrey Hepburn in the leading role.

On the other hand, the Golem myth reminds us that interpersonal expectations can be a source of negative social phenomena. According to Hasidic tradition, in the mid-sixteenth century, in Prague, the venerable rabbi Judah Loew ben Bezalel creates a human figure out of clay, which he animates by mysterious spells and rituals. Despite the rabbi's intentions, the clay Golem does not serve its creator, but grows into a destructive monster that must be "restored to dust."

Stimulus/outcome expectancies

The concept of expectancy is crucial in so-called neo-behavioristic theories of learning. In contrast to classical behaviorists, especially to the founder of behaviorism, Watson (1913, 1919), they state that stimuli that precede behavior (antecedents) do not automatically elicit responses, but have an effect on responses by creating or changing expectations. In other words, from that perspective, stimuli do not directly elicit responses but when stimuli are present, people (and animals) acquire or change expectancies, and on that basis elicit the response or – quite opposite – withhold the response. Similarly, from such a neo-behavioristic perspective, the consequences of behavior have an effect not on future behaviors, but expectancies of a specific consequence of the behavior have an effect on emission or suppression of that behavior. Although in radical behaviorism, founded by Skinner (1938, 1974), people (and animals) behave in a given manner now because this specific behavior was reinforced in the past, from a neo-behavioristic point of view, people (and animals) behave in a given manner now because they expect that they will receive a reinforcer after their behavior, or they withhold their behavior when expecting that it would be punished if emitted.

Although Tolman (1932, 1949) seems to be first to have noticed that expectancy was the basic thing acquired in a learning experiment, Bolles (1972) proposed the laws of learning that are an account of both classical (Pavlovian) conditioning (the primary law of learning) and operant (instrumental) learning (the secondary law of learning) from an expectancy point of view. According to the primary law of learning, "what is learned is that certain events, cues, (S), predict certain other, biologically important events, consequences (S*). An animal may incidently show new responses, but what it learns is an expectancy that represents and corresponds to the S-S★ contingency" (Bolles, 1972, p. 402). His secondary law of learning states that "animals can learn R-S★ expectancies that represent and correspond to the R-S★ contingencies in their environment. These expectancies, together with S-S★ expectancies, constitute all of what is learned in most instrumental learning experiments" (Bolles, 1972, p. 403). From this perspective, classical conditioning produces expectancies that certain stimuli will be followed by other stimuli, and operant conditioning produces expectancies that particular behavior will produce particular outcomes. Similar views of the role of expectancies (cognitions) in both classical and operant (instrumental) learning have been suggested since Bolles's (1972) proposal (Brewer, 1974; Kirsch *et al.*, 2004; Rescorla, 1988, 1991).

Expectancies have become an important part of social learning theories of personality. For example, Rotter (1954) proposed a predictive formula stating that behavior potential is a function of expectancy and reinforcement value. In other words, the probability of exhibiting a given behavior is a function of the likelihood that that behavior will lead to a particular reinforcer and the desirability of that reinforcer. In Rotter's (1954) theory, expectancy is the subjective likelihood that a particular behavior will lead to a particular reinforcer. However, Rotter is best known as the author of the concept of generalized expectancies for control of reinforcement – i.e. locus of control (Rotter, 1966). Locus of control is a general, cross-situational belief about what determines whether or not people are reinforced. According to Rotter (1966, p. 1):

> when a reinforcement is perceived by the subject as following some action of his own but not being entirely contingent upon his action, then, in our culture, it is typically perceived as the result of luck, chance, fate, as under the control of powerful others, or as unpredictable because of the great complexity of the forces surrounding him. When the event is interpreted in this way by an individual, we have labeled this a belief in *external control*. If the person perceives that the event is contingent upon his own behavior or his own relatively permanent characteristics, we have termed this a belief in *internal control*.

In his approach to personality, Mischel (1973) differentiates between behavior-outcome expectancy and stimulus-outcome expectancy. The former "represent the 'if ___; then ___' relations between behavioral alternatives and probable outcomes anticipated with regard to particular behavioral possibilities in particular situations. In any given situation, the person will generate the response pattern which he expects is most likely to lead to the most subjectively valuable outcomes (consequences) in that situation" (Mischel, 1973, p. 270). On the other hand, "the outcomes expected for any behavior hinge on a multitude of stimulus conditions that moderate the probable consequences of any pattern of behavior. These stimuli ('signs') essentially 'predict' for the person other events that are likely to occur" (Mischel, 1973, p. 271) (cf. S-S★ expectancy; Bolles, 1972).

4   S. Trusz and P. Bąbel

Bandura (1977b) also included expectancies in his social learning theory. Similarly to most of the neo-behaviorists, he states that reinforcement serves as an incentive – people behave to get a reinforcer rather than behave because they were reinforced in the past. In other words, reinforcement affects behavior by creating expectations that behaving in a certain way will produce an anticipated reinforcer. Moreover, Bandura (1977a) incorporates into his theory the idea of self-efficacy as an expectancy of what an individual can accomplish using their skills. Self-efficacy determines whether behavior will be initiated, how much effort will be expended and how long it will be sustained in the face of obstacles and aversive experiences. Bandura (1977a) distinguished between two types of expectancies: outcome and efficacy. An outcome expectancy is "a person's estimate that a given behavior will lead to certain outcomes. An efficacy expectation is the conviction that one can successfully execute the behavior required to produce the outcomes" (p. 193). They were differentiated because it is possible to believe that a particular behavior will produce certain reinforcers (high outcome expectancy) together with being convinced of not being able to perform this behavior (low efficacy expectancy).

Bandura's (1977a) account of expectancies – i.e. self-efficacy – helps to understand the mechanisms of behavior change. More generally, expectancies are listed among the main therapeutic factors in psychotherapy (Frank, 1961, 1971). Expectancies have been also used to explain the development and reduction of specific symptoms – e.g. depression and fear. The theory of learned helplessness developed by Maier and Seligman (1976) uses the concept of expectancy, similar to Bandura's (1977a) outcome expectancy. They state that as a result of being subjected to uncontrollable aversive events (punishers), organisms acquire expectancies that their behavior does not affect outcomes:

> the incentive to initiate voluntary responses in a traumatic situation is partly produced by the expectation that responding produces relief. In the absence of this incentive, voluntary responding will decrease in likelihood. When a person or animal has learned that relief is independent of responding, the expectation that responding produces relief is negated, and therefore response initiation is reduced.
>
> (Maier & Seligman, 1976, p. 18)

Although the attributional reformulation of learned helplessness theory (Abramson *et al.*, 1978) incorporates the concept of explanatory style, expectancies are still an important part of the new theory. Abramson and colleagues (1978) explicitly state that "when highly desired outcomes are believed improbable or highly aversive outcomes are believed probable, and the individual expects that no response in his repertoire will change their likelihood, (helplessness) depression results" (p. 68).

The above-mentioned theories as well as most social learning theories deal with outcome expectancy or – in other words – stimulus expectancies – i.e. expectancies of the occurrence of external stimuli – both reinforces and punishes. They cannot be recognized either as intrapersonal or interpersonal, but they seem to be in some way similar to interpersonal expectancies, as they deal with external stimuli as well as interpersonal expectancies deal with people or animals that are external. However, the main difference is that stimulus expectancies do not change the stimulus, but interpersonal expectancies do change the behavior of other humans as well as animals.

Intrapersonal expectancies

Reiss (1980, 1991) proposed an expectancy model of the effect of classical conditioning on human fear. According to the model, what is learned in classical conditioning is an expectation regarding the occurrence or nonoccurrence of the unconditional stimulus. From this perspective, fear is in part a function of the expectancy of fear as well as fear reduction may be the effect of changing the expectancy of its occurrence. This conception may be recognized as a link between stimulus expectancies and intrapersonal expectancies. Although it still deals with stimulus expectancies (i.e. expectancies of the occurrence of dangerous stimuli which produce fear responses), fear is indeed an intrapersonal response.

The most influential theory of intrapersonal expectancies is the one proposed by Kirsch (1985). It extends Rotter's (1954) social learning theory which predicts voluntary behavior by outcome expectancies. In contrast, Kirsch's (1985, 1997a) theory is an account of response expectancies – i.e. the expectancies of one's nonvolitional reactions to situational cues. Response expectancies predict the occurrence of involuntary behavior. However, according to this theory voluntary behavior may also be affected by response expectancies, as nonvolitional responses may have reinforcement value. In contrast to outcome expectancies, response expectancies are directly self-confirming – i.e. response expectancy for a particular experience generates this experience. Similar to neo-behaviorists, Kirsch (1985, 1997a) suggested that classical conditioning might be one method by which response expectancies are acquired. The other methods of forming and changing expectancies include verbal persuasion, attributional processes, modeling, and self-observation. It has been proposed that placebo effects, fear reduction (as well as the experience of fear), and the effects of hypnosis, among others, operate via the mechanism of response expectancies (Kirsch, 1985, 1997a, 1999). Generally, expectancy is one of the main mechanisms that have been proposed to produce placebo effects (Bootzin, 1985; Bootzin & Caspi, 2002; Evans, 1985; Kirsch, 1997b; Ross & Olson, 1981).

Intrapersonal expectancies are a key factor in Hahn's (1985) sociocultural model of illness and healing. Although Hahn (1997b) defines expectation as "a sense or a specific belief that some event will occur" (p. 57), he states that "expectations are not simply logical and cognitive statements but are commonly associated with emotional states that reflect or underlie the bearer's feelings about the expectation" (p. 59). On the basis of an expectancy (positive or negative) and an outcome (positive

6 S. Trusz and P. Bąbel

and negative), he distinguishes between four different effects of a placebo: placebo effects (positive expectations and a positive outcome), placebo side-effects (positive expectations and a negative outcome), nocebo effects (negative expectations and a negative outcome), and nocebo side-effects (negative expectations and a positive outcome). Hahn's (1985) model is the most influential account of the nocebo effect (Hahn, 1997a, 1997b, 1999), defined as "the causation of sickness (or death) by expectations of sickness (or death) and by associated emotional states" (Hahn, 1997a, p. 607; 1997b, p. 56).

Similar to Hahn's conception (1997a, 1997b, 1999), Benson (1997) lists three components that make up the placebo and nocebo effect: expectancy of a patient, expectancy of a physician and other members of the staff – e.g. nurses – and expectancy that is engendered by the relationship between the first two. According to Spiegel (1997), the nocebo effect is activated in three different ways, including negative messages from the healthcare system or an individual in the system, and negative messages from the patient's social and psychological environment. These messages are, of course, the sources of expectancies. It seems clear from both Benson's (1997) and Spiegel's (1997) accounts that not only intrapersonal expectancies (on the patient side) but also interpersonal expectancies (on the medical staff side) have an effect of both healing and illness.

Interpersonal expectancies

Within scientific reflection, the issue of interpersonal expectancies is raised for the first time by a sociologist William Isaac Thomas, and then by Robert Merton. The former, in his work *The Relation of Research to the Social Process* (1931), presents a penetrating analysis of the relations between social perception and behavior. He illustrates the significance of these relations through a story of a mentally ill patient, who

> has killed several persons who had the unfortunate habit of talking to themselves on the street. From the movement of their lips he imagined that they were calling him vile names, and he behaved as if this were true. If men define those situations as real, they are real in their consequences.
>
> (Thomas, p. 189)

Thomas's ideas were developed by Robert Merton, who, in his influential paper *The Self-fulfilling Prophecy* (1948), introduced a formal definition of a self-fulfilling prophecy, discussing economic, political, social, and educational phenomena – e.g. bank failures, armed conflicts, race relations, and students' achievements in tests. According to the author,

> the self-fulfilling prophecy is, in the beginning, a false definition of the situation evoking a new behavior which makes the originally false conception come true. The specious validity of the self-fulfilling prophecy perpetuates

a reign of error. For the prophet will cite the actual course of events as proof that he was right from the very beginning.

(Thomas, p. 195)

Until today, this definition has been a reference point for the majority of studies that analyze the process of confirming originally inaccurate interpersonal expectancies (Brophy, 1983; Darley & Fazio, 1980; Good, 1987; Jussim, 1986, 2012; Rosenthal, 2002). The most spectacular studies on the mechanism of self-fulfilling prophecy turned out to be the works by Robert Rosenthal and his colleagues on the experimenter expectancy effect (Rosenthal, 1969, 1997, 2002, 2003; Rosenthal & Rubin, 1978) and the Pygmalion effect (interpersonal expectancies in education, see Babad, 1993; Harris & Rosenthal, 1985; Rosenthal & Jacobson, 1968; Rubie-Davies, 2015). As for the former effect, the authors managed to prove that under favorable conditions the experimenter's expectancies significantly influence the behavior of people and animals in the direction consistent with the one previously assumed in the research hypothesis. In the Pygmalion experiment carried out in one of the American elementary schools, eight months after the manipulation of the teachers' expectations concerning "alleged intellectual blooming" of a particular group of students, the researchers noted a significant increase in their IQ scores, compared to students from a control group (on average by 15.4 and 9.4 points, respectively, among first and second graders).

Rosenthal's studies, especially the Pygmalion experiment, aroused great public interest and divided the academic community for the next sixty years (Jussim, 2012; Jussim & Harber, 2005; Spitz, 1999; Wineburg, 1987). According to their advocates, interpersonal expectancies are a powerful source of social problems, such as prejudices, discriminations, and diverse achievements within a large group of people (see e.g. Madon & Wilard in this volume). According to their critics, interpersonal expectancies are usually accurate, and therefore they correlate with other people's behavior, but they do not cause it (see, e.g. Jussim & Stevens in this volume). It is estimated that by the mid-1980s there were around 400 published studies that tried to replicate the results obtained in the Pygmalion experiment (Wineburg, 1987), and in the collective analysis published in 1997, Rosenthal included 479 studies.

Ultimately, in a series of meta-analyses (Harris & Rosenthal, 1985, 1986; Rosenthal, 1997; Rosenthal & Rubin, 1978) it was demonstrated that the interpersonal expectancy effects are a real phenomenon that can be brought about in a lab and observed in natural settings, such as school, workplace, therapeutic and consulting room, court, and the military. The average size of the expectancy effect has a Cohen's d value of .60, which, according to the BESD measure, means an increase of the success probability (success rate) in predicting the object's response from 35 percent to 65 percent, after taking into account diverse expectancies in the analysis (Rosnow & Rosenthal, 2003). In one of the most recent meta-analyses, covering 674 experimental and naturalistic studies and 784 teacher expectancy effects, Hattie (2009) calculated an overall effect size of $d = 0.43$.

8 S. Trusz and P. Bąbel

A mechanism of confirming false interpersonal expectancies can be described, following Merton (1948), in three points: (1) observers form unjustified beliefs about objects. These beliefs can be derived from cognitive schemas, e.g. gender stereotypes, social status, external appearance, etc., and concern the objects' characteristics and behavior (Dusek & Joseph, 1983; Jussim, 2012); (2) observers convey their unjustified beliefs to the objects through their verbal behaviors – e.g. comments such as "women are more stupid than men," "redheads are dishonest," etc., and through their nonverbal behaviors – e.g. gestures, eye contacts, touch, etc. (Harris, 1989, 1993; Harris & Rosenthal, 1985); and (3) the observer's originally unjustified beliefs are confirmed by the object's behaviors. This confirmation can occur at the real (behavioral) level, or only at the perceptual level, when the observer, as a result of cognitive distortions, interprets the objects' behaviors as consistent with his or her earlier expectations (Miller & Turnbull, 1986; Snyder & Klein, 2005).

Merton's idea is developed within various models of expectancy effects. The most interesting of them, considering the possibility of integrating the intrapersonal perspective (expectancy about self) and interpersonal perspective (expectancy about others), were proposed by Rosenthal (1981, as cited in Harris & Rosenthal, 1985), Darley and Fazio (1980), Jussim (1986), and more recently by Olson and collaborators, (1996). Some elements of these models can be easily associated with intrapersonal expectancy effects – namely, mediator and/or moderator variables – i.e. factors influencing the size and/or direction of the process of confirming expectations concerning one's own responses and/or the behavior of other people or animals.

Within the 10 Arrow Model, Rosenthal proposes one basic element (*component A*) containing the distal independent variables that can be equated with pre-existing moderator variables – e.g. stable attributes of the expecter and expectee, such as their personalities, motivation, cognitive abilities, and emotionality, which affect the level of susceptibility of observers and targets, respectively, to the creation of expectancies and their subsequent confirmation.

Similarly, in three stages of the self-fulfilling prophecy model, Jussim draws attention to the mediator variables for effects. Among them, on the expecters' side, he names such factors as: (1) perceptions of control; (2) perception of similarity; (3) cognitive dissonance; (4) attributions; and (5) affect. Each of the indicated variables is either a significant correlate of intrapersonal expectancies, or a factor interacting with them, which can ultimately differentiate the expecters' behavior towards the expectees. For example, when analyzing the role of perception of control, Jussim notes:

> because teachers perceive high-expectancy students as having a greater comprehension of a broader range of topics, they also feel more able to direct, control, and reach understandings with these students . . . teachers consider their own control to be a more important determinant of lows' performance than of highs' performance. Therefore, teachers feel a greater need to assert their control over lows' behavior than over highs' behavior.
>
> (1986, p. 435)

On the expectees' side, the author distinguishes the following factors: (1) perceptions of control; (2) values; (3) self-schemas; and (4) self-esteem. These factors can also be considered as important correlates of intrapersonal expectancies or factors modifying objects' susceptibility to confirmation of observers' beliefs. Again, discussing the significance of perceptions of control, Jussim stresses that

> by providing noncontingent feedback to lows . . . teachers will lead many lows to believe that performance is not contingent on effort. As a consequence, lows will not try as hard, persist as long, or, more generally, understand which behaviors lead to scholastic success. Ultimately, this leads to lower levels of performance
>
> (Jussim, 1986, p. 439)

Darley and Fazio (1980), characterizing the mechanism of confirming interpersonal expectancies, draw attention to the targets' cognitive processes accompanying this phenomenon. The target actively participates in the process of verifying the accuracy of interpersonal expectancies, making attributions to his or her own behaviors and the observer's behaviors. Thus, the target can identify with their own responses or reject them, assuming that these responses have been provoked entirely by the observer; the target can remember them or not, regarding them as incidental and not significant. As a result, the target can actively resist the process of self-fulfilling prophecy, or act in accordance with the definition of situation imposed by the observer.

Concluding their perceptive analysis of expectancy confirmation processes arising in the social interaction sequence, the authors (Darley & Fazio, 1980) state:

> if the target regards something about himself or herself or his or her category membership as a cause of the perceiver's behavior, then this needs to be dealt with in future interactions with the perceiver. On one hand, the target may not accept the validity of that conclusion. Therefore, the target may attempt to counteract and change the perceiver's initial impressions. Or . . . the target may come to accept the self mirror in the perceiver's actions.
>
> (p. 873)

Since the mid-1960s, researchers in various domains of social and behavioral sciences have discussed and tested models of intrapersonal and interpersonal expectancy phenomena. Despite such a long tradition, except for a few exceptions (e.g. Harris, 1993; Jussim, 1986, 2012; Neuberg, 1994; Olson *et al.*, 1996; Roese & Sherman, 2007), these two perspectives on expectancy effects have developed independently. A good example of such an exception is Olson and collaborators' (1996) model which takes into account factors influencing the process of generating, expression, and confirmation vs. falsification of intra- and interpersonal expectancies. For example, the authors identify the determinants of certainty, accessibility, clarity, and meaning – i.e. basic dimensions, in which predictions about oneself

10 S. Trusz and P. Bąbel

and others can be characterized. Among them, special attention should be paid to the processes of memory, learning, motivation, and the expecters' attributions concerning their own responses and the responses of their interaction partners. Moreover, within the model there are comprehensively described cognitive (i.e. processes of attention, encoding, and interpretation of information reaching the observer, attribution, counterfactual thinking, and memory), affective (i.e. prejudices, anxiety-depression, sense of humor, positive and negative emotions associated with confirming vs. questioning the accuracy of expectations), behavioral (i.e. hypotheses testing and self-fulfilling prophecy), and physiological (i.e. the placebo vs. nocebo effect) consequences of intra- and interpersonal expectancies.

Although some exceptions exist, the psychology of intrapersonal expectancies and the psychology of interpersonal expectancies are still developing independently. The main aim of our book is to open the discussion between researchers and theoreticians representing both perspectives.

Overview of the book

The book, which we are extremely happy to put into our readers' hands, contains chapters written by the most eminent experts from the world's leading academic institutions dealing with problems of intrapersonal expectancies – i.e. (in alphabetical order): Jessica Baltman, Thomas H. Brandon, Salvatore J. Catanzaro, Luana Colloca, Peter S. Hendricks, Michael E. Hyland, Irving Kirsch, Steven J. Lynn, James Maddux, Zev M. Medoff, Jack Mearns, Guy H. Montgomery, Madalina Sucala, and Julie Schnur, as well as interpersonal expectancies – i.e. Elisha Babad, Hester de Boer, Jennifer K. Bosson, Lee Jussim, Stephanie Madon, Steven L. Neuberg, Christine Rubie-Davies, Mark Snyder, Sean T. Stevens, William B. Swann, Jr., Rhona Weinstein, Margaretha P. C. van der Werf, Charles K. West, and Jennifer Willard.

We asked the contributors to prepare review chapters on the topics that they have been studying extensively, integrating them in four main issues – i.e.: (1) the beginnings (genesis) of the research (what and why the authors wanted to know about intra- and/or interpersonal expectancy effects?); (2) the current state of the art (what is already known about intra- and/or interpersonal expectancy effects); (3) the future directions of the research (what the authors still want to know about intra- and/or interpersonal expectancy effects); and (4) the applications of the results (how can we apply the results of the authors' research on intra- and/or interpersonal expectancy effects?).

The book is divided into two parts. Part 1 contains chapters dealing with intrapersonal expectancy effects, while Part 2 deals with interpersonal expectancies.

In Chapter 2, Irving Kirsch presents his own theory of response expectancy, which is the most important theoretical account of the effects of intrapersonal expectancies. Response expectancies are expectations about our own automatic reactions to events. The author presents the genesis and the most fundamental theses of his theory, but also the results of his own and other researchers' studies that support his assumptions. He concludes that response expectancies tend to be self-confirming and can produce an unmediated, intrapersonal, self-fulfilling prophecy. He then reviews data showing this in three research domains in which he is an expert – i.e. fear, placebo effects, and the treatment of depression. In conclusion, Kirsch points out future directions in the studies on response expectancy as well as clinical applications of their results.

In Chapter 3, Michael E. Hyland describes the beginnings of his criticism of response expectancy theory, especially the data that is inconsistent with Kirsch's theory. He assumes that the association between expectancy and outcome could be an epiphenomenon and that the results could be explained by an extension of self-determination theory in the therapeutic domain: intrinsic goal satisfaction leads to improved health outcomes. Hyland proposes the theory that long-term therapeutic benefit was the result of concordance between a participant's goals and the motivational features of the therapeutic ritual. This new perspective provides an alternative perspective of placebo responding. According to Hyland, fundamentally different mechanisms apply in the short-term, laboratory analogue situation compared with "real life" therapeutic effects. The mechanism primarily relevant to the former is response expectancy, whereas the mechanism primarily relevant to the latter is motivational concordance. The author discusses the results of the research supporting his theory and points out both future directions for the studies on the motivational concordance theory and practical application of the theory.

Chapter 4, by James E. Maddux, deals with self-efficacy beliefs, which are people's beliefs about their ability to produce desired outcomes through their own actions. These beliefs are among the most important determinants of behavior that people choose to engage in and how much they persevere in their efforts in the face of obstacles and challenges. Therefore, they also are among the most important determinants of psychological well-being and adjustment. Maddux discusses the genesis of the concept of self-efficacy and reviews the current state of theory and research on this concept: defining, measuring, origins of self-efficacy, as well as the relationships between personality and self-efficacy. Also discussed are the applications of self-efficacy in psychological health and well-being, physical health and well-being, self-regulation, psychotherapy, education, career, and work. Maddux concludes with future directions in the research on self-efficacy.

In Chapter 5, Jessica Baltman and Steven Jay Lynn discuss the relationships between hypnosis, memory, and expectation. They notice that although participants who experience a hypnotic induction often report more recollections during recall tests than participants who do not experience an induction, increases in accurate recollections reported during hypnosis are almost always accompanied by either a comparable or greater increase in the number of inaccurate recollections. However, hypnosis inflates recall confidence, which may be especially problematic in forensic settings in which confidence in inaccurate recollections can be misleading. Baltman and Lynn note that expectations regarding hypnosis are one of the determinants of hypnotic responding, and people may adopt a lax criterion to guess or report vague recollections as memories due to the widely held expectation that hypnosis improves memory. The authors discuss the implications and applications of the effects of expectations regarding hypnosis on memory as well as future directions of the studies on the relationships between expectancies, hypnosis, and memory.

Chapter 6, by Salvatore J. Catanzaro and Jack Mearns, answers the question why some people seem to maintain their equanimity even while experiencing strong negative emotions, while others prolong negative emotional states by engaging in negative meta-appraisals and hopeless attributions. They discuss the theoretical development and measurement of negative mood regulation expectancies. Catanzaro and Mearns review the results of the research on the relationships between stress, coping, negative mood regulation expectancies, and mood. They present data showing that negative mood regulation expectancies are associated with more active and less avoidant coping responses, more effective mood repair, more positive behavioral responses under stress, fewer or less intense symptoms of emotional distress, and physical illness. Moreover, negative mood regulation expectancies have been proven to buffer the impact of other variables that increase the risk of problematic drinking and mediate psychotherapeutic changes in symptoms. Finally, Catanzaro and Mearns point out future directions in the studies on response expectancy as well as applications of their results.

In Chapter 7, Peter S. Hendricks and Thomas H. Brandon describe the genesis of their interest in smoking-related expectancies and review the results of the research on the role of smoking-related expectancies in cigarette use behavior. Hendricks and Brandon discuss the measurement of smoking-related expectancies and the results of two lines of study on the relationship between expectancies and smoking behavior: (1) cross-sectional and longitudinal associations of smoking-related expectancies with cigarette use behavior and (2) manipulation of smoking-related expectancies. Generally, the results of the studies provide support for the thesis that one's decision to engage in smoking behavior is determined by the consequences one expects from doing so, otherwise known as expectancies. Those who hold positive expectancies for cigarette use are more likely to smoke than those who hold primarily negative expectancies. Similarly, those who hold positive expectancies for smoking cessation are more likely to quit than those who hold negative expectancies. In conclusion, the authors point out both future directions for studies on smoking-related expectancies and practical applications of their results.

Chapter 8, by Madalina Sucala, Julie Schnur, and Guy H. Montgomery, presents the authors' program of response expectancy research in cancer care. Sucala, Schnur, and Montgomery start with the state of the art and present their early foundational research on the role of response expectancies in the production of placebo effects. They then continue with applied research on the role of response expectancies in patients' experiences of cancer treatment-related side-effects – i.e. nausea, fatigue, pain, emotional distress – and in psychosocial interventions – i.e. hypnosis – in cancer care to reduce such side-effects. The chapter concludes with a discussion of applications of the results of the authors' studies and future research directions.

In Chapter 9, Zev M. Medoff and Luana Colloca start with a discussion of placebo effects due to intrapersonal expectancies, both conscious and unconscious. According to Colloca and Miller's model verbal instructions, conditioning and social observational learning contribute to create expectations which, in turn, shape the placebo effect. Social observational learning is the main subject of the chapter. Medoff and Colloca review the results of the research on placebo effects induced by social observational learning. It has been found that people who observe pain reduction in other people are more likely to exhibit analgesia themselves. The effect of observation also applies to the nocebo effect, where negative expectations can increase a subject's perceived experience of pain. The chapter concludes with a discussion of future research directions as well as implications of the results for patient–clinician interactions. This chapter was chosen as the last one of the first part of the book because its topic links intrapersonal and interpersonal expectancies, as both types of expectancies seem to play a role in the effects of social observational learning.

The second part of the book contains articles addressing interpersonal expectancy effects. Interpersonal expectancy effects manifest themselves most spectacularly in the form of the self-fulfilling prophecy phenomenon, with the originally false expectancies of observers – e.g. the expectancies of teachers towards students, parents towards children, doctors/therapists towards patients/clients, investigators towards objects, employers towards employees, and even judges towards defendants – being transformed into actual, better, or worse performance – e.g. school tests results (Rosenthal & Jacobson, 1968; Dusek, 1985; Rubie-Davies, 2015), the effects of therapy in a doctor's or therapist's office (Rosenthal, 2002), results in a laboratory (Rosenthal, 1969), sales results (Eden, 1990), and length of sentences (Blanck, 1993), etc.

In the first five chapters of a more general nature, the authors discuss the conditions in which interpersonal expectancies effects occur, and they identify personal and nonpersonal factors that affect the size and direction of these effects. In the remaining chapters, the authors characterize the self-fulfilling prophecy phenomenon in specific contexts, mainly in a classroom setting.

Thus, in Chapter 10, Mark Snyder considers the conditions in which interpersonal expectancies create social reality, and presents the phenomenon of behavioral confirmation of a wide range of false beliefs in various types of social interactions. On the other hand, the author stresses that the scenario of behavioral confirmation is not a universal phenomenon and identifies *intrapersonal* and *contextual* conditions in which it is limited and/or eliminated.

In Chapter 11, William B. Swann, Jr and Jennifer K. Bosson characterize the identity negotiation process in social interaction. Considering the research findings referred to above, the authors discuss the nature and consequences of the tendency to behavioral confirmation of an observer's beliefs about personal characteristics of a given object vs. confirmation of self-views by an object in various social contexts, especially in a work group setting.

In Chapter 12, Steven L. Neuberg identifies and discusses goals/motivations of the observers and targets that influence a mediating mechanism between

14 S. Trusz and P. Bąbel

stereotype-tinged expectancies and level of behavioral confirmation process. The most important ones include observer accuracy motivation and observer vs. target self-presentational goals.

The authors of Chapter 13, Lee Jussim and Sean T. Stevens, argue that the prevailing conviction in social psychology that social perception is dominated by self-fulfilling prophecy, error, and bias is not justified. On the contrary, numerous classical and contemporary tests in the field of social sciences show that interpersonal expectancy effects tend to be weak and fleeting, and perceptions of individuals and groups tend to be highly accurate.

The opposite position is presented by Jennifer Willard and Stephanie Madon. In Chapter 14, the authors review the power of self-fulfilling prophecies among individuals who are highly susceptible to their effects and the potential for small self-fulfilling prophecy effects to be rendered powerful through two types of accumulation process – i.e. accumulation over time and across people.

Drawing attention to issues specific to the phenomenon of self-fulfilling prophecy in the classroom, in Chapter 15 Elisha Babad describes the study program in which he and his colleagues for fifty years have focused on the documentation of teachers' expectancy-related differential verbal and nonverbal behavior toward high- and low-expectancy students in the classroom. Moreover, the author discusses the social/emotional outcomes of teacher differentiality in the classroom.

In Chapter 16, Rhona Weinstein characterizes her proprietary "child-mediated model of teacher expectancy effects." She argues that the impact of educational self-fulfilling prophecy, on one hand, could be modified by the level of accuracy of teachers' expectancies about students' competences, and, on the other hand, by students' awareness of differential teachers' treatment.

In Chapter 17, Charles K. West presents the history of research on the educational self-fulfilling prophecy, in which a statistical procedure called cross-lagged panel analysis was first applied. Subsequently, the author discusses strengths and limitations of the indicated statistical tool.

In Chapter 18, Christine Rubie-Davies presents the history of research on the Pygmalion effect, and in this context the author characterizes her own program of studies on expectancy effects, aimed at identifying high and low biased teachers. Finally, estimating a practical value of the research in this area, Rubie-Davis characterizes her intervention program for teachers called "The Teacher Expectation Project."

In Chapter 19, Hester de Boer and Margaretha P. C. van der Werf present the results of research on long-term teacher expectations, currently conducted in the Netherlands on large samples of students in primary and secondary schools. It is worth emphasizing that the authors managed to determine the scope of the phenomenon and identify several student characteristics related to bias in teachers' expectations, and factors weakening the relationship between teachers' bias and student achievement.

We are convinced that without taking into consideration both perspectives – i.e. intra- and interpersonal ones – analysis of the phenomenon of expectancies would be incomplete, and therefore inadequate (see Olson *et al.*, 1996; Roese & Sherman, 2007). That is why, in the final chapter of the book, we make an attempt to integrate these two perspectives. Intra- and interpersonal expectancy effects may interpenetrate, overlap, and interact, thus influencing people's behavior in different contexts, including school, workplace, a therapist's or doctor's office, etc. (Jussim, 1986, 2012). Self-efficacy, for instance, may affect the direction and force of a self-fulfilling prophecy, acting as a significant moderator and/or mediator (Dweck & Master, 2009), while the process of perceptual/behavioral confirmation of false social beliefs may affect the memory of an observer and an object, their self-schemas and self-esteem, etc., acting as a moderator and/or mediator of intrapersonal expectancy effects.

In summary, the book provides a theory, research review, and summary of the current knowledge on intra- and interpersonal expectancy effects and related phenomena. It is to be stressed that our book presents the most recent knowledge on social and psychological mechanisms of forming both intra- and interpersonal expectancies, their sustainment and results, as well as discusses the latest theoretical concepts and the results of studies concerning expectancy effects, focusing on their application value. It is the first review of the phenomenon of interpersonal expectancies in over twenty years, the second book that has been ever published on intrapersonal expectancies (the first was edited by Kirsch and published seventeen years ago, in 1999), and the only publication presenting a complementary view of expectancies – i.e. focused on both intra- and interpersonal perspectives on the causes and effects of expectancies, as well as the factors influencing expectancy effects. In our opinion, only such a complementary approach allows to adequately describe, explain, and predict phenomena associated with expectancies, so important in terms of the quality of people's functioning, their health, well-being, and educational and professional achievements, etc.

Note

1 Preparation of this chapter was supported by the National Science Centre in Poland under grant number 2012/05/D/HS6/03350 awarded to the first author and under grant number 2014/14/E/HS6/00415 awarded to the second author.

References

Abramson, L. Y., Seligman, M. E. P., & Teasdale, J. D. (1978). Learned helplessness in humans: Critique and reformulation. *Journal of Abnormal Psychology*, *87*, 49–74.

Babad, E. (1993). Pygmalion – 25 Years after interpersonal expectations in the classroom. In P. D. Blanck (ed.), *Interpersonal Expectations: Theory, Research and Applications* (125–153). New York: Cambridge University Press.

Bacon, F. (1902). *Novum Organum*. New York: P. F. Collier & Son.

Bandura, A. (1977a). Self-efficacy: Toward a unifying theory of behavioral change. *Psychological Review*, *84*, 191–215.

Bandura, A. (1977b). *Social Learning Theory*. New York: General Learning Press.

16 S. Trusz and P. Bąbel

Benson, H. (1997). The nocebo effect: History and physiology. *Preventive Medicine, 26,* 612–615.

Blanck, P. D. (ed.). (1993). *Interpersonal Expectations: Theory, Research and Applications.* New York: Cambridge University Press.

Bolles, R. C. (1972). Reinforcement, expectancy, and learning. *Psychological Review, 79,* 394–409.

Bootzin, R. R. (1985). The role of expectancy in behavior change. In L. White, B. Tursky & G. E. Schwartz (eds), *Placebo: Theory, Research and Mechanisms* (196–210). New York: The Guilford Press.

Bootzin, R. R. & Caspi, O. (2002). Explanatory mechanisms for placebo effects: Cognition, personality and social learning. In H. A. Guess, A. Kleinman, J. W. Kusek & L. W. Engel (eds), *The Science of the Placebo: Toward an Interdisciplinary Research Agenda* (108–132). London: BMJ Books.

Brewer, W. F. (1974). There is no convincing evidence for operant or classical conditioning in adult humans. In W. B. Weimer & D. S. Palermo (eds), *Cognition and the Symbolic Processes* (1–42). Hillsdale, NJ: Lawrence Erlbaum Associates.

Brophy, J. (1983). Research on the self-fulfilling prophecy and teacher expectations. *Journal of Educational Psychology, 75,* 631–661.

Darley, J. M. & Fazio, R. H. (1980). Expectancy confirmation processes arising in the social interaction sequence. *American Psychologist, 35,* 867–881.

Dusek, J. (ed.). (1985). *Teacher Expectancies.* Hillsdale, NJ: Erlbaum.

Dusek, J. & Joseph, G. (1983). The bases of teacher expectancies: A meta-analysis. *Journal of Educational Psychology, 75,* 327–346.

Dweck, C. & Master, A. (2009). Self-theories motivate self-regulated learning. In D. H. Schunk & B. J. Zimmerman (eds) *Motivation and Self-regulated Learning: Theory, Research, and Application* (pp. 31–51). New York: Routledge.

Eden, D. (1990). *Pygmalion in Management: Productivity as a Self-fulfilling Prophecy.* Lexington, MA: Lexington Books.

Evans, F. J. (1985). Expectancy, therapeutic instructions, and the placebo response. In L. White, B. Tursky & G. E. Schwartz (eds), *Placebo: Theory, Research and Mechanisms* (215–228). New York: The Guilford Press.

Frank, J. D. (1961). *Persuasion and Healing: A Comparative Study of Psychotherapy.* Baltimore, MD: Johns Hopkins University Press.

Frank, J. D. (1971). Therapeutic factors in psychotherapy. *American Journal of Psychotherapy, 25,* 350–361.

Good, T. (1987). Two decades of research on teacher expectations: Findings and future directions. *Journal of Teacher Education, 38,* 32–47.

Hahn, R. A. (1999). Expectations of sickness: Concept and evidence of the nocebo phenomenon. In I. Kirsch (ed.), *How Expectancies Shape Experience* (333–356). Washington, DC: American Psychological Association.

Hahn, R. A. (1985). A sociocultural model of illness and healing. In L. White, B. Tursky & G. E. Schwartz (eds), *Placebo: Theory, Research and Mechanisms* (167–195). New York: The Guilford Press.

Hahn, R. A. (1997a). The nocebo phenomenon: Concept, evidence, and implications for public health. *Preventive Medicine, 26,* 607–611.

Hahn, R. A. (1997b). The nocebo phenomenon: Scope and foundations. In A. Harrington (ed.), *The Placebo Effect: An Interdisciplinary Exploration* (pp. 56–76). Cambridge, MA: Harvard University Press.

Harris, M. J. (1989). Personality moderators of interpersonal effects: Replication of Harris and Rosenthal (1986). *Journal of Research in Personality, 23,* 381–397.

Harris, M. J. (1993). Issues in studying the mediation of expectancy effects: A taxonomy of expectancy situations. In P. D. Blanck (ed.), *Interpersonal Expectations: Theory, Research and Applications* (350–378). New York: Cambridge University Press.

Harris, M. J. & Rosenthal, R. (1985). Mediation of interpersonal expectancy effects: 31 metaanalyses. *Psychological Bulletin, 97,* 363–386.

Harris, M. J. & Rosenthal, R. (1986b). Four factors in the mediation of teacher expectancy effects. In R. S. Feldman (ed.), *The Social Psychology of Education. Current Research and Theory* (91–114). Cambridge: Cambridge University Press.

Hattie, J. (2009). *Visible Learning: A Synthesis of over 800 Meta-analyses Relating to Achievement.* London: Routledge.

Jussim, L. (1986). Self-fulfilling Prophecies: A Theoretical and Integrative Review. *Psychological Review, 93,* 429–445.

Jussim, L. (2012). *Social Perception and Social Reality: Why Accuracy Dominates Bias and Self-fulfilling Prophecy.* New York: Oxford University Press.

Jussim, L. & Harber, K. D. (2005). Teacher expectations and self-fulfilling prophecies: Knowns and unknowns, resolved and unresolved controversies. *Personality and Social Psychology Review, 9,* 131–155.

Kirsch, I. (1985). Response expectancy as a determinant of experience and behavior. *American Psychologist, 40,* 1189–1202.

Kirsch, I. (1997a). Response expectancy theory and application: A decennial review. *Applied & Preventive Psychology, 6,* 69–79.

Kirsch, I. (1997b). Specifying nonspecifics: Psychological mechanisms of placebo effects. In A. Harrington (ed.), *The Placebo Effect: An Interdisciplinary Exploration* (166–186). Cambridge: Harvard University Press.

Kirsch, I. (ed.). (1999). *How Expectancies Shape Experience.* Washington, DC: American Psychological Association.

Kirsch I., Lynn, S. J., Vigorito, M. & Miller, R. R. (2004). The role of cognition in classical and operant conditioning. *Journal of Clinical Psychology, 60,* 369–392.

Klopfer, B. (1957). Psychological variables in human cancer. *Journal of Projective Techniques, 21,* 331–340.

Maier, S. F. & Seligman, M. E. (1976). Learned helplessness: Theory and evidence. *Journal of Experimental Psychology, 105,* 3–46.

Merton, R. K. (1948). The self-fulfilling prophecy. *Antioch Review, 8,* 193–210.

Miller, D. T. & Turnbull, W. (1986). Expectancies and interpersonal processes. *Annual Review of Psychology, 37,* 233–256.

Mischel, W. (1973). Toward a cognitive social reconceptualization of personality. *Psychological Review, 80,* 252–283.

Neuberg, S. L. (1994). Expectancy-confirmation processes in stereotype-tinged social encounters: The moderating role of social goals. In M. P. Zanna & J. M. Olson (eds), *The Psychology of Prejudice: The Ontario Symposium* (Vol. 7, 103–130). Hillsdale, NJ: Erlbaum.

Olson, J. M., Roese, N. J. & Zanna, M. P. (1996). Expectancies. In E. T. Higgins & A. W. Kruglanski (eds), *Social Psychology: Handbook of Basic Principles* (211–238). New York: The Guilford Press.

Reiss, S. (1980). Pavlovian conditioning and human fear: An expectancy model. *Behavior Therapy, 11,* 380–396.

Reiss, S. (1991). Expectancy model of fear, anxiety, and panic. *Clinical Psychology Review, 11,* 141–153.

Rescorla, R. A. (1988). Pavlovian conditioning: It's not what you think it is. *American Psychologist, 43,* 151–160.

Rescorla, R. A. (1991). Associative relations in instrumental learning: The eighteenth Bartlett memorial lecture. *Quarterly Journal of Experimental Psychology Section B: Comparative and Physiological Psychology*, *43*, 1–23.

Roese, N. J. & Sherman, J. W. (2007). Expectancy. In A. W. & E. T. Higgins (eds), *Social Psychology: Handbook of Basic Principles (2nd edn)* (91–115). New York and London: Guilford Press.

Rosenthal, R. (1969). Interpersonal expectations: Effects of the experimenter's hypothesis. In R. Rosenthal & R. L. Rosnow (eds), *Artifact in Behavioral Research* (181–277). New York: Academic Press.

Rosenthal, R. (1997). Interpersonal expectancy effects: A forty year perspective. Meeting paper presented at the American Psychological Association Convention, Chicago, 16 August.

Rosenthal, R. (2002). Covert communication in classrooms, clinics, courtrooms, and cubicles. *American Psychologist*, *57*, 839–849.

Rosenthal, R. (2003). Covert communication in laboratories, classrooms, and the truly real world. *Current Directions in Psychological Science*, *12*, 151–154.

Rosenthal, R. & Jacobson, L. (1968). *Pygmalion in the Classroom: Teacher Expectation and Pupils' Intellectual Development*. New York: Irvington.

Rosenthal, R. & Rubin, D. B. (1978). Interpersonal expectancy effects: The first 345 studies. *Behavioral and Brain Sciences*, *3*, 377–386.

Rosnow, R. L. & Rosenthal, R. (2003). Effect sizes for experimenting psychologists. *Canadian Journal of Experimental Psychology*, *57*, 221–237.

Ross, M. & Olson, J. M. (1981). An expectancy-attribution model of the effects of placebos. *Psychological Review*, *88*, 408–437.

Rotter, J. B. (1954). *Social Learning and Clinical Psychology*. Englewood Cliffs, NJ: Prentice Hall.

Rotter, J. B. (1966). Generalized expectancies for internal versus external control of reinforcement. *Psychological Monographs: General and Applied*, *80*, 1–28.

Rubie-Davies, C. (2015). *Becoming a High Expectation Teacher: Raising the Bar*. London and New York: Routledge.

Skinner, B. F. (1938). *The Behavior of Organisms: An Experimental Analysis*. New York: Appleton-Century.

Skinner, B. F. (1974). *About Behaviorism*. New York: Knopf.

Snyder, M. & Klein, O. (2005). Construing and constructing others: On the reality and the generality of the behavioral confirmation scenario. *Interaction Studies*, *6*, 53–67.

Spiegel, H. (1997). Nocebo: The power of suggestibility. *Preventive Medicine*, *26*, 616–621.

Spitz, H. H. (1999). Beleaguered Pygmalion: History of the controversy over claims that teacher expectancy raises intelligence. *Intelligence*, *27*, 199–234.

Thomas, W. I. (1931). The relation of research to the social process. In W. I. Thomas (ed.), *Essays on Research in the Social Sciences: Papers Presented in a General Seminar Conducted by the Committee on Training of the Brookings Institution, 1930–31* (75–194). Washington, DC: Kennikat Press.

Tolman, E. C. (1932). *Purposive Behavior in Animals and Men*. New York: Appleton-Century-Crofts.

Tolman, E. C. (1949). There is more than one kind of learning. *Psychological Review*, *56*, 144–155.

Watson, J. B. (1913). Psychology as the behaviorist views it. *Psychological Review*, *20*, 158–177.

Watson, J. B. (1919). *Psychology from the Standpoint of a Behaviorist*. Philadelphia, PA: J.B. Lippincott.

Weinberger, J. & Eig, A. (1999). Expectancies: The ignored common factor in psychotherapy. In I. Kirsch (ed.), *How Expectancies Shape Experience* (pp. 357–382). Washington, DC: American Psychological Association.

Wineburg, S. S. (1987). The self-fulfillment of the self-fulfilling prophecy: A critical appraisal. *Educational Researcher, 16*, 28–37.

PART I
Intrapersonal expectancies

PREFACE

Expectancy about self

Irving Kirsch

Although distinct concepts, expectancies about the self and expectancies about others share much in common, and a consideration of them in the same volume is long overdue. Their principal commonality is that they are both self-confirming, but the difference in the object of the expectancy (self or other) has implications for understanding the psychological mechanisms underlying that effect. Unless we posit psychic processes, we must assume that the self-confirming effect of interpersonal expectancies are mediated by their effect on the expecter's behavior toward the target person. The expecter's behavior then affects the target's behavior. With expectancies about the self, the process is necessarily more direct, because the expecter and the target are the same person.

Part I of this book concerns expectancies about the self. Chapter I considers response expectancies, which are expectancies of the occurrence of automatic reactions, perceptions, experiences, and behavior, the prototype being the expectancies associated with placebo effects. Some of the effects or response expectancies on experience are mediated by behavior. Expecting to experience a therapeutic outcome, for example, might lead people to more actively engage in the treatment process, and this might in turn promote the anticipated outcome. But the self-confirming effects of response expectancies can be even more direct. I have posited that the expectancy of a subjective experience can have an immediate (i.e. unmediated) self-confirming effect (Kirsch, 1985).

Some of the areas in which important effects of response expectancies are presented in depth is this book. These include hypnosis (Baltman and Lynn), negative mood regulation (Catanzaro and Mearns), smoking (Hendricks and Brandon), and cancer (Scula, Schnur and Montgomery). This first part of the book also explicates important self-related constructs that are distinct from response expectancies, specifically self-efficacy (Maddux) and motivational concordance (Hyland). Finally, the last chapter of part I (Medoff and Colloca) bridges expectancies about the self (i.e. intrapersonal expectancies) and expectancies about others (i.e. interpersonal expectancies). It concerns the effects of observation of others (modeling) on one's own subjective experience, mediated by response expectancies. Thus, interpersonal observation affects intrapersonal expectancies in the production of placebo effects.

Daniel Dennett (1993) once described the brain as an expectancy machine. Its purpose is to anticipate events so that one can behave in a way that maximizes positive outcomes and avoids negative ones. It also affects perception, allowing the organism to disambiguate ambiguous stimuli so that it can react quickly (Kirsch, 1999). This is the underlying basis of the self-confirming effects of response expectancies.

References

Dennett, D. C. (1993). *Consciousness Explained*. London: Penguin,

Kirsch, I. (1985). Response expectancy as a determinant of experience and behavior. *American Psychologist, 40*, 1189–1202.

Kirsch, I. (1999). Response expectancy: An introduction. In I. Kirsch (ed.), *How Expectancies Shape Experience* (3–13). Washington, DC: American Psychological Association.

2

RESPONSE EXPECTANCY

Irving Kirsch

Genesis

As an undergraduate psychology major in the early 1970s, I became enamored of learning theory, in particular the cognitive behavioral learning theory of Edward C. Tolman (1932). Tolman was a self-proclaimed behaviorist, but he was a behaviorist of a different stripe from most other behaviorists. Although he agreed with John B. Watson (1913) that introspection had to be abandoned as a research methodology, he nevertheless believed that people – and other animals – thought. While most behaviorists before and after him conceived of classical and instrumental conditioning as automatic processes linking stimuli to responses, Tolman argued that their effects were mediated by cognition. He and his colleagues conducted an impressive series of studies demonstrating that in instrumental learning, rats developed cognitive maps of their environment, expectancies about where food was located, and based on their observation of changed conditions of a maze they had learned in, were capable of displaying insight leading to behavior that conflicted with their reinforcement history.

The next step in the genesis of the idea of response expectancy was my introduction to behavior therapy. The data convinced me that systematic desensitization was an effective treatment for phobias, but I doubted the theoretical rationales that had been used to explain it. All of these were based on non-cognitive, automatic conditioning models. Wolpe (1958), who originated the technique, based it on the idea of reciprocal inhibition. The idea was that phobias were classically conditioned learned responses. The treatment aimed to use conditioning to associate the phobic stimulus with a response that was incompatible with anxiety – for example, relaxation or sexual arousal. The new conditioned response would then inhibit the anxiety response. A hierarchy going gradually from a low-intensity version of the phobic stimulus (e.g. looking at a picture of a snake) to a very high-intensity image (e.g. handling a live snake) was deemed necessary so that the

26 I. Kirsch

relaxation would inhibit the anxiety, rather than the anxiety inhibiting the relaxation. Other conditioning-based explanations of systematic desensitization included counterconditioning, habituation, and extinction (Davison, 1968; Lader & Mathews, 1968).

As a disciple of Tolman, it was natural for me to doubt these mechanistic conceptions of systematic desensitization. Instead, it seemed reasonable to suspect that the therapeutic effects were cognitively mediated. A number of researchers hypothesized that phobic disorders were in effect due to a fear of fear (Goldstein & Chambless, 1978; Kirsch & Henry, 1977; Kirsch et al., 1983; Reiss & McNally, 1985). What phobic individuals fear are not snakes, heights, water, supermarkets, and the other stimuli they so desperately avoid; rather, they fear the experience of fear and panic that they anticipate experiencing when in their presence. Desensitization and other behavior therapies for phobias alter these expectations, leading people to conceive of themselves as no longer phobic. This conception led me to conduct a series of studies challenging automatic conditioning explanations of systematic desensitization.

The expectancy-based theory of phobias and their treatment led to an interest in placebo effects. Here was another arena in which the expectancy of a therapeutic change produced that change as a self-fulfilling prophecy. But there is an important difference between expectancy-based fears and placebo effects. People fear and avoid situations in which they expect aversive consequences (Beck, 1976; Rotter, 1954). Because fear is aversive, the expectancy of its occurrence produces the anticipated fear and the reduction of the expectancy leads to the reduction of the fear. But why should the belief that one is taking an analgesic produce a reduction in pain, why should the belief that one has taken a tranquilizer produce relaxation, and why should the belief that one has taken a stimulant produce arousal? This consideration led me to develop the concept of the self-confirming response expectancies (Kirsch, 1985, 1990).

What we know

Most of our expectations refer to things that are outside ourselves. We expect good or bad weather, high or low scores on a test, changes in stock prices, good or bad behavior on the part of others. These are stimulus expectancies. Response expectancies are expectations about our own automatic reactions to events. We expect to feel tired if we don't get enough sleep, to feel less pain if we take a pain medication, and to feel fear or excitement on a roller coaster. Stimulus and response expectancies shape our behavior because they both refer to expected outcomes. We generally behave in such a way as to enhance the likelihood of positive outcomes and decrease the likelihood of negative outcomes. So we might bring along an umbrella, study for a test, or change our investment strategy, depending on the particular stimulus expectancies we have. Similarly, we might go to bed early, take an aspirin, or avoid a particularly high roller coaster, depending on the response expectancies we hold.

There is an important difference between stimulus expectancies and response expectancies. For the most part, stimulus expectancies have no direct effect on whether the expected outcome will occur. They affect the outcome only by changing our behavior. In contrast, response expectancies can affect the expected outcome directly. This is most clearly seen with respect to placebo and nocebo effects. For example, expecting a diminution of pain is often sufficient to produce a reduction in experienced pain, even though the intensity of the stimulus is the same and nothing has been done to relieve the pain (Montgomery & Kirsch, 1996). Thus, response expectancies tend to be self-confirming. They can produce an unmediated, intrapersonal, self-fulfilling prophecy. In the sections below, I review data showing this in a number of research domains.

The expectancy model of fear

Response expectancy theory was born of suspicions that phobic anxiety is maintained by anxiety expectancies and that systematic desensitization achieves its effects by altering those expectancies. These suspicions have been confirmed by data. The effects of desensitization can be duplicated by credible control treatments, including one in which imaged exposure to the phobic stimulus is paired with painful electric shock (Kirsch & Henry, 1977), an effect that is directly opposite to that predicted by conditioning theory. Other research established that phobic anxiety is very highly correlated with anxiety expectancy and that the degree of improvement that is expected to occur after desensitization treatment is very highly correlated with actual improvement (Kirsch *et al.*, 1983; Schoenberger *et al.*,1991; Southworth & Kirsch, 1988).

Independently of my work in this area, Reiss and McNally (Reiss & McNally, 1985) developed an expectancy-based model for understanding normal and pathological fear. They hypothesized that fear is produced by danger expectancy (i.e. the perception of threat), anxiety expectancy, and the degree to which danger and anxiety are experienced as aversive (respectively termed *danger sensitivity* and *anxiety sensitivity*). They also developed the Anxiety Sensitivity Index (Reiss *et al.*, 1986), which has proved to be a useful construct in predicting fear and avoidance. The model hypothesizes that fear varies as a multiplicative function of expected negative outcomes and the perceived aversiveness of those outcomes, with the important proviso that anxiety or panic are among the aversive outcomes that may be expected.

Besides their practical importance, the concepts of anxiety sensitivity, danger sensitivity, and social evaluation sensitivity are theoretically interesting because of their fit with social learning theory (Rotter, 1954) and other expectancy-value models (Ajzen & Fishbein, 1980). In these theories, intentional behavior is predicted as a multiplicative function of expected outcomes and the values of those outcomes to the individual. Sensitivities to anxiety, danger, and social evaluation can be thought of as reinforcement values. They measure the degree to which people find anxiety and danger aversive and the importance that people attach to social evaluation. In this way, these constructs extend the expectancy-value hypothesis to emotional reactions.

28 I. Kirsch

The relation of anxiety sensitivity to fear varies from one anxiety disorder to another (Taylor *et al.*, 1992). Because fear of fear is central to current conceptions of panic disorder with and without agoraphobia, it is not surprising that anxiety sensitivity scores are especially high among people with this disorder. Conversely, anxiety sensitivity is not a significant predictor of fear in people with simple phobias (Schoenberger *et al.*, 1991; Taylor *et al.*, 1992). In contrast to anxiety sensitivity, anxiety expectancy appears to predict fear and avoidance across all types of phobias. Typical correlations between anxiety expectancy and fear are in the range of .75 (Kirsch *et al.*, 1983; Southworth & Kirsch, 1988), and a substantial association (Beta = .55) remains even when danger sensitivity, anxiety sensitivity, danger expectancy, and self-efficacy are controlled statistically (Schoenberger *et al.*, 1991).

Although unexpected panic attacks is a definitional component of panic disorders (American Psychiatric Association, 2013), a causal role for expectancy as a trigger of panic attacks is indicated by data (Kenardy *et al.*, 1992). In this study, women diagnosed with a panic disorder rated anxiety, perceived danger, control, and expected panic at hourly intervals for one week. Of these variables, expectancy was the only reliable precursor of panic attacks.

If the correlation between anxiety expectancy and fear is causal, changing those expectancies should be an essential part of treatment. Data from treatment outcome studies are consistent with this hypothesis. They indicate that the effects of desensitization treatments can be duplicated by sufficiently credible control procedures and that expectancy change covaries with anxiety change (e.g. Kirsch *et al.*, 1983). However, the most direct test of this hypothesis was provided in a study of the effects of *in vivo* exposure on agoraphobia (Southworth & Kirsch, 1988). Over a two-week period, participants in this study were given ten sessions of *in vivo* exposure, during which they were asked to walk away from their homes until they became anxious and then to turn around and return. Half of the participants were told that the purpose of this was to lower their anxiety. The others were told that the purpose was to assess their anxiety and that treatment would not begin until after the two-week period. Clients provided with therapeutic expectancies showed substantially greater improvement and improved more rapidly than those who were led to believe that *in vivo* exposure was for the purpose of assessment. These data indicate that the therapeutic effects of *in vivo* exposure can be suppressed by disguising its therapeutic intent.

Placebo effects

The placebo effect is the prototype of response expectancy effects. Largely ignored for centuries, then recognized as a nuisance variable that needed to be controlled in clinical trials, placebo effects are now being ever more widely recognized as a phenomenon that needs to be understood and exploited.

In 1955, the *Journal of the American Medical Association* (*JAMA*) published Henry K. Beecher's classic article *The Powerful Placebo*, in which he claimed that approximately one-third of people exhibited a placebo effect across a wide variety of conditions. However, Beecher neglected to take into account the fact that much of this change might be due to factors other than the administration of a placebo. They might be due, for example, to the natural history of the condition being treated or the statistical artifact of regression toward the mean. Almost a half century later, Hróbjartsson and Gøtzsche (2001) conducted a meta-analysis of clinical trials in which there were no-treatment control groups as well as placebo groups. They reported finding little evidence of a powerful placebo effect.

There is good reason to believe that the Hróbjartsson and Gøtzsche (2001) meta-analysis grossly underestimates the placebo effect. They analyzed clinical trials of treatments for a motley collection of disorders, including the common cold, alcohol abuse, smoking, poor oral hygiene, herpes simplex infection, infertility, mental retardation, marital discord, fecal soiling, Alzheimer's disease, carpal tunnel syndrome, and "undiagnosed ailments." The "placebos" in these clinical trials were not limited to conventional pill placebos, but instead included relaxation (classified as a treatment in some of the studies and as a placebo in others); leisure reading; answering questions about hobbies, newspapers, magazines, favorite foods, and favorite sports teams; and talking about daily events, family activities, football, vacation activities, pets, hobbies, books, movies, and television shows. Not surprisingly, the most reliable finding in the Hróbjartsson and Gøtzsche (2001) meta-analysis was that there was substantial and significant heterogeneity in the outcomes produced by placebo. In other words, either some placebos were significantly more effective than others, some disorders were more amenable to placebo treatment than others, or both.

In fact, there are considerable data indicating placebo effects that are powerful and long lasting. Wampold *et al.* (2005) reanalyzed the Hróbjartsson and Gøtzsche (2001) data set and concluded that "when disorders are amenable to placebos and the design is adequate to detect the effects, the placebo effect is robust and approaches the treatment effect." Elsewhere (Kirsch, 2006), I have summarized the data indicating significant placebo effects for a variety of conditions (Parkinson's disease, rheumatoid arthritis, asthma, contact dermatitis, gastric function, pain, anxiety, and depression). In the remainder of this section, I review data on the magnitude of the placebo effect in the treatment of depression, a condition for which Hróbjartsson and Gøtzsche claimed that placebos were ineffective.

Placebo effects in the treatment of depression

In 1998, Guy Sapirstein and I published a meta-analysis aimed at assessing the placebo effect in the treatment of depression. In so doing, we were careful to distinguish between the placebo response and the placebo effect. In 1965, Seymour Fisher and colleagues drew attention to the distinction between a drug response and a drug effect (Fisher *et al.*, 1965). A drug response is the change observed following the administration of a drug. A drug effect is assessed as the difference between response to the drug and the response to a placebo. Analogously, a placebo response is the change that occurs following administration of a placebo, which

30 I. Kirsch

may include such factors as spontaneous remission, the natural history of the condition being treated, and regression toward the mean. A placebo effect is the difference in outcome that can be attributed to the provision of the placebo, which can only be assessed with reference to an untreated control group. This was the basis for Hróbjartsson and Gøtzsche's (2001) critique of Beecher's (1955) claim about the power of placebos.

The problem that Sapirstein and I had was that we were unable to find any depression trials that included both placebo pills and no-treatment controls (Kirsch & Sapirstein, 1998). So what we did was to compare the placebo response in anti-depressant trials to changes in no-treatment control groups in psychotherapy trials (Kirsch & Sapirstein, 1998). We found a pre-post effect size (Cohen's d) of 1.16 in the placebo groups and an effect size of 0.37 in the no-treatment groups. In other words, improvement on placebo was three times as great as improvement without placebo, and simple subtraction gives a d of 0.79 for this placebo effect. This is more than double the effect size reported for the antidepressant drug effect typically reported in meta-analyses (Kirsch et al., 2008; NICE, 2004; Turner et al., 2008).

More recently, my colleagues and I have replicated this finding on a substantially more extensive data base (Khan et al., 2012). Patients given placebos showed a 38 percent reduction in symptoms, compared to a 13 percent reduction in untreated patients. Patients given antidepressants drugs showed a 46 percent reduction in symptoms. Thus, the placebo effect (i.e. the placebo response vs. natural history) consisted of a 25 percent reduction in symptoms, whereas the drug effect (drug vs. placebo) was only an 8 percent reduction. The placebo effect was three times as great as the drug effect.

Future directions

The data are clear that the placebo effect can be very powerful indeed. This, however, depends on the condition being treated. Placebo effects are very strong for depression, anxiety, irritable bowel syndrome (IBS), and Parkinson's disease (Goetz et al., 2008; Kaptchuk et al., 2008; Kirsch et al., 2008; Sugarman et al., 2014), although they are nonexistent for bone density or infertility (Harrison et al., 1975; Schneider et al., 1999). The powerful effect of placebos in some clinical conditions makes it imperative to understand how it is produced.

There is much that we already know. One hypothesized causal factor in most placebo effects is response expectancy – specifically, the expectation that one will experience a particular change (Kirsch, 1985). This is supported in studies showing a strong association between rated expectancies and subsequent placebo responding (Montgomery & Kirsch, 1997; Price et al., 1999; Vase et al., 2005). Although correlations do not imply causation, a causal relation is supported by studies in which experimental manipulations that alter expectancies also alter the magnitude of the placebo response, and when expectancy change is held constant, the effect of these manipulations disappear (Kirsch et al., 2014; Montgomery & Kirsch, 1997). The procedures used to enhance placebo-related expectations and outcomes in these studies is based on classical conditioning. This raises the possibility that expectancy is an epiphenomenon rather than a causal factor. However, expectancy mediation is clearly demonstrated by findings showing that the placebo-enhancing effects of classical conditioning can be blocked by verbal information (Benedetti *et al.*, 2003; Montgomery & Kirsch, 1997; Watson *et al.*, 2006, 2007).

Another causal factor producing placebo effects is the therapeutic relationship. This was demonstrated in a study on irritable bowel syndrome (Kaptchuk *et al.*, 2008). We randomized patients to three groups: a wait-list control group, a group which received placebo treatment with a neutral, matter-of-fact clinician, and a group that received the same placebo treatment augmented by a warm, empathic, and enthusiastic clinician. Enhancing the therapeutic relationship increased the magnitude of the placebo effect significantly.

An important question that needs to be answered is the relationship between expectancy and the therapeutic relationship. Are they additive? Do they affect each other? That is, does a good therapeutic relationship enhance outcome expectations, and do positive expectations lead patients to be more likely to bond with the clinician? Finally, to what extent can a warm therapeutic relationship produce positive outcomes in the absence of positive expectations?

Clinical applications

The administration of placebos can produce clinically meaningful changes in many clinical conditions, and it generally does so without serious side effects or health risks. However, it is widely thought that placebos must be administered deceptively in order to be effective. If patients know that the pills they have been given are placebos, they won't expect to change, and therefore will not experience a therapeutic benefit. This presents an ethical dilemma. How can we harness the placebo effect without deception?

One method is to tell patients they are being given a placebo, but to do so in a manner that enhances their expectations for improvement. We tested this possibility in a second study on irritable bowel syndrome (Kaptchuk *et al.*, 2010). We told patients suffering from IBS that placebos have been shown to be effective for their condition, that their effects are induced at least in part by a well-known mechanism (that of classical conditioning), and that for that reason, the act of taking a placebo pill could work as a new mind–body treatment that could reduce IBS symptoms. We found that the patients in our study accepted this rationale, took their placebo pills as prescribed (two pills twice a day), and got better in comparison to patients in a control group that were not given the placebo pills. The effect was as large as that produced by commonly prescribed medication for IBS. Furthermore, it could not be completely accounted for by the therapeutic relationship, because time and attention were held constant across the two groups. Instead, it was produced via the self-confirming attribute of response expectancies.

A second means of enhancing therapeutic response expectancies without deception is through the use of hypnosis. Indeed, I have characterized hypnosis as a non-deceptive placebo (Kirsch, 1990). There are a number of striking similarities between hypnosis and the placebo effect. They are both based on suggestion and linked to expectancy, they both can be enhanced by expectancy-enhancing conditioning procedures (Kirsch *et al.*, 1999; Wickless & Kirsch, 1989), they affect the same clinical conditions – for example, pain and IBS (Patterson & Jensen, 2003; Wilson *et al.*, 2006), and neither require the induction of a trance to be effective (Braffman & Kirsch, 1999; Milling *et al.*, 2005). Indeed, the hypnotic induction is non-specific (Kirsch, 2001). Among the procedures used successfully to induce hypnosis are having the hypnotic subject relax or stay wide awake and alert. They may be asked to close their eyes or keep them open. Gongs can be sounded or lights flashed or pressure applied to the forehead. In short, anything that is accepted by the subject has a hypnotic induction can be used as a hypnotic induction. But although the induction is a placebo, direct suggestions for therapeutic changes can be very powerful, as shown – for example, by the successful use of suggestion as the sole anesthesia during surgical and otherwise painful dental procedures (Hammond, 2008; Kleinhauz & Eli, 1993).

References

Ajzen, I. & Fishbein, M. (1980). *Understanding Attitudes and Predicting Social Behaviour.* Englewood Cliffs, NJ: Prentice Hall.

American Psychiatric Association. (2013). *Diagnostic and Statistical Manual of Mental Disorders: DSM-5(tm)* (5th edn). Arlington, VA: American Psychiatric.

Beck, A. T. (1976). *Cognitive Therapy and the Emotional Disorders.* New York: International Universities Press.

Beecher, H. K. (1955). The powerful placebo. *The Journal of the American Medical Association, 159*, 1602–1606.

Benedetti, F., Pollo, A., Lopiano, L., Lanotte, M., Vighetti, S. & Rainero, I. (2003). Conscious expectation and unconscious conditioning in analgesic, motor, and hormonal placebo/nocebo responses. *Journal of Neuroscience, 23*, 4315–4323.

Braffman, W. & Kirsch, I. (1999). Imaginative suggestibility and hypnotizability: An empirical analysis. *Journal of Personality and Social Psychology, 77*, 578–587.

Davison, G. (1968). Systematic desensitization as a counter-conditioning process. *Journal of Abnormal Psychology, 73*, 91–99.

Fisher, S., Lipman, R. S., Uhlenhuth, E., Rickels, K. & Park, L. C. (1965). Drug effects and initial severity of symptomatology. *Psychopharmacologia, 7*, 57–60.

Goetz, C. G., Wuu, J., McDermott, M. P., Adler, C. H., Fahn, S., Freed, C. R., & Leurgans, S. (2008). Placebo response in Parkinson's disease: Comparisons among 11 trials covering medical and surgical interventions. *Movement Disorders, 5*, 690–699.

Goldstein, A. J. & Chambless, D. L. (1978). A reanalysis of agoraphobia. *Behavior Therapy, 9*, 47–59.

Hammond, D. C. (2008). Hypnosis as sole anesthesia for major surgeries: Historical & contemporary perspectives. *American Journal of Clinical Hypnosis, 51*, 101–121.

Harrison, R. F., Blades, M., De Louvois, J. & Hurley, R. (1975). Doxycycline treatment and human infertility. *The Lancet, 7907*, 605–607.

Hróbjartsson, A. & Gøtzsche, P. C. (2001). An analysis of clinical trials comparing placebo with no treatment. *New England Journal of Medicine, 344*, 1594–1602.

Kaptchuk, T. J., Friedlander, E., Kelley, J. M., Sanchez, M. N., Kokkotou, E., Singer, J. P. & Lembo, A. J. (2010). Placebos without deception: A randomized controlled trial in irritable bowel syndrome. *PLoS One*, *12*, e15591.

Kaptchuk, T. J., Kelley, J. M., Conboy, L. A., Davis, R. B., Kerr, C. E., Jacobson, E. E. & Lembo, A. J. (2008). Components of the placebo effect: A randomized controlled trial in irritable bowel syndrome. *British Medical Journal*, *336*, 998–1003.

Kenardy, J., Fried, L., Kraemer, H. C. & Taylor, C. B. (1992). Psychological precursors of panic attacks. *The British Journal of Psychiatry*, *160*, 668–673.

Khan, A., Faucett, J., Lichtenberg, P., Kirsch, I. & Brown, W. A. (2012). A systematic review of comparative efficacy of treatments and controls for depression. *PLoS One*, *7*, e41778.

Kirsch, I. (1985). Response expectancy as a determinant of experience and behavior. *American Psychologist*, *40*, 1189–1202.

Kirsch, I. (1990). *Changing Expectations: A Key to Effective Psychotherapy*. Belmont, CA: Brooks/Cole.

Kirsch, I. (2001). The altered states hypnosis. *Social Research*, *68*, 795–807.

Kirsch, I. (2006). Placebo: The role of expectancies in the generation and alleviation of illness. In P. Halligan, A. Mansel (eds), *The Power of Belief: Psychosocial Influence on Illness, Disability and Medicine* (55–67). Oxford: Oxford University Press.

Kirsch, I. & Henry, D. (1977). Extinction versus credibility in the desensitization of speech anxiety. *Journal of Consulting and Clinical Psychology*, *45*, 1052–1059.

Kirsch, I. & Sapirstein, G. (1998). Listening to Prozac but hearing placebo: A meta-analysis of antidepressant medication. *Prevention and Treatment*, *1* (Article 0002a). Retrieved from: http://psycnet.apa.org/journals/pre/1/2/2a/

Kirsch, I., Wickless, C. & Moffitt, K. H. (1999). Expectancy and suggestibility: Are the effects of environmental enhancement due to detection? *International Journal of Clinical and Experimental Hypnosis*, *47*, 40–45.

Kirsch, I., Tennen, H., Wickless, C., Saccone, A. J. & Cody, S. (1983). The role of expectancy in fear reduction. *Behavior Therapy*, *14*, 520–533.

Kirsch, I., Deacon, B. J., Huedo-Medina, T. B., Scoboria, A., Moore, T. J. & Johnson, B. T. (2008). Initial severity and antidepressant benefits: A meta-analysis of data submitted to the Food and Drug Administration. *PLoS Medicine*, *5*. Retrieved from: http://medicine. plosjournals.org/perlserv/?request=get-document&doi=10.1371/journal.pmed.0050045

Kirsch, I., Kong, J., Sadler, P., Spaeth, R., Cook, A., Kaptchuk, T. J. & Gollub, R. (2014). Expectancy and conditioning in placebo analgesia: Separate or connected processes? *Psychology of Consciousness: Theory, Research, and Practice*, *1*, 51–59.

Kleinhauz, M. & Eli, I. (1993). When pharmacologic anesthesia is precluded: The value of hypnosis as a sole anesthetic agent in dentistry. *Special Care in Dentistry*, *13*, 15–18.

Lader, M. & Mathews, A. (1968). A physiological model of phobic anxiety and desensitization. *Behaviour Research and Therapy*, *6*, 411–421.

Milling, L. S., Kirsch, I., Allen, G. J. & Reutenauer, E. L. (2005). The effects of hypnotic and nonhypnotic imaginative suggestion on pain. *Annals of Behavioral Medicine*, *29*, 116–127.

Montgomery, G. H. & Kirsch, I. (1996). Mechanisms of placebo pain reduction: An empirical investigation. *Psychological Science*, *7*, 174–176.

Montgomery, G. H. & Kirsch, I. (1997). Classical conditioning and the placebo effect. *Pain*, 72, 107–113.

NICE. (2004). Depression: Management of depression in primary and secondary care. Clinical practice guideline No. 23. Retrieved from: www.nice.org.uk/page.aspx?o=235213 (24 May 2005).

34 I. Kirsch

Patterson, D. R. & Jensen, M. P. (2003). Hypnosis and clinical pain. *Psychological Bulletin*, *129*, 495–521.

Price, D. D., Milling, L. S., Kirsch, I., Duff, A., Montgomery, G. H. & Nicholls, S. S. (1999). An analysis of factors that contribute to the magnitude of placebo analgesia in an experimental paradigm. *Pain*, *83*, 147–156.

Reiss, S. & McNally, R. J. (1985). The expectancy model of fear. In S. Reiss & R. R. Bootzin (eds), *Theoretical Issues in Behavior Therapy* (107–121). New York: Academic Press.

Reiss, S., Peterson, R. A., Gursky, D. M. & McNally, R. J. (1986). Anxiety sensitivity, anxiety frequency and the prediction of fearfulness. *Behaviour Research and Therapy*, 24, 1–8.

Rotter, J. B. (1954). *Social Learning and Clinical Psychology*. Englewood Cliffs, NJ: Prentice Hall.

Schneider, P. F., Fischer, M., Allolio, B., Felsenberg, D., Schröder, U., Semler, J. & Ittner, J. R. (1999). Alendronate increases bone density and bone strength at the distal radius in postmenopausal women. *Journal of Bone and Mineral Research*, *14*, 1387–1393.

Schoenberger, N. E., Kirsch, I. & Rosengard, C. (1991). Cognitive theories of human fear: An empirically derived integration. *Anxiety Research*, *4*, 1–13.

Southworth, S. & Kirsch, I. (1988). The role of expectancy in exposure-generated fear reduction in agoraphobia. *Behaviour Research and Therapy*, *26*, 113–120.

Sugarman, M. A., Loree, A. M., Baltes, B. B., Grekin, E. R. & Kirsch, I. (2014). The efficacy of paroxetine and placebo in treating anxiety and depression: A meta-analysis of change on the Hamilton Rating Scales. *PLoS One*, 9 (8): e106337.

Taylor, S., Koch, W. J. & McNally, R. J. (1992). How does anxiety sensitivity vary across the anxiety disorders? *Journal of Anxiety Disorders*, *6*, 249–259.

Tolman, E. C. (1932). *Purposive Behavior in Animals and Men*. Oxford: Appleton-Century.

Turner, E. H., Matthews, A. M., Linardatos, E., Tell, R. A. & Rosenthal, R. (2008). Selective publication of antidepressant trials and its influence on apparent efficacy. *New England Journal of Medicine*, *358*, 252–260.

Vase, L., Robinson, M. E., Verne, G. N. & Price, D. D. (2005). Increased placebo analgesia over time in irritable bowel syndrome (IBS) patients is associated with desire and expectation but not endogenous opioid mechanisms. *Pain*, *115*, 338–347.

Wampold, B. E., Minami, T., Tierney, S. C., Baskin, T. W. & Bhati, K. S. (2005). The placebo is powerful: Estimating placebo effects in medicine and psychotherapy from randomized clinical trials. *Journal of Clinical Psychology*, *61*, 835–854.

Watson, A., El-Deredy, W., Bentley, D. E., Vogt, B. A. & Jones, A. K. P. (2006). Categories of placebo response in the absence of site-specific expectation of analgesia. *Pain*, *126*, 115–122.

Watson, A., El-Deredy, W., Vogt, B. A. & Jones, A. K. P. (2007). Placebo analgesia is not due to compliance or habituation: EEG and behavioural evidence. *NeuroReport*, *18*, 771–775.

Watson, J. B. (1913). Psychology as the behaviorist views it. *Psychological Review*, *20*, 158–177.

Wickless, C. & Kirsch, I. (1989). Effects of verbal and experiential expectancy manipulations on hypnotic-susceptibility. *Journal of Personality and Social Psychology*, *57*, 762–768.

Wilson, S., Maddison, T., Roberts, L., Greenfield, S., Singh, S. & On Behalf of The Birmingham Ibs Research, G. (2006). Systematic review: The effectiveness of hypnotherapy in the management of irritable bowel syndrome. *Alimentary Pharmacology & Therapeutics*, *24*, 769–780.

Wolpe, J. (1958). *Psychotherapy by Reciprocal Inhibition*. Palo Alto, CA: Stanford University Press.

3

THE STORY OF MOTIVATIONAL CONCORDANCE

Michael E. Hyland

How the research started

In 1985, I published a theoretical paper on the relationship between psychological and physiological theories (Hyland, 1985) in the same year and journal that Irving Kirsch published his seminal paper on response expectancy theory (Kirsch, 1985). Because my paper dealt with the underlying assumptions on which his theory was based, Irving contacted me – emails had just been invented – and we started corresponding and eventually publishing on a theoretical principle, which we called methodological complementarity (Hyland & Kirsch, 1988; Kirsch & Hyland, 1987, 1988). In brief, the principle states that both psychological and physiological theories are needed as they are complementary descriptions. Our paths then diverged (although we kept in personal contact), and I started working as a respiratory psychologist, work that included the development of an asthma-specific quality of life scale, while Irving worked, among other things, on placebos.

One of the consequences of my work on asthma assessment was that I was invited to collaborate on a large clinical trial to investigate the efficacy of homeopathy for asthma. Because of the possibility that homeopathy was a placebo, I asked that there should be a baseline measure of belief in complementary and alternative medicine, as this could provide results consistent with response expectancy theory. The results showed that homeopathy was no different from a placebo (Lewith *et al.*, 2002b), but also that beliefs did *not* predict outcome (Lewith *et al.*, 2002a). This was my first experience with data that seemed to be inconsistent with response expectancy theory.

My research continued in respiratory medicine, but my interest in complementary and alternative medicine (CAM) had been awakened. I knew that trait absorption and spirituality predicted CAM usage. With the help of undergraduate students, I conducted a highly speculative study examining to test to what extent expectancy, spirituality, and absorption predicted outcome in a study of flower

36 M. E. Hyland

essences (a treatment related to homeopathy and for which evidence has indicated is a placebo). The results provided some surprising insights, one of which was the very strong correlation ($r = .58$) between baseline expectancy and spirituality, and somewhat weaker but still significant relationship ($r = .25$) between absorption and expectancy (Hyland *et al.*, 2006). Although all three variables predicted outcome, spirituality was the strongest predictor. This finding led me to question previous research linking expectancy with placebo outcome. It seemed to me entirely possible that the association between expectancy and outcome could be an epiphenomenon, and that expectancy correlated with the intrinsic satisfaction of the therapeutic ritual.

The most obvious explanation for the association between spirituality and outcome in the flower essence study came from motivation theory, and more specifically self-determination theory. It seemed that the results could be explained by an extension of self-determination theory in the therapeutic domain: intrinsic goal satisfaction leads to improved health outcomes.

Over the next few years I investigated the theory that long-term therapeutic benefit was the result of concordance between participants' goals and the motivational features of the therapeutic ritual. The investigations were carried out with the help of three excellent Ph.D. students – Adam Geraghty, Ben Whalley and Carolina Gaitan-Sierra – all of whom made major contributions to the research programme. Although all my Ph.D. students received governmental funding, grants submitted to research councils were unsuccessful.

The current state of knowledge

Research showed that spirituality was a better predictor of outcome from flower essence treatment compared with expectancy even when multiple expectancy measures were taken (Hyland *et al.*, 2007), but spirituality predicted outcome *only* when flower essence treatment was presented as a spiritual therapy. When flower essences were presented as a therapy working through suggestion, then the association disappeared, or was negative when other variables were taken into account (Hyland & Whalley, 2008). Further research showed the importance of perceived effort to outcome – i.e. the more effort put into a therapeutic ritual, the better the outcome (Gaitan-Sierra & Hyland, 2011, 2014a). More recent research supports the affect expectation hypothesis, that if high positive expectations are disconfirmed, then people experience poorer outcome – despite the high positive expectations (Gaitan-Sierra & Hyland, 2014b).

The various findings have been integrated into a theoretical framework that provides an alternative perspective of placebo responding (Hyland, 2011a, 2011b). Current placebo research is predicated on an assumption that this something called a 'placebo response' and that the mechanisms underlying this placebo response are the same irrespective of whether there is a short-term physiological or psychological response to the presentation of a placebo or whether there is a long-term therapeutic response to a placebo. The alternative perspective is that fundamentally different mechanisms apply in the short-term, laboratory analogue situation compared with

The story of motivational concordance **37**

'real life' therapeutic effects. The mechanism primarily relevant to the former is response expectancy, whereas the mechanism primarily relevant to the latter is motivational concordance.

Like expectancy theory, mine also starts from an assumption. The assumption is that the body is a complex, parallel distributed processing system that responds to the external environment in two ways. First, there is short-term adaptation to the presenting situation, where the presenting situation is detected through both psychologically mediated (e.g. through cognitive processing) and biological mediated (e.g. through infection) routes. The adaptation to the acute situation is then based on a program (i.e. set of rules) encoded in the parallel processing system that determines an optimal response to the situation. Short-term adaptation is already represented in existing theory, such as the acute stress response where the body makes numerous psychological, autonomic and immune adaptations to a stressor, and perception of pain as illustrated by the integration of information in the neuromatrix theory of pain (Melzack, 2001). According to my theoretical perspective, the effect of cognitions such as expectation is simply one additional input into this acute adaptive system. The effect of expectations – and response expectancy theory – should therefore not be considered a special 'placebo theory' but rather one mechanism of influence of the short-term adaptation system. Cognitions are combined with affect, and the numerous other psychological and biological inputs so as to produce an adaptation in terms of symptomatology and biology that the parallel processing system is programmed to produce.

The second form of adaptation is long term, and involves self-organisational change. Self-organisation refers to the ability of some self-regulating systems to become more effective at self-regulation – i.e. to adaptively change its program. The integrative theory suggests that the body self-organises in response to chronic inputs such that its programming is altered. This altered programming then alters the way the body responds to any ongoing input. The system has 'learned' from prior exposure and now functions differently due to the new set of rules or program that has been acquired from 'experience'. As with acute responses, long-term self-organisation is represented in existing theories, such as the epigenetic changes that take place during 'fetal programming', a concept introduced in the Barker hypothesis (Godfrey & Barker, 2001) and the epigenetic changes associated with early life trauma (Miller *et al.*, 2011). I use the term 'body programming' to refer to the more general tendency of the body to become programmed through long-term exposure to events – and to use the term 'body *re*programming' to refer to therapeutic interventions that are intended to counteract the programming that can occur, for example, from exposure to long-term stress. According to my theory, long-term placebo effects are not the result of some long-term placebo mechanism, but rather just part of the tendency for the body to self-organise – and to become reprogrammed – when exposed to therapeutic inputs.

Underlying both the short-term and long-term placebo effects is a simple message. The idea of a 'placebo response' is misguided. There are responses to inert or placebo substances, but the inertness of the substance does not convey some special property

38   M. E. Hyland

over the response. The placebo response is simply a psychologically mediated (psychological and biological) response. It just happens to be caused by an inert substance on one occasion. However, it is exactly the same mechanism or mechanisms that occur in response to other psychologically mediated information. It makes more sense to refer to psychologically mediated responses rather than placebo responses. My proposal has some similarities to that of Kirsch (2005) who suggested that it is meaningless to use the term 'placebo psychotherapy', because all psychotherapy involves placebo mechanisms. Equally, it seems to me that psychotherapy and response to inert substances are all psychologically mediated mechanisms. They all involve some kind of therapeutic ritual, and what is important is not the presence or absence of a therapist or of an inert substance, but rather the psychological mechanisms that result from that ritual.

Future directions for research

The conceptual model I have presented is best thought of as a theoretical framework for investigation rather than a fully fledged theory. It leaves much unknown. There are two principal types of question that require addressing.

The first question is: what is the kind of information that the body encodes over the long term and how is that information formed from the combination of the numerous inputs the body receives? I have suggested (Hyland, 2011a) that there is a superordinate dimension that represents safety versus threat, but there must be other subordinate dimensions. If the body becomes 'programmed' by events, as I suggest, what exactly is this programming and what dimensions does it take? I believe that there are answers that come in part from personality theory (Hyland, 2011a), but this is only part of the story. We know next to nothing about the way that consciously mediated information is combined with unconscious primes, or how biological information (such as infection) is combined with psychological mediated information. The issue of information combination is almost entirely unexplored, because empirical research has tended to focus on one type of input at a time. So, for example, there is research on the effects of long-term stress and there is research on the long-term effects of psychologically mediated inputs. But how do these different types of input combine?

My perspective leads to the recommendation of a more holistic perspective. Rather than examine particular lifestyle events in isolation, we should take into account how the body integrates and responds to the numerous inputs it receives during the lifespan. I suggest that the concept of 'the unconscious' should be replaced by the concept of 'encoded body information' – that is, information which is not directly available to consciousness but is nevertheless encoded in some yet to be discovered way – in a body that functions in the remarkable way it does because it is a distributed parallel processing system.

The second kind of question is this: what are the effects of different types of encoded information in terms of physiological and psychological consequences? It is clear that chronic adverse circumstances, such as stress, lead to increases in systemic inflammatory mediators and to dysphoric psychological states, but it would be helpful to have a more precise idea about the way particular types of body programming have pathological consequences, and to what extent those pathological consequences can be undone through body reprogramming.

Practical applications

There is a clear message from the theoretical perspective I have developed. It is that lifestyle is far more important to health outcome than is often thought, and that lifestyle has both pathology inducing and therapeutic effects – with or without the benefit of a therapist and with or without an inert substance. My guess is that if it were better able to understand the relationship between lifestyle and the body's underlying programming, then the importance of lifestyle would be more apparent. The emphasis on lifestyle is consistent with other researchers who have shown that psychologically mediated and biologically mediated stress throughout the lifespan has an adverse effect on health. It is consistent with research showing that positive psychological and biological interventions can have beneficial effects on health.

The concepts of body programming and body reprogramming have challenging practical implications. Health providers will often pay for a psychotherapist, whereas they may not pay for spa treatment or for a holiday. My perspective is that exactly the same mechanisms are involved in all three, so it is illogical to pay for one and not the other. Not only may it make sense in terms of health economics to provide holidays, but it might also make sense to provide pregnant women with free spa treatment, due to the important programming that takes place during the fetal stage, and the long-term health implications of early fetal stress. Of course, while health services are primarily disease services, this recommendation is likely to get a frosty reception!

References

Gaitan-Sierra, C. & Hyland, M. E. (2011). Non-specific mechanisms that enhance well-being in health promoting behaviors. *Health Psychology*, *30*, 793–796.

Gaitan-Sierra, C. & Hyland, M. E. (2014a). Mood enhancement in health-promoting non-aerobic exercise: The role of non-specific mechanisms. *Journal of Health Psychology*, *19*, 918–930.

Gaitan-Sierra, C. & Hyland, M. E. (2014b). Common factor mechanisms in clinical practice and their relationship with outcome. *Clinical Psychology and Psychotherapy*, *19*, 918–930.

Godfrey, K. M. & Barker, D. J. (2001). Fetal programming and adult health. *Public Health Nutrition*, *4*, 611–624.

Hyland, M. E. (1985). Do person variables exist in different ways? *American Psychologist*, 40, 1003–1010.

Hyland, M. E. (2011a). *The Origins of Health and Disease*. Cambridge: Cambridge University Press.

Hyland, M. E. (2011b). Motivation and placebos: Do different mechanisms occur in different contexts? *Philosophical Transactions B*, *366*, 1828–1837.

Hyland, M. E., Geraghty, A. D. W., Joy, O. E. T. & Turner, S. I. (2006). Spirituality predicts outcome independently of expectancy following flower essence self-treatment. *Journal of Psychosomatic Research*, *60*, 53–58.

Hyland, M. E. & Whalley, B. (2008). Motivational concordance: An important mechanism in self-help therapeutic rituals involving inert (placebo) substances. *Journal of Psychosomatic Research*, *65*, 405–413.

Hyland, M. E. Whalley, B. & Geraghty, A. W. A. (2007). Dispositional predictors of placebo responding: A motivational interpretation of flower essence and gratitude therapy. *Journal of Psychosomatic Research*, *62*, 331–340.

Hyland, M. E. & Kirsch, I. (1988). Methodological complementarity with and without reductionism. *Journal of Mind and Behavior*, *9*, 5–12.

Kirsch, I. (1985). Response expectancy as a determinant of experience and behavior. *American Psychologist*, *40*, 1189–1202.

Kirsch, I. (2005). Placebo psychotherapy: Synonym or oxymoron? *Journal of Clinical Psychology*, *61*, 791–803.

Kirsch, I. & Hyland, M. E. (1988). Complementarity, causal isomorphism and the mind–body problem. In W. Baker, L. Mos, H. Stam, H. V. Rappard (eds), *Recent Trends in Theoretical Psychology* (77–85). New York: Springer-Verlag.

Kirsch, I. & Hyland, M. E. (1987). How thoughts affect the body: A metatheoretical framework. *Journal of Mind and Behavior*, *8*, 417–434.

Lewith, G. T., Hyland, M. E. & Shaw, S. (2002a). Do attitudes and beliefs about complementary medicine affect treatment outcome? *American Journal of Public Health*, *92*, 8–10.

Lewith, G. T., Watkins, A. D., Hyland, M. E., Shaw, S., Broomfield, J., Dolan, G. & Holgate, S. T. (2002b). Use of ultramolecular potencies of allergen to treat asthmatic people allergic to house dust mite: Double blind randomised controlled clinical trial. *British Medical Journal*, *324*, 520–523.

Melzack, R. (2001). Pain and the neuromatrix in the brain. *Journal of Dental Education*, *65*, 1378–1382.

Miller, G. E., Chen, E. & Parker, K. J. (2011). Psychological stress in childhood and susceptibility to the chronic diseases of aging: Moving toward a model of behavioral and biological mechanisms. *Psychological Bulletin*, *137*, 959–997.

4

SELF-EFFICACY

James E. Maddux

Self-efficacy

Self-efficacy beliefs are people's beliefs about their ability to produce desired outcomes through their own actions. These beliefs are among the most important determinants of the behaviors people choose to engage in and how much they persevere in their efforts in the face of obstacles and challenges. Therefore, they also are among the most important determinants of psychological well-being and adjustment.

Beginnings

Although self-efficacy beliefs had been alluded to in other theories, they were not explored extensively until Albert Bandura's 1977 *Psychological Review* article, "Self-Efficacy: Toward a Unifying Theory of Behavior Change." Since that time, thousands of studies have been published on the role of self-efficacy beliefs in practically every imaginable domain and topic. (See, for example, Bandura, 1995, 1997, 2006b; Maddux & Gosselin, 2011, 2012: Maddux & Volkmann, 2010.) My own research has been concerned with both theoretical issues (e.g. the relationship between self-efficacy beliefs and other beliefs and expectancies) and attempts to self-efficacy theory to better understand a variety of problems and behaviors in both clinical psychology and health psychology.

Current state of theory and research

Defining self-efficacy

Self-efficacy beliefs are not predictions or intentions about behavior; they are concerned not with what one believes one *will* do but with what one believes one

42 J. E. Maddux

can do. Self-efficacy is not a motive, drive, or need for control. Self-efficacy is not a personality trait. Although measures of general self-efficacy have been developed and are used frequently in research, they have not been as useful as specific self-efficacy measures in predicting how people will behave under specific conditions (Bandura, 1997; Maddux & Gosselin, 2011, 2012).

Measuring self-efficacy

Measures of self-efficacy beliefs should be specific to the domain of interest (e.g. social skills, exercise, dieting, safe sex, arithmetic skills). Within a given domain, self-efficacy beliefs can be measured with varying degrees of behavioral and situational specificity, depending on what one is trying to predict. Thus, the measurement of self-efficacy should be designed to capture the multiple characteristics of the behavior of interest and the situations in which it occurs. Specifying behaviors and situations improves the power of self-efficacy measures to predict behavior (Bandura, 2006a, 2006b; Maddux & Gosselin, 2012).

Origins of self-efficacy beliefs

The early development of self-efficacy beliefs is influenced primarily by two interacting factors. The first is the development of the capacity for symbolic thought, particularly capacities for understanding cause-and-effect relationships and for self-observation and self-reflection. Second, the development of self-efficacy beliefs is influenced by the responsiveness of environments to the child's attempts at manipulation and control. Environments that are responsive to the child's actions facilitate the development of self-efficacy beliefs, whereas situations that do not respond to the child's actions hinder their development. The development of self-efficacy beliefs encourages exploration, which typically leads to actions that produce results, which in turn strengthens the self-efficacy beliefs (Maddux & Gosselin, 2012).

Self-efficacy beliefs develop throughout the lifespan as people continually integrate information from five primary sources. The most powerful influences on self-efficacy beliefs are *performance experiences*—one's own attempts to control one's environment. Successful attempts at control that one attributes to one's own efforts will strengthen self-efficacy beliefs for that behavior or domain. Self-efficacy beliefs also are influenced by *vicarious experiences*—observations of the behavior of others and the consequences of those behaviors. People use these observations to form expectancies about their own behavior and its consequences. People can also influence their self-efficacy beliefs by *imagining* themselves or others behaving effectively or ineffectively in hypothetical situations. Self-efficacy beliefs also are influenced by *verbal persuasion*—*what* others say to a person about what they believe that person can or cannot do. *Physiological and emotional states* influence self-efficacy when a person learns to associate poor performance or perceived failure with aversive physiological arousal (e.g. fear, sadness, pain) and success with pleasant feeling states (e.g. satisfaction, pride, joy) (Bandura, 1997; Maddux & Gosselin, 2012).

Self-efficacy and personality

Although self-efficacy is not a personality trait, the capacity for developing strong self-efficacy beliefs may be influenced by personality. Research on the five-factor model of personality suggests that people higher in conscientiousness, higher in extroversion, and lower in neuroticism more easily develop strong self-efficacy beliefs. People higher in conscientiousness are more likely to set more explicit and more challenging goals, and setting explicit and challenging goals is associated with goal attainment, which enhances self-efficacy beliefs. People higher in neuroticism —because they are motivated largely to avoid failure—may set goals that are poorly defined and less challenging than do people lower in neuroticism, goals that are less likely to result in stronger self-efficacy beliefs. People who are higher in neuroticism also may view their goals as more stressful and less meaningful, and feel less efficacious about attaining them. People higher in extraversion and conscientiousness also report stronger efficacy beliefs regarding their goals. People higher in conscientiousness are less likely to procrastinate, are more likely to persist in the face of challenges, and are better able to delay or suppress gratification. Individuals who are *both* high in conscientiousness and low in neuroticism tend to have clear goals and tend to persist under unfavorable conditions. Setting clear goals, persisting under challenging conditions, delaying gratification, and not procrastinating increase the probably of success and therefore the probability that self-efficacy beliefs will be enhanced (McCrae & Loeckenhoff, 2010; Maddux & Volkmann, 2010).

Applications of self-efficacy theory

Psychological health and well-being

Most theories of psychological health and well-being agree that a sense of control over one's behavior, one's environment, and one's own thoughts and feelings is essential to psychological well-being. Self-efficacy beliefs play a major role in a number of common psychological problems. Low self-efficacy expectancies are an important feature of depression in that depressed people usually believe they are less capable than other people of behaving effectively in many important areas of life. Dysfunctional anxiety and avoidance behavior can be the direct result of low self-efficacy beliefs for managing threatening situations. Self-efficacy beliefs also play a powerful role in substance abuse problems, sexual problems, and eating disorders. Common characteristics of unhappy marriages and other romantic relationships are weak self-efficacy beliefs for accomplishing shared goals and for resolving conflicts. Self-efficacy beliefs also predict successful coping with traumatic life events such as homelessness, natural disasters, terrorist attacks, and criminal assaults (Bandura, 1997; Maddux & Gosselin, 2011, 2012).

Physical health and well-being

Self-efficacy beliefs influence physical health in two ways. First, they influence the adoption of healthy behaviors, the cessation of unhealthy behaviors, and the maintenance of behavioral changes in the face of challenges and difficulties. Enhancing self-efficacy beliefs is a part of successful change and maintenance of virtually every behavior crucial to health, including exercise, eating a healthy diet, managing stress, engaging in safe sex practices, giving up smoking, overcoming alcohol abuse, complying with medical treatment and prevention regimens, and disease detection behaviors such as breast self-examinations (Bandura, 1997; Maddux & Gosselin, 2011, 2012).

Second, self-efficacy beliefs influence a number of biological processes that, in turn, influence health and disease. Self-efficacy beliefs affect the body's physiological responses to stress, including the immune system. Lack of perceived control over environmental demands can increase susceptibility to infections and hasten the progression of disease. Self-efficacy beliefs also influence the activation of catecholamines, a family of neurotransmitters (chemicals in the nervous system) important to the management of stress and perceived threat, along with endogenous (naturally occurring) painkillers referred to as endorphins (Bandura, 1997; Maddux & Gosselin, 2011, 2012).

Self-regulation

The vast majority of psychological disorders and unhealthy behaviors (e.g. smoking, poor eating habits) can be viewed as the result of the failures in self-regulation of thought, emotion, and behavior. Self-efficacy beliefs influence self-regulation in several ways. First, they influence the goals people set for themselves. A person with stronger self-efficacy beliefs in a specific achievement domain will set more ambitious goals in that domain. Second, they influence the activities people attempt in pursuit of their goals, how much effort they expend, expenditure, and how much they persevere in the face of challenge and obstacles. Third, they influence how efficiently and effectively people solve problems and make decisions. People who have confidence in their ability to solve problems and make decisions remain calm and focused, and use their cognitive resources more effectively than people who doubt their abilities. This usually leads to better solutions and decisions and greater achievements (Bandura, 1997; Maddux & Gosselin, 2012).

Psychotherapy

Different psychological interventions, or different components of an intervention, may be equally effective because they equally enhance self-efficacy for crucial behavioral and cognitive skills. The success of psychological interventions can be enhanced by arranging experiences designed to strengthen self-efficacy beliefs for specific behaviors in specific problematic and challenging situations. Getting clients to engage in successful *performance experience* is an important goal of most types of psychotherapy, especially cognitive and behavioral interventions. *Vicarious experiences* (observational learning) can be used to teach clients new skills and strengthen their self-efficacy beliefs for those skills. For example, films and videotapes that show other people overcoming their fears have been used successfully with people who have phobias. Psychotherapists sometimes use *imagined experience* to help clients strengthen self-efficacy beliefs by having clients imagine themselves engaging in feared behaviors or overcoming difficulties. For example, cognitive therapy of anxiety and fear problems often involves modifying the client's visual images of danger and anxiety, including images of coping effectively with the feared situation. Most psychological interventions rely strongly on *verbal persuasion* to enhance a client's self-efficacy and encourage the client to take small risks that may lead to small successes. Finally, because *physiological and emotional states* also can influence self-efficacy, teaching clients strategies for controlling and reducing emotional arousal (specifically anxiety) while attempting new behaviors should enhance self-efficacy beliefs and increase the likelihood of successful implementation (Bandura, 1997; Maddux & Lewis, 1995; Maddux & Gosselin, 2012).

Education

Research on self-efficacy theory has explored the contribution of students' ever-evolving perceptions of their academic abilities, confidence that they can complete specific academic tasks, predictions about academic outcomes, and interpretation of success and failure experiences (Pajares, 2006). Students with higher levels of academic self-efficacy demonstrate higher academic goal-setting, value academic achievement more, spend twice as much time studying, earn higher grades, and report greater concentration and control while completing homework, when compared to students with lower academic self-efficacy (Bassi *et al.*, 2007). Students often compare their performance to that of their peers, seek feedback and approval from teachers and caregivers, and choose models to emulate that carry academic implications; all of these processes can affect self-efficacy and academic performance (Pajares, 2005; Schunk & Meece, 2005). Classroom environments that promote learning and mastery goals over performance goals, specific feedback over general feedback, and effort over ability tend to result in higher levels of self-efficacy and perseverance (Pajares, 2005).

Career and work

Self-efficacy beliefs are important predictors of which occupations people choose to enter and how people go about making their occupational choices (Betz, 2007). In addition, higher job-related self-efficacy predicts both occupational success and occupational satisfaction. Individuals who believe they can perform the behaviors required for a particular job are more likely to believe that these job-related behaviors will lead to success and are more likely to be interested in that line of work (Betz, 2007; Maddux & Gosselin, 2011, 2012).

Future directions

Research on self-efficacy will continue to explore the role that self-efficacy beliefs play in psychological adjustment, psychological interventions for psychological

46 J. E. Maddux

problems, and facilitating behavior related to physical health and well-being and educational and occupational success. Crucial to these efforts will be continued exploration of the role that self-efficacy plays in the complex process of self-regulation, which is crucial to psychological and physical health and achievement and attainment in school and on the job. In addition, work will also continue to explore the notion of *collective efficacy*—a group's shared beliefs in its ability to collectively accomplish its goals—and the role that it plays in the success of couples, families, school, organizations, communities, and societies (Bandura, 1997; Maddux & Gosselin, 2011, 2012).

References

Bandura, A. (1977). Self-efficacy: Toward a unifying theory of behavior change. *Psychological Review, 84*, 191–215.

Bandura, A. (ed.) (1995). *Self-efficacy in Changing Societies*. New York: Cambridge University Press.

Bandura, A. (1997). *Self-Efficacy: The Exercise of Control*. New York: Freeman Press.

Bandura, A. (2006a). Guide for constructing self-efficacy scales. In F. Pajares & T. Urdan (eds), *Self-efficacy Beliefs of Adolescents* (307–337). Charlotte, NC: Information Age.

Bandura, A. (2006b). Toward a psychology of human agency. *Perspectives on Psychological Science, 1*, 164–180.

Bassi, M., Steca, P., Delle Fave, A. & Caprara, G. V. (2007). Academic self-efficacy beliefs and quality of experience in learning. *Journal of Youth and Adolescence, 36*, 301–312.

Betz, N. E. (2007). Career self-efficacy: Exemplary recent research and emerging directions. *Journal of Career Assessment, 15*, 403–422.

McCrae, R. R. & Löckenhoff, C. E. (2010). Self-regulation and the five-factor model of personality traits. In R. H. Hoyle (ed.), *The Handbook of Self-regulation and Personality* (145–168). Malden, MA: Blackwell Publishing.

Maddux, J. E. & Gosselin, J. T. (2011). Self-efficacy. In D. S. Dunn (ed.), *Oxford Bibliographies Online: Psychology*. New York: Oxford University Press. Retrieved from: www.oxford bibliographies.com/view/document/obo-9780199828340/obo-9780199828340-0088.xml?rskey=twCabi&result=105

Maddux, J. E. & Gosselin, J. T. (2012). Self-efficacy. In M. R. Leary & J. P. Tangney (eds), *Handbook of Self and Identity* (2nd edn) (401–418). New York: Guilford.

Maddux, J. E. & Lewis, J. (1995). Self-efficacy and adjustment: Basic principles and issues. In J. E. Maddux (ed.), *Self-efficacy, Adaptation, and Adjustment: Theory, Research, and Application* (37–68). New York: Plenum.

Maddux, J. E. & Volkmann, J. R. (2010). Self-efficacy and self-regulation. In R. Hoyle (ed.), *Handbook of Personality and Self-regulation* (315–321). New York: Wiley-Blackwell.

Pajares, F. (2006). Self-efficacy during adolescence: Implications for teachers and parents. In F. Pajares & T. Urdan (eds), *Self-Efficacy Beliefs of Adolescents* (339–367). Charlotte, NC: Information Age Publishing.

Pajares, F. & Schunk, D. H. (2001). Self-beliefs and school success: Self-efficacy, self-concept, and school achievement. In R. Riding & S. Rayner (eds), *Self-perception* (239–266). London: Ablex Publishing.

5

HYPNOSIS, MEMORY, AND EXPECTATIONS

Jessica Baltman and Steven Jay Lynn

Introduction

In the United States, the role of hypnotically elicited testimony in court has been vigorously debated. Although hypnotically elicited testimony was inadmissible to most courts during the first half of the twentieth century, it was admitted as evidence in many courts in the 1980s and 1990s. This shift reflected an increased acceptance of the video recorder model of memory and the belief that "repressed" memories could be "recovered" with the use of specific memory recovery techniques. Nevertheless, as research over the last thirty years has revealed, memory is reconstructive and memories elicited during hypnosis are less likely or no more likely to be accurate than recollections reported when hypnosis is not employed. Accordingly, today most states bar hypnotically elicited testimony in court. Specifically, 27 states have adopted a per se inadmissible rule, 4 have adopted a per se admissible rule, and 13 have ruled that admissibility of hypnotically elicited testimony should be determined on a case-by-case basis.

The current state of research

Participants who experience a hypnotic induction often report more recollections during recall tests than do participants who do not experience an induction. However, increases in accurate recollections reported during hypnosis are almost always accompanied by either a comparable or greater increase in the number of inaccurate recollections (Klatzky & Erdelyi, 1985). For example, Dywan and Bowers (1983) reported that participants reported twice as many accurate hypnotically elicited recollections and three times as many inaccurate hypnotically elicited recollections than non-hypnotized participants.

48 J. Baltman and S. J. Lynn

Based on a review of 36 empirical articles, Erdelyi (1994) concluded that hypnosis led to greater reporting of memories during recall for high-sense stimuli (e.g. meaningful pictures) but not low-sense stimuli (e.g. nonsense syllables). However, none of the studies reviewed controlled for response productivity, precluding a determination of whether increases in accurate recollections reflect enhanced recall accuracy versus increases in overall reporting. Moreover, most of the studies did not include non-hypnosis controls, also precluding evaluation of the effects of repeated testing. When studies control for productivity (e.g. requiring a set number of recollections), they generally report comparable or diminisished recall accuracy across hypnotic versus nonhypnotic conditions (e.g. Whitehouse *et al.*, 1988). In most studies in which no differences in recall accuracy emerge between hypnotic and nonhypnotic conditions, subjects in nonhypnotic conditions are exposed to suggestive procedures such as misleading questions (Lynn *et al.*, 2009).

A significant concern regarding hypnosis is that it inflates recall confidence. Lynn *et al.* (2009) reported that in twenty-three studies, hypnotized subjects either expressed greater confidence in recollections during or after hypnosis compared with subjects in nonhypnotic conditions, or hypnotized subjects expressed confidence in the validity of pseudomemories they had previously denied. In nine studies, hypnotic and nonhypnotic conditions were comparable in terms of recall confidence. Inflated memory confidence can be especially problematic in forensic settings in which confidence in inaccurate recollections can be misleading, as eyewitness testimony is often the most influential consideration in jury decision-making (Smith *et al.*, 2004). In a 2009 survey of the general population, 37.1 percent of respondents responded "Strongly agree" or "Mostly agree" to the statement, "In my opinion, the testimony of one confident eyewitness should be enough evidence to convict a defendant of a crime" (Simons & Chabris, 2011).

Expectations regarding hypnosis is second only to responsiveness to nonhypnotic suggestions as a determinant of hypnotic responding (Kirsch, 2000). Indeed, people may adopt a lax criterion to guess or report vague recollections as memories due to the widely held expectation that hypnosis improves memory, a belief that may also account for inflated levels of confidence in hypnotically elicited memories (Wagstaff *et al.*, 2008). Surveys confirm the pervasive expectation/belief that hypnosis improves memory. In a 2009 online survey of a sample (n=1500) demographically representative of the US population, 54 percent of respondents indicated that they "Strongly agree" or that they "Mostly agree" with the statement, "Hypnosis is useful in helping witnesses accurately recall details of crimes" (Simons & Chabris, 2011). When this survey was administered to a sample of "experts" (attendees at the 2010 annual meeting of the Psychonomic Society), not one respondent indicated any level of agreement with this statement. Yet in a 2011–2012 survey of Ph.D. level board certified psychologists ($n = 53$) (Patihis *et al.*, 2014), 11.3 percent of respondents agreed with the statement, "When someone has a memory of trauma while in hypnosis, it objectively must have occurred." Although this percentage is considerably lower than Yapko (1994) obtained (47 percent expressed greater faith in details of traumatic event when hypnotized) decades earlier based on Ph.D. level psychotherapists' survey responses, it is nevertheless alarmingly high.

Several studies have manipulated expectations regarding the effects of hypnosis on memory. Young and Cooper (1972) found that responses to a post-hypnotic suggestion for amnesia varied as a function of what participants were told about whether post-hypnotic amnesia was indicative of a genuine hypnotic response. Silva and Kirsch (1987) provided highly hypnotizable college students, who had already demonstrated the ability to experience hypnotic amnesia, with expectations that they would not be able to (a) recall a memorized list of six words during deep hypnosis, or (b) not recall the target words during the initial part of hypnosis but would be able to do so after the suggestion to enter a deeper hypnotic state. Subjects with the amnesia expectations for "deep hypnosis" recalled one word from the list, whereas subjects with positive recall expectations recalled five words, on average.

Warning participants about the effects of hypnosis on memory may mitigate the negative effects of hypnosis on recall accuracy and confidence. Burgess and Kirsch (1999) showed college students high and low in hypnotizability forty lines of images and tested their recall. Before the hypnotic induction, subjects in the positive expectancy condition were told that hypnosis improves memory accuracy, whereas subjects in the negative expectancy condition were warned that hypnosis can decrease memory accuracy and inflate confidence in inaccurate memories. Subjects in the nonhypnotic condition were not provided with information about the effects of hypnosis on memory. No differences were evident in correct recollections as a function of experimental condition or hypnotizability. Nevertheless, in the positive expectancy condition, highly hypnotizable participants reported more recall errors during the hypnosis and post-hypnosis recall tests than participants in the negative expectancy and nonhypnotic control conditions.

Future directions

One of the most exciting current and future directions of research is the study of the types of instructions and hypnotic suggestions that may improve, rather than hinder memory. Wagstaff *et al.* (2008) investigated whether the expectation that hypnosis can help discriminate accurate from inaccurate memories can vitiate the negative effects of hypnosis on memory. Participants listened to an audio recording of a conversation and later listened to a recording of a woman recounting the original conversation but with some of the details changed. Finally, participants recalled details of the first conversation. Before listening to the second audiotape, some subjects were warned that the second audiotape contained misleading information discrepant from the first conversation. They were also told that if they concentrate in their relaxed hypnotic state, they would find it easier to distinguish correct and incorrect information. Participants in the hypnotic warning group reported more correct responses and fewer errors than participants who did not receive hypnosis/warnings. Wagstaff contended that these instructions engendered the expectation that participants would be able to discriminate previously seen from new material during hypnosis, which stimulated greater effort to evaluate the accuracy of recollections prior to selecting answers.

Still, some studies suggest that the culturally based expectation that hypnosis improves memory may be so influential that warnings are not sufficient to nullify the negative effects of hypnosis on memory and recall confidence (Green *et al.*, 1998; Neuschatz *et al.*, 2003). Clearly, additional research is called for that specifies the conditions of hypnotic and nonhypnotic recall associated with increases and decreases in memory performance.

Applications and implications

The research reviewed can provide guidance to courts in determining whether to admit or bar hypnotically elicited testimony. The extant research implies that hypnosis should not be used to enhance eyewitness testimony, given the risks involved. Indeed, nonhypnotic methods, such as the cognitive interview, which use a variety of mnemonic devices to facilitate recall may not pose as significant risks (Memon *et al.*, 2010). Nevertheless, nonhypnotic suggestive procedures may degrade recall accuracy as much or more so than hypnosis (Scoboria *et al.*, 2006), raising difficult questions about whether hypnotic procedures should be singled out for exclusion in the courtroom. It is incumbent on experts who testify regarding the admissibility of hypnotically elicited testimony to present a comprehensive, balanced, and up-to-date description of the latest research findings, such as those reported by Wagstaff, to facilitate decisions regarding the admissibility of hypnotically augmented testimony.

References

Burgess, C. A. & Kirsch, I. (1999). Expectancy information as a moderator of the effects of hypnosis on memory. *Contemporary Hypnosis, 16*, 22–31.

Dywan, J. & Bowers, K. (1983). The use of hypnosis to enhance recall. *Science, 4620*, 184–185.

Erdelyi, M. H. (1994). Hypnotic hypermnesia: The empty set of hypermnesia. *International Journal of Clinical and Experimental Hypnosis, 42*, 379–390.

Green, J. P., Lynn, S. J. & Malinoski, P. (1998). Hypnotic pseudomemories, prehypnotic warnings, and the malleability of suggested memories. *Applied Cognitive Psychology, 12*, 431–444.

Kirsch, I. (2000). The response set theory of hypnosis. *American Journal of Clinical Hypnosis, 42*, 274–292.

Klatzky, R. L. & Erdelyi, M. H. (1985). The response criterion problem in tests of hypnosis and memory. *The International Journal of Clinical and Experimental Hypnosis, 33*, 246–257.

Lynn, S. J., Barnes, S. & Matthews, A. (2009). Hypnosis and memory: From Bernheim to the present. In K. Markman, W. Klein, & J. Suhr (eds). *Handbook of Imagination and Mental Simulation* (pp. 103–118). New York: Psychology Press.

Mazzoni, G., Laurence, J. & Heap, M. (2014). Hypnosis and memory: Two hundred years of adventures and still going! *Psychology of Consciousness: Theory, Research, and Practice, 2*, 153.

Memon, A., Meissner, C. A. & Fraser, J. (2010). The Cognitive Interview: A meta-analytic review and study space analysis of the past 25 years. *Psychology, Public Policy, and Law, 16*, 340.

Neuschatz, J., Lynn, S. J., Benoit, G. & Fite, R. (2003). Hypnosis and memory illusions: An investigation using the Deese/Roediger paradigm. *Imagination, Cognition and Personality*, *22*, 3–12.

Patihis, L., Ho, L. Y., Tingen, I. W., Lilienfeld, S. O. & Loftus, E. F. (2014). Are the "memory wars" over? A scientist-practitioner gap in beliefs about repressed memory. *Psychological Science*, *25*, 519–530.

Scoboria, A., Mazzoni, G. & Kirsch, I. (2006). Effects of misleading questions and hypnotic memory suggestion on memory reports: A signal-detection analysis. *International Journal of Clinical and Experimental Hypnosis*, *54*, 340–359.

Silva, C. E. & Kirsch, I. (1987). Breaching hypnotic amnesia by manipulating expectancy. *Journal of Abnormal Psychology*, 96(4), 325–329.

Simons, D. J. & Chabris, C. F. (2011). What people believe about how memory works: A representative survey of the US population. *PLoS One*, *8*, e22757.

Smith, S. M., Stinson, V. & Prosser, M. A. (2004). Do they all look alike? An exploration of decision-making strategies in cross-race facial identifications. *Canadian Journal of Behavioural Science*, *36*, 146.

Wagstaff, G. F., Cole, J., Wheatcroft, J., Anderton, A. & Madden, H. (2008). Reducing and reversing pseudomemories with hypnosis. *Contemporary Hypnosis*, *25*, 178–191.

Whitehouse, W. G., Dinges, D. F., Orne, E. C. & Orne, M. T. (1988). Hypnotic hypermnesia: Enhanced memory accessibility or report bias? *Journal of Abnormal Psychology*, *97*, 289.

Yapko, M. D. (1994). Suggestibility and repressed memories of abuse: A survey of psychotherapists' beliefs. *American Journal of Clinical Hypnosis*, *36*, 194–208.

Young, J. & Cooper, L. M. (1972). Hypnotic recall amnesia as a function of manipulated expectancy. Paper presented at the *Proceedings of the Annual Convention of the American Psychological Association*.

6

GENERALIZED EXPECTANCIES FOR NEGATIVE MOOD REGULATION

Development, assessment, and implications of a construct

Salvatore J. Catanzaro and Jack Mearns

Theoretical development and measurement

Why do some people seem to maintain their equanimity even while experiencing strong negative emotions, while others prolong negative emotional states by engaging in negative meta-appraisals and hopeless attributions? Converging theoretical and empirical lines of work have identified people's cognitions about what they can do to feel better, and suggested that the effectiveness of such actions is linked to one's confidence in them (Burns *et al.*,1987; Doerfler & Richards, 1981; Rippere, 1976, 1977). For example, Teasdale (1985) proposed that "depression about depression"– a vicious circle in which depressed mood produces thoughts about personal inadequacy and hopelessness, which further depress mood – is an important target for therapeutic intervention. Similarly, Reiss *et al.* (1986) focused on "fear of fear" as producing anxiety and panic disorders. Mayer and colleagues' work on "meta-experience" of mood grew into the concept of emotional intelligence (Mayer & Gaschke, 1988; Salovey & Mayer, 1990).

Franko *et al.* (1985) noted that even young children were aware of strategies they use when feeling unhappy, sad, or angry. Franko *et al.* conceptualized these strategies within Rotter's social learning theory (SLT; Rotter, 1954, 1982) as generalized expectancies for problem-solving. Generalized expectancies influence behavior cross-situationally. Because Rotter's SLT provides a powerful framework for conceptualizing the interplay of relatively stable individual differences with situational factors as influences on behavior and cognition, we framed negative mood regulation expectancies (NMRE) within SLT as people's beliefs about their ability to do something to make themselves feel better when they feel upset (Catanzaro & Mearns, 1990).

NMRE are response expectancies (Kirsch, 1985), beliefs about non-volitional emotional outcomes of behavior. Like the placebo effect, NMRE are self-confirming: simply expecting to be in a better mood results in improved mood, irrespective of actual attempts to change one's mood. We conceptualized strong NMRE as facilitating healthy mood regulation and protecting individuals against emotional distress in three ways: (a) by enhancing the likelihood that an individual will engage in adaptive, effortful behaviors to change negative moods; (b) by reducing the likelihood that an individual will engage in maladaptive attempts to cope; and (c) by directly repairing a negative mood. We anticipated that strong NMRE might buffer the effects of stress or mitigate the impact of other risk factors on mood and health.

Measurement of NMRE

The NMR scale (Catanzaro & Mearns, 1990) is a thirty-item self-report measure with high internal consistency and a unidimensional factor structure. Twenty-five years of research support the validity of the NMR scale as a measure of NMRE in a variety of populations across the lifespan. A youth form for use with children as young as nine years old has been developed (Laurent *et al.*, 2016). There is mounting evidence that NMRE can be measured validly in a variety of languages and across cultures (Backenstrass *et al.*, 2008; Mearns *et al.*, 2012, 2013, 2016; Pfeiffer *et al.*, 2012).

Stress, coping, NMRE, and mood

Coping with stressful events

NMRE are associated with more active and less avoidant coping responses (e.g. Brashares & Catanzaro, 1994; Catanzaro *et al.*, 2000; Mearns & Mauch, 1998). Catanzaro and Greenwood (1994) prospectively examined NMRE as a predictor of coping and symptoms at two assessments separated by six to eight weeks. NMRE were positively associated with active coping and negatively associated with avoidant responses. An intriguing finding is that active coping and depressive symptoms were uncorrelated, but they became positively related when NMRE were statistically controlled. Thus, one's confidence that one's coping attempts will be successful is an important determinant of how effective coping actually is.

Dynamics of mood states

NMRE have been associated with more effective mood repair in laboratory studies (e.g. Hemenover, 2003; Smith & Petty, 1995). For example, Hemenover *et al.* (2008) used video clips to induce negative mood, then instructed participants to engage in mood repair or a control activity. Stronger NMRE predicted better affect repair across both conditions, but the impact of NMRE was especially strong when participants recalled and wrote positive memories. Rusting and DeHart (2000) induced a negative mood, instructed participants to engage in either positive reappraisal or to focus on their negative mood, and then assessed the positivity of memories they generated. Individuals with stronger NMRE generated more mood-incongruent memories when using positive reappraisal. Those with weak NMRE were especially susceptible to the deleterious effects of focusing on a negative mood, suggesting a vicious circle in which individuals with weak NMRE experience prolonged negative moods, further weakening their NMRE. This work supports the view of mood regulation efforts as especially effective when individuals are confident in them.

Behavioral performance under stress or distress

NMRE are associated with more positive behavioral responses under stress. Catanzaro (1996) assessed NMRE among a group of college students at the beginning of a course; at the end of the term, he assessed their state anxiety immediately before an exam. With previous course performance controlled, higher anxiety was associated with poorer performance only among those who had reported weaker NMRE months earlier. In contrast, for those with strong NMRE, the more anxious they were, the better they performed on the exam.

Symptoms of emotional distress and ill health

NMRE are associated with fewer or less intense symptoms of emotional distress and physical illness (e.g. Mearns & Mauch, 1998). Further, NMRE prospectively predict symptoms of anxiety and depression (e.g. Catanzaro et al., 2000; Kassel et al., 2007). Mearns (1991) showed that stronger NMRE were associated with fewer depressive symptoms following the end of a romantic relationship. Catanzaro et al. (2014) conducted studies in two countries showing that NMRE predict depressive and anxiety symptoms independently of affective traits. NMRE, but not traits, predicted change in symptoms over time, replicating Davis et al. (2005). It is important to note that associations between NMRE and emotional distress are at least partly independent of mediation by coping responses, consistent with the response expectancy hypothesis.

Individuals with weaker NMRE show elevated levels of self-injurious behavior and associated risk factors, such as suicidal ideation and attraction to death (Orbach et al. 2007; Tresno et al., 2012, 2013). In a group of high-risk veterans diagnosed with both substance dependence and major depressive disorder, Mrnak-Meyer et al. (2011) reported that NMRE independently predicted suicide attempts requiring hospitalization during a six-month treatment period, whereas previous suicide attempts, depressive symptoms, and pre-treatment drug and alcohol use did not. In fact, Mrnak-Meyer et al. calculated that each point increase in the average response to NMR scale items was associated with a 73 percent reduction in the probability of suicidal hospitalization. This finding highlights the role of NMRE in the development of suicidal and parasuicidal behavior, and also highlights that whether clinical interventions designed to enhance mood regulation skills are successful depends in part on people's faith that new mood regulation strategies will work for them.

Weaker NMRE have been associated with attachment difficulties and poor conflict management in romantic relationships (e.g. Creasey & Ladd, 2004; Thorberg & Lyvers, 2010). NMRE mediate relations between parental attachment and stress-related outcomes (McCarthy *et al.*, 2006). Courbasson *et al.* (2012) assessed NMRE in their evaluation of the effectiveness of dialectical behavior therapy (DBT) for individuals diagnosed with both eating and substance use disorders. DBT appeared to strengthen NMRE, and increases in NMRE were associated with decreases in emotional eating and increases in expectancies for resisting substance use. Similarly, Ben-Porath *et al.* (2009) reported that diagnosis of a comorbid borderline personality disorder in eating disordered individuals was associated with especially weak NMRE. A DBT-informed treatment increased NMRE among such individuals.

Alcohol use

Researchers have been particularly interested in the role of NMRE in problematic alcohol use, given the increasing support for the stressor-vulnerability model and related approaches that emphasize coping motives in alcohol abuse (Kassel *et al.*, 2000; Lyvers *et al.*, 2010). It appears that NMRE buffer the impact of other variables that increase risk for problematic drinking. A particularly interesting set of findings was reported by Catanzaro and Laurent (2004) in a sample of high school students. Strong NMRE buffered the adverse impact of adolescents' perception of weak family support on levels of drinking to cope and self-reported drunkenness. However, the combination of strong NMRE and strong tendencies to rely on avoidant coping responses was unexpectedly associated with increased levels of drinking to cope and drunkenness. Catanzaro and Laurent argued that, among adolescents, superficially adaptive beliefs that one can regulate a negative mood in general might include maladaptive beliefs about specific options that reflect their immaturity.

Psychotherapy and NMRE

A variety of cognitively oriented treatments, such as DBT, enhance NMRE. Several studies show that strengthening NMRE mediates psychotherapeutic changes in symptoms (Backenstrass *et al.*, 2006). Cloitre and colleagues have developed and tested treatment packages for post-traumatic stress disorder that emphasize enhancement of mood regulation skills early in treatment to help clients cope with the challenges of exposure to traumatic experiences later in therapy. Their work has repeatedly documented the importance of enhancing NMRE for recovery from traumatic events, such as childhood sexual abuse or the 9/11 terrorist attack (e.g. Cloitre *et al.*, 2004, 2005; Levitt *et al.*, 2007).

Future directions in research on NMRE

Specific emotions

We intentionally conceptualized NMRE very generally to apply to a wide variety of negative emotional states. This is why the stem for NMR scale items refers broadly to being "upset." While the NMR scale measures people's cross-affective generalized expectancies, individuals may vary in their specific expectancies for regulating particular negative emotions. Therefore, for some research questions, it might prove useful to alter instructions to focus on expectancies for regulating specific emotional states, clarifying the role of NMRE as a stress buffer or risk moderator. Evidence for a stress-moderating role of NMRE is inconsistent; only a few studies report a buffering effect (e.g. Mearns & Mauch, 1998). Experimental findings regarding the effects of negative mood states on cognition and behavior suggest buffering, in that negative mood inductions have adverse effects only on those with weaker NMRE (e.g. Hemenover et al., 2008; Rusting & DeHart, 2000). Researchers may have more success documenting a stress-moderating role for NMRE with more precise conceptualization and measurement of stressors and distress.

Translations and cross-cultural research

The NMR scale has been translated into several languages: German (Backenstrass et al., 2008); Hebrew (Gilboa-Schechtman et al., 2006); Spanish (Pfeiffer et al., 2012); Indonesian (Tresno et al., 2012); Japanese (Mearns et al., 2016); Korean (Mearns et al., 2013); and Chinese (Wang et al., 2014). Associations of NMRE with variables such as coping responses, depressive symptoms, and self-injurious behavior have been consistent across diverse populations.

The German, Spanish, Hebrew, and Indonesian scales are direct translations of the thirty-item English version. In contrast, the Japanese, Chinese, and Korean scales include new items created to measure aspects of mood regulation that are more salient in Asian cultures. To advance understanding of cultural differences in NMRE, research is needed in which multilingual individuals complete the NMR scale in multiple languages (cf. Benet-Martinez, 2007).

Development of NMRE

No research has directly investigated the child-rearing practices that foster stronger NMRE, though it is clear that greater NMRE are associated with positive parental attachment and strong family support among adolescents and young adults (e.g. Creasey & Ladd, 2004). Investigation of parenting practices and childhood experiences that foster the development of NMRE will be important (cf. Tough, 2012).

Interpersonal consequences

Many studies have examined the interpersonal consequences of displays of negative mood (e.g. Joiner *et al.*, 1992), and some have examined the interpersonal consequences of specific emotion regulation strategies, with reappraisal being associated with better interpersonal functioning than suppression (e.g. Gross & John, 2003). Given the cultural value in the United States of emotional self-control, we hypothesize that Americans who profess stronger NMRE will be perceived favorably by others. We speculate that exhibiting weak NMRE will be associated with negative social evaluations, independent of actual displays of negative emotion. Cross-cultural examination of the interpersonal consequence of stronger and weaker NMRE will also be valuable.

Mindfulness meditation and other contemplative practices

Over the last decade, Western psychologists have become increasingly interested in the benefits of Eastern traditions. These traditions approach mood regulation within a broader framework of developing magnanimity in the face of difficulties, understanding adverse events as transitory, and conceptualizing awareness of experience as distinct from experience. Such practices appear to foster strong mood regulation expectancies. Jiminez, Niles, and Park (2010) reported that stronger dispositional mindfulness was associated with stronger NMRE, which in turn partially mediated the negative association between mindfulness and depressive symptoms.

Neuropsychological and physiological correlates

Recent advances in imaging technology have spurred an explosion of research illuminating the correlations between psychological phenomena and activity in the brain. For example, experienced meditators show distinctive EEG patterns (Ferrarelli *et al.*, 2013), and an eight-week program in meditation produced beneficial changes in brain activity and immune functioning (Davidson *et al.*, 2003). Given the important role of NMRE in adaptation, we anticipate that NMRE-induced inhibition of negative affect and promotion of positive affect will be accompanied by identifiable patterns of brain activity.

Applications of research on NMRE

Role in prevention programs and psychotherapeutic treatment

Changes in NMRE demonstrably mediate the effectiveness of treatment for at least two disorders: depression (Backenstrass *et al.*, 2006) and PTSD (Cloitre *et al.*, 2004). Courbasson *et al.* (2010) suggest a similar role for eating disorders with comorbid substance abuse. Given the wide range of life problems that result from impaired mood regulation, we anticipate that treatments specifically designed to enhance mood regulation skills will be developed for a variety of disorders. It is critical for treatment approaches to include methods that explicitly enhance NMRE, and to evaluate the role that changes in NMRE play in treatment effectiveness. Stress and anger management and other prevention programs should include modules to maximize the effectiveness of new mood regulation skills.

Fostering development of strong NMRE in family and school contexts

As more is learned about how strong NMRE can be fostered, practical, research-based advice for parents, teachers, and others entrusted with facilitating the healthy development of children can be devised. Given the present state of knowledge, it seems clear that simply teaching children concrete methods to "calm down" or "cheer up" is necessary, but not sufficient. It is as important to ensure that children come to believe strongly that they can regulate the upsetting emotions they might experience to help them develop into resilient adults.

References

Backenstrass, M., Pfeiffer, N., Schwarz, T., Catanzaro, S. J. & Mearns, J. (2008). Reliabilitaet und Validitaet der Deutschsprachigen Version der Generalized expectancies for negative mood regulation (NMR) scale [Reliability and validity of the German version of the Generalized expectancies for negative mood regulation (NMR) scale]. *Diagnostica, 54*, 43–51.

Backenstrass, M., Schwarz, T., Fiedler, P., Joest, K., Reck, C., Mundt, C. & Kronmueller, K. T. (2006). Negative mood regulation expectancies, self-efficacy beliefs, and locus of control orientation: Moderators or mediators of change in the treatment of depression? *Psychotherapy Research, 16*, 250–258.

Ben-Porath, D. D., Wisniewski, L. & Warren, M. (2009). Differential treatment response for eating disordered patients with and without a comorbid borderline personality diagnosis using a dialectical behavior therapy (DBT)-informed approach. *Eating Disorders, 17*, 225–241.

Benet-Martinez, V. (2007). Cross-cultural personality research: Conceptual and methodological issues. In R. W. Robins, R. C. Fraley & R. F. Krueger (eds), *Handbook of Research Methods in Personality Psychology* (170–189). New York: Guilford.

Brashares, H. J. & Catanzaro, S. J. (1994). Mood regulation expectancies, coping responses, depression, and burden among female caregivers to dementia patients. *Journal of Nervous and Mental Disease, 182*, 437–442.

Burns, D. D., Shaw, B. F. & Croker, W. (1987). Thinking styles and coping strategies of depressed women: An empirical investigation. *Behaviour Research and Therapy, 25*, 223–225.

Catanzaro, S. J. (1996). Negative mood regulation expectancies, emotional distress, and examination performance. *Personality and Social Psychology Bulletin, 22*, 1023–1029.

Catanzaro, S. J. & Greenwood, G. (1994). Expectancies for negative mood regulation, coping, and dysphoria among college students. *Journal of Counseling Psychology, 41*, 34–44.

Catanzaro, S. J. & Laurent, J. (2004). Perceived family support, negative mood regulation expectancies, coping, and adolescent alcohol use: Evidence of mediation and moderation effects. *Addictive Behaviors, 29*, 1779–1797.

Catanzaro, S. J. & Mearns, J. (1990). Measuring generalized expectancies for negative mood regulation: Initial scale development and implications. *Journal of Personality Assessment*, *54*, 546–563.

Catanzaro, S. J., Wasch, H. H., Kirsch, I. & Mearns, J. (2000). Coping-related expectancies and dispositions as prospective predictors of coping responses and symptoms. *Journal of Personality*, *68*, 757–788.

Catanzaro, S. J., Backenstrass, M., Mearns, J., Pfeiffer, N. & Brendalen, S. M. (2014). Prediction of symptoms of emotional distress by mood regulation expectancies and affective traits. *International Journal of Psychology*, *49*, 471–479.

Cloitre, M., Miranda, R., Stovall-McClough, K. C. & Han, H. (2005). Beyond PTSD: Emotion regulation and interpersonal problems as predictors of functional impairment in survivors of childhood abuse. *Behavior Therapy*, *36*, 119–124.

Cloitre, M., Stovall-McClough, K. C., Miranda, R. & Chemtob, C. M. (2004). Therapeutic alliance, negative mood regulation, and treatment outcome in child abuse-related posttraumatic stress disorder. *Journal of Consulting and Clinical Psychology*, *72*, 411–416.

Courbasson, C., Nishikawa, Y. & Dixon, L. (2012). Outcome of dialectical behaviour therapy for concurrent eating and substance use disorders. *Clinical Psychology & Psychotherapy*, *19*, 434–449.

Creasey, G. & Ladd, A. (2004). Negative mood regulation expectancies and conflict behaviors in late adolescent college student romantic relationships: The moderating role of generalized attachment representations. *Journal of Research on Adolescence*, *14*, 325–355.

Davidson, R. J., Kabat-Zinn, J., Schumacher, J., Rosenkranz, M., Muller, D. & Sheridan, J. F. (2003). Alterations in brain and immune function produced by mindfulness meditation. *Psychosomatic Medicine*, *65*, 564–570.

Davis, R. N., Andresen, E. N., Trosko, M., Massman, P. J. & Lovejoy, M. C. (2005). Negative mood regulation (NMR) expectancies: A test of incremental validity. *Personality & Individual Differences*, *39*, 263–270.

Doerfler, L. A. & Richards, C. S. (1981). Self-initiated attempts to cope with depression. *Cognitive Therapy and Research*, *5*, 367–371.

Ferrarelli, F., Smith, R., Dentico, D., Riedner, B. A., Zennig, C., Benca, R. M. & Tononi, G. (2013). Experienced mindfulness meditators exhibit higher parietal-occipital EEG gamma activity during NREM sleep. *PLoS One*, *8*, e73417.

Franko, D. L., Powers, T. A., Zuroff, D. C. & Moskowitz, D. S. (1985). Children and affect: Strategies for self-regulation and sex differences in sadness. *American Journal of Orthopsychiatry*, *55*, 210–219.

Gilboa-Schechtman, E., Avnon, L., Zubery, E. & Jeczmien, P. (2006). Emotional processing in eating disorders: Specific impairment or general distress related deficiency? *Depression and Anxiety*, *23*, 331–339.

Gross, J. J. & John, O. P. (2003). Individual differences in two emotion regulation processes: Implications for affect, relationships, and well-being. *Journal of Personality and Social Psychology*, *85*, 348–362.

Hemenover, S. H. (2003). Individual differences in rate of affect change: Studies in affective chronometry. *Journal of Personality and Social Psychology*, *85*, 121–131.

Hemenover, S. H., Augustine, A. A., Shulman, T., Tran, T. Q. & Barlett, C. P. (2008). Individual differences in negative affect repair. *Emotion*, *8*, 468–478.

Jimenez, S. S., Niles, B. L. & Park, C. L. (2010). A mindfulness model of affect regulation and depressive symptoms: Positive emotions, mood regulation expectancies, and self-acceptance as regulatory mechanisms. *Personality and Individual Differences*, *49*, 645–650.

Joiner, T. E., Jr., Alfano, M. S. & Metalsky, G. I. (1992). When depression breeds contempt: Reassurance-seeking, self-esteem, and rejection of depressed college students by their roommates. *Journal of Abnormal Psychology*, *101*, 165–173.

Kassel, J. D., Bornovalova, M. & Mehta, N. (2007). Generalized expectancies for negative mood regulation predict change in anxiety and depression among college students. *Behaviour Research and Therapy, 45*, 939–950.

Kassel, J. D., Jackson, S. I. & Unrod, M. (2000). Generalized expectancies for negative mood regulation and problem drinking among college students. *Journal of Studies on Alcohol, 61*, 332–340.

Kirsch, I. (1985). Response expectancies as a determinant of experience and behavior. *American Psychologist, 40*, 1189–1202.

Laurent, J., Roome, A., Catanzaro, S. J., Mearns, J. & Harbke, C. H. (2016). *Generalized Expectancies for Negative Mood Regulation Among Youths in Grades 4–8*. Manuscript in preparation.

Levitt, J. T., Malta, L., Martin, A., Davis, L. & Cloitre, M. (2007). The flexible application of a manualized treatment for PTSD symptoms and functional impairment related to the 9/11 World Trade Center attack. *Behaviour Research and Therapy, 45*, 1419–1433.

Lyvers, M., Thorberg, F. A., Ellul, A., Turner, J. & Bahr, M. (2010). Negative mood regulation expectancies, frontal lobe related behaviors and alcohol use. *Personality and Individual Differences, 48*, 332–337.

McCarthy, C. J., Lambert, R. G. & Moller, N. P. (2006). Preventive resources and emotion regulation expectancies as mediators between attachment and college students' stress outcomes. *International Journal of Stress Management, 13*, 1–22.

Mayer, J. D. & Gaschke, Y. N. (1988). The experience and meta-experience of mood. *Journal of Personality and Social Psychology, 55*, 102–111.

Mearns, J. (1991). Coping with a breakup: Negative mood regulation expectancies and depression following the end of a romantic relationship. *Journal of Personality and Social Psychology, 60*, 327–334.

Mearns, J. & Mauch, T. G. (1998). Negative mood regulation expectancies predict anger among police officers and buffer the effects of job stress. *Journal of Nervous and Mental Disease, 186*, 120–125.

Mearns, J., Park, J.-H. & Catanzaro, S. J. (2013). Developing a Korean language measure of generalized expectancies for negative mood regulation. *Journal of Asia Pacific Counseling, 3*, 91–99.

Mearns, J., Wang, G., Yang, X., Han, P. & Catanzaro, S. J. (2012, May). A new Chinese measure of generalized expectancies for negative mood regulation. Paper presented at the annual APS convention, Chicago.

Mearns, J., Self, E., Kono, K., Sato, T., Takashima, E., Tresno, F., Watabe, Y. & Catanzaro, S. J. (2016). Measuring generalized expectancies for negative mood regulation in Japan: The Japanese language NMR scale. *International Journal of Quantitative Research in Education, 3, 109–127*.

Mrnak-Meyer, J., Tate, S. R., Tripp, J. C., Worley, M. J., Jajodia, A. & McQuaid, J. R. (2011). Predictors of suicide-related hospitalization among U.S. veterans receiving treatment for comorbid depression and substance dependence: Who is the riskiest of the risky? *Suicide and Life-Threatening Behavior, 41*, 532–542.

Orbach, I., Blomenson, R., Mikulincer, M., Gilboa-Schechtman, E., Rogolsky, M. & Retzoni, G. (2007). Perceiving a problem-solving task as a threat and suicidal behavior in adolescents. *Journal of Social and Clinical Psychology, 26*, 1010–1034.

Pfeiffer, N., Martínez, V., Mearns, J., Catanzaro, S. J., Rojas G., Backenstrass M. & Kaemmerer, A. (2012). Preliminary reliability and validity of the Spanish generalized expectancies for negative mood regulation scale. *Revista Panamericana de Salud Pública, 31*, 129–134.

Reiss, S., Peterson, R. A., Gursky, D. M. & McNally, R. J. (1986). Anxiety sensitivity, anxiety frequency, and the prediction of fearfulness. *Behaviour Research and Therapy, 24*, 1–8.

Rippere, V. (1976). Antidepressive behaviour: A preliminary report. *Behaviour Research and Therapy*, *14*, 289–299.

Rippere, V. (1977). What's the thing to do when you're feeling depressed: A pilot study. *Behaviour Research and Therapy*, *15*, 185–191.

Rotter, J. B. (1954). *Social Learning and Clinical Psychology*. Englewood Cliffs, NJ: Prentice Hall.

Rotter, J. B. (1982). *The Development and Application of Social Learning Theory*. New York: Praeger.

Rusting, C. L. & DeHart, T. L. (2000). Retrieving positive memories to regulate negative mood: Consequences for mood-congruent memory. *Journal of Personality and Social Psychology*, *78*, 737–752.

Salovey, P. & Mayer, J. D. (1990). Emotional intelligence. *Imagination, Cognition, and Personality*, *9*, 185–211.

Smith, S. M. & Petty, R. E. (1995). Personality moderators of mood congruency effects on cognition: The role of self-esteem and negative mood regulation. *Journal of Personality and Social Psychology*, *68*, 1092–1107.

Teasdale, J. D. (1985). Psychological treatments for depression: How do they really work? *Behaviour Research and Therapy*, *23*, 157–165.

Thorberg, F. A. & Lyvers, M. (2010). Attachment in relation to affect regulation and interpersonal functioning among substance use disorder in patients. *Addiction Research & Theory*, *18*, 464–478.

Tough, P. (2012). *How Children Succeed: Grit, Curiosity, and the Hidden Power of Character*. Boston, MA: Houghton Mifflin Harcourt.

Tresno, F., Ito, Y. & Mearns, J. (2012). Self-injurious behavior and suicide attempts among college students in Indonesia. *Death Studies*, *36*, 627–639.

Tresno, F., Ito, Y. & Mearns, J. (2013). Risk factors for non-suicidal self-injury in Japanese college students: The moderating role of mood regulation expectancies. *International Journal of Psychology*, *48*, 1009–1017.

Wang, G. F., Yang, X. H. & Mearns, J. (2014). The Chinese version of the Negative Mood Regulation Scale: An examination of reliability and validity. *Chinese Mental Health Journal*, *28*, 875–880.

7

SMOKING-RELATED EXPECTANCIES

Peter S. Hendricks and Thomas H. Brandon

Genesis

Whether the product of adolescent experimentation, intermittent use at social gatherings, or ingrained addiction, smoking represents a choice. To be sure, those who use tobacco make a decision—conscious or unconscious—to light and inhale the smoke from their cigarette. The same can be said of smoking cessation; those who quit smoking choose to abstain from cigarette use. What, then, drives these choices? Logic suggests that one's decision to engage in a given behavior is determined by the consequences he or she expects from doing so, otherwise known as expectancies. For instance, those who hold chiefly positive expectancies for cigarette use (e.g. "Smoking will make me look cool and rebellious") would be more likely to smoke than those who hold primarily negative expectancies (e.g. "Smoking will make me smell bad and cause lung cancer"). Similarly, those who hold predominantly positive expectancies for smoking cessation (e.g. "If I quit smoking, my social life would improve and I would live longer") would be more likely to quit than those who hold largely negative expectancies (e.g. "If I quit smoking, I would feel short-tempered and I would gain weight"). See Brandon *et al.* (1999) for a more comprehensive description of a tobacco expectancies model.

Given the clarity of this logic, it is no surprise that the expectancy construct has enjoyed an extensive history in the addiction field. Some of the earliest models of addiction were heavily influenced by Julian Rotter's (1954) and Albert Bandura's (1977) social learning theories, both of which featured expectancies prominently. Bandura's venerable theory proposed two types of expectancies: "outcome expectancies," or beliefs that a behavior will produce positive outcomes; and "self-efficacy expectations," or beliefs that one can successfully accomplish a particular behavior. According to this theory, when both outcome expectancies and self-efficacy expectations are strong, an individual is likely to engage in the behavior.

For years, smoking research primarily focused on the role of self-efficacy in cigarette use behavior, with the alcohol field devoting comparatively more attention

Smoking-related expectancies **63**

to outcome expectancies. Prompted by this gap in the tobacco literature, the authors' collective efforts have systematically evaluated the role of smoking-related expectancies in cigarette use behavior since the early 1990s. This chapter briefly describes the results, future directions, and applications of the authors' work.

State of the art

Measurement of smoking-related expectancies

Before systematically investigating the role of smoking-related expectancies in cigarette use behavior, standardized and valid instruments were required to assess these constructs. Following the lead of alcohol researchers (e.g. Brown *et al.*, 1980), the authors developed the Smoking Consequences Questionnaire (SCQ; Brandon & Baker, 1991), the Smoking Consequences Questionnaire-Adult (SCQ-A; Copeland *et al.*, 1995), and the Smoking Abstinence Questionnaire (Hendricks *et al.*, 2011; SCQ). The original SCQ was developed to measure cigarette use expectancies among college smokers. Principal components analysis (PCA) identified four broad scales: (1) expectancies for the negative consequences associated with smoking (i.e. health risks, unpleasant physical feelings, and negative social impression); (2) expectancies for the negative reinforcement value of smoking (i.e. the ability of cigarettes to reduce negative affect); (3) expectancies for the positive reinforcement value of smoking (i.e. the ability of cigarettes to induce positive affect, provide enjoyable sensorimotor experiences, and facilitate social interaction); and (4) expectancies for the appetite/weight control properties of smoking.

The SCQ-A followed a similar developmental process but among more experienced adult smokers. PCA revealed ten scales of more homogeneous content than the SCQ. This difference followed similar findings in the alcohol field, suggesting that as substance users gain experience, they develop more specific and refined expectancies about the effects of their substance (Brown *et al.*, 1990). Both the SCQ and the SCQ-A were originally developed with separate ratings of probability and desirability of smoking consequences. Although the desirability ratings contribute additional variance (Copeland & Brandon, 2002), only the probability ratings are typically used today. Other investigators have developed versions of the SCQ in Spanish (Cepida-Benito & Ferrer, 2000), for children (Copeland *et al.*, 2007) and for adolescents (Lewis-Esquirre *et al.*, 2005), as well as brief forms for adults (Rash & Copelend, 2008) and adolescents (Myers *et al.*, 2003). The SAQ reversed the behavioral target of smoking expectancies. Instead of focusing on expectancies related to smoking behaviors, it focuses on expectancies for smoking abstinence (i.e. abstinence-related expectancies) among adult smokers. PCA revealed 10 scales: (1) expectancies for post-cessation withdrawal effects; (2) expectancies for gains in social functioning; (3) expectancies for adverse outcomes (e.g. increased use of illicit substances); (4) expectancies for the effectiveness of smoking cessation treatments (e.g. pharmacotherapy); (5) expectancies for commonly offered reasons to quit smoking (e.g. improved health outcomes); (6) expectancies about barrers to treatment (e.g., cost of medications; (7) expectancies for abstinence-specific

64 P. S. Hendricks and T. H. Brandon

social support; (8) expectancies that quitting would be uncomplicated and easy; (9) expectancies that one's experience with coffee drinking would be altered; and (10) expectancies for weight gain.

Expectancies and smoking behavior

In the construct validation of the SCQ, Brandon & Baker (1991) found that daily smokers held the most positive expectancies for cigarette use, followed by occasional smokers, triers, and never smokers. Wetter *et al.* (1994) extended these results in a study of treatment-seeking smokers and found that greater expectancies for positive outcomes predicted greater post-cessation withdrawal symptom severity, negative affect, and stress. Furthermore, weaker expectancies for negative outcomes and greater expectancies for positive outcomes predicted a greater likelihood of smoking cessation treatment failure, above and beyond a range of demographic, treatment, and smoking-related variables.

Using the SCQ-A, Copeland *et al.* (1995) found that treatment-seeking smokers reported greater expectancies for negative outcomes than non-treatment-seeking smokers and that greater expectancies for positive outcomes were associated with greater cigarette dependence and reduced odds of smoking cessation treatment success.

An alternative approach to examining the role of substance use expectancies upon behavior utilizes a laboratory manipulation. The "balanced placebo design" has a long history in the alcohol field (e.g. Marlatt *et al.*, 1973), but could not be used with smoking until the development of placebo (denicotinized) cigarettes. The design involves two crossed experimental factors: whether participants are told they are receiving active drug versus placebo; and whether they actually receive an active drug or placebo. This allows for testing the independent effects of both pharmacology (actual drug dose) and expectancy (told drug dose), as well as their interaction. Moreover, further evidence of expectancy effects are revealed if the degree of expectancy effect is moderated by a baseline measure of relevant expectancies. Juliano and Brandon (2002) performed the first balanced placebo study of smoking. They found evidence of both pharmacological and expectancy effects on anxiety reduction, and that the expectancy effect was moderated by negative reinforcement expectancy scores of the SCQ – that is, nicotine dosing instructions affected anxiety primarily among smokers who held expectancies for the negative reinforcement value of smoking. This design has since been utilized by other researchers to test the role of expectancies upon a range of smoking effects (e.g. Perkins *et al.*, 2008).

Smokers' abstinence-related expectancies have only recently become the subject of scientific inquiry. In the first study of the association between abstinence-related expectancies as measured by the SAQ and cigarette use behavior, Hendricks *et al.* (2011) reported robust correlations between the SAQ scales and cigarette dependence, motivation to quit, abstinence self-efficacy, and withdrawal symptoms. The SAQ predicted these constructs above and beyond the SCQ-A, suggesting that abstinence-related expectancies and cigarette use expectancies are distinct concepts. In a follow-up study, Hendricks and Leventhal (2013) found that greater expectancies for post-cessation withdrawal symptoms and weight gain, and weaker expectancies that quitting would be uncomplicated and easy, prospectively predicted greater overnight abstinence-induced withdrawal symptoms above and beyond cigarette dependence. Moreover, in two additional studies, abstinence-related expectancies mediated the relationship between drug involvement and motivation to quit smoking (Hendricks *et al.*, 2014) as well as the relationships of race and gender with motivation to quit smoking and abstinence self-efficacy (Hendricks *et al.*, 2014). Research further exploring the utility of abstinence-related expectancies is ongoing.

Expectancy manipulation

Although investigations have evaluated both the cross-sectional and longitudinal associations of smoking-related expectancies with cigarette use behavior, stronger causal evidence requires the experimental manipulation of expectancies. Once again, the alcohol field has led the way with "expectancy challenge" studies that attempt to disavow drinkers of their positive alcohol expectancies (e.g. that alcohol makes one more social; see Darkes & Goldman, 1993). This design is more difficult with smoking because smokers' expectancies appear to be more accurate than many of the alcohol-related expectancies (Hendricks & Brandon, 2008). Nevertheless, Copeland and Brandon (2000) used videotaped messages from current and former smokers designed to increase expectancies about the negative health effects of smoking and decrease expectancies about negative affect reduction by smoking. They found that only the latter manipulation increased smokers' motivation to quit smoking and reduced their cigarette consumption.

Ditre *et al.* (2010) focused on the use of smoking to manage acute pain. They found that contesting the expectancy that smoking relives pain produced decreased urge and longer latencies to smoke in an experimental laboratory design.

The authors also took expectancy manipulation in a different direction as a means to evaluate and enhance the effects of personally tailored smoking cessation materials. First, Webb, Simmons, and Brandon (2005) demonstrated that "placebo-tailored" self-help materials (untailored materials presented to smokers as personally tailored to their needs) yielded more favorable smoking cessation outcomes relative to standard self-help materials. Then, Webb, Hendricks, and Brandon (2007) showed that smokers' expectancies for tailored materials could be augmented prior to the intervention, further improving outcomes.

Future directions and applications

Smoking-related outcome expectancies have proven to be robust and reliably predictive constructs with respect to a range of behaviors and outcomes associated with smoking as well as other substances of abuse. In addition to the self-report

66 P. S. Hendricks and T. H. Brandon

measures described above, more implicit measures of expectancies have yielded impressive, albeit less robust, findings (see Hendricks & Brandon, 2008). Expectancies may very well represent motivational pathways toward smoking that draw upon numerous influences, including direct and vicarious smoking experience, parental influence, and exposure to media such as tobacco marketing and counter-marketing. The world is now experiencing the rapid introduction and uptake of numerous novel tobacco products and nicotine delivery systems, most notably electronic cigarettes (e-cigarettes).

The long-term consequences of e-cigarette use are as yet unknown. Nevertheless, the systematic development of expectancy measures for these new products would aid in the prediction of use onset by adolescents as well as the possible harm-reducing switch in use by current cigarette smokers. Consistent with this notion, Juliano and Brandon (2004) previously compared expectancies for cigarettes versus therapeutic nicotine replacement therapies to identify barriers to the latter's uptake. And Hendricks and Brandon (2008) delineated the differences between expectancies for smoking versus nicotine per se. Moreover, expectancy assessment could be used to evaluate the effects of both industry marketing and public health counter-marketing efforts, as well as the development of tobacco dependence interventions (Brandon et al., 2004). Such data would be of value to regulatory agencies.

Finally, there have been relatively few efforts to target smoking-related or abstinence-related expectancies via clinical interventions. There are challenges associated with this approach, but it merits more aggressive and systematic research as a component of the campaign against the worldwide tobacco epidemic.

References

Bandura, A. (1977). *Social Learning Theory*. Englewood Cliffs, NJ: Prentice Hall.

Brandon, T. H. & Baker, T. B. (1991). The smoking consequences questionnaire: The subjective expected utility of smoking in college students. *Psychological Assessment: A Journal of Consulting and Clinical Psychology, 3*, 484–491.

Brandon, T. H., Juliano, L. M. & Copeland, A. L. (1999). Expectancies for tobacco smoking. In I. Kirsch (ed.), *How Expectancies Shape Experience* (263–299). Washington, DC: American Psychological Association.

Brandon, T. H., Herzog, T. A., Irvin, J. E. & Gwaltney, C. J. (2004). Cognitive and social learning models of drug dependence: Implications for the assessment of tobacco dependence in adolescents. *Addiction, 99* (1), 51–77.

Brown, S. A., Goldman, M. S., Inn, A. & Anderson, L. R. (1980). Expectations of reinforcement from alcohol: Their domain and relation to drinking patterns. *Journal of Consulting and Clinical Psychology, 50*, 336–344.

Cepeda-Benito, A. & Ferrer, A. R. (2000). Smoking consequences questionnaire –Spanish. *Psychology of Addictive Behaviors, 14*, 219–230.

Copeland, A. L. & Brandon, T. H. (2000). Testing the causal role of expectancies in smoking motivation and behavior. *Addictive Behaviors, 25*, 451–454.

Copeland, A. L. & Brandon, T. H. (2002). Do desirability ratings moderate the validity of probability ratings on the Smoking Consequences Questionnaire-Adult (SCQ-A)? A reanalysis using regression. *Psychological Assessment, 14*, 353–359.

Copeland, A. L., Brandon, T. H. & Quinn, E. P. (1995). The Smoking Consequences Questionnaire-Adult: Measurement of smoking outcome expectancies of experienced smokers. *Psychological Assessment*, *7*, 484–494.

Copeland, A. L., Diefendorff, J. M., Kendzor, D. E., Rash, C. J., Businelle, M. S., Patterson, S. M. & Williamson, D. A. (2007). Measurement of smoking outcome expectancies in children: The Smoking Consequences Questionnaire-Child. *Psychology of Addictive Behaviors*, *21*, 469–477.

Darkes, J. & Goldman, M. S. (1993). Expectancy challenge and drinking reduction: Experimental evidence for a mediational process. *Journal of Consulting and Clinical Psychology*, *61*, 344–353.

Ditre, J. W., Heckman, B. W., Butts, E. A. & Brandon, T. H. (2010). Effects of expectancies and coping on pain-induced motivation to smoke. *Journal of Abnormal Psychology*, *119*, 524–533.

Hendricks, P. S. & Brandon, T. H. (2008). Smokers' expectancies for smoking versus nicotine. *Psychology of Addictive Behaviors*, *22*, 135–140.

Hendricks, P. S. & Leventhal A. M. (2013). Abstinence-related expectancies predict smoking withdrawal effects: Implications for possible causal mechanisms. *Psychopharmacology*, *230*, 363–373.

Hendricks, P. S., Peters, E. N., Thorne, C. B., Delucchi, K. L. & Hall, S. M. (2014). Expectancies for smoking cessation among drug-involved smokers: Implications for clinical practice. *Journal of Substance Abuse Treatment*, *46*, 320–324.

Hendricks, P. S., Wood, S. B., Baker, M. R., Delucchi, K. L. & Hall, S. M. (2011). The Smoking Abstinence Questionnaire: Measurement of smokers' abstinence-related expectancies. *Addiction*, *106*, 716–728.

Hendricks, P. S., Westmaas, J. L., Ta Park, V. M., Thorne, C. B., Wood, S. B., Baker, M. R., Lawler, M. R., Webb Hooper, M., Delucchi, K. L. & Hall, S. M. (2014). Smoking abstinence-related expectancies among American Indians, African Americans, and women: Potential mechanisms of disparities in cigarette use. *Psychology of Addictive Behaviors*, *28*, 193–205.

Juliano, L. M. & Brandon, T. H. (2002). Effects of nicotine dose, instructional set, and outcome expectancies on the subjective effects of smoking in the presence of a stressor. *Journal of Abnormal Psychology*, *111*, 88–97.

Juliano, L. M. & Brandon, T. H. (2004). Smokers' expectancies for nicotine replacement therapy versus cigarettes. *Nicotine & Tobacco Research*, *6*, 569–574.

Lewis-Esquerre, J. M., Rodrigue, J. R. & Kahler, C. W. (2005). Development and validation of an adolescent smoking consequences questionnaire. *Nicotine and Tobacco Research*, *7*, 81–90.

Marlatt, G. A., Deming, B. & Reid, J. B. (1973). Loss of control drinking in alcoholics: An experimental analogue. *Journal of Abnormal Psychology*, *81*, 233–241.

Myers M. G., McCarthy, D. M., MacPherson, L. & Brown, S. A. (2003). Constructing a short form of the Smoking Consequences Questionnaire with adolescents and young adults. *Psychological Assessment*, *15*, 163–172.

Perkins, K. A., Ciccocioppo, M., Conklin, C. A., Milanak, M. E., Grottenthaler, A. & Sayette, M. A. (2008). Mood influences on acute smoking responses are independent of nicotine intake and dose expectancy. *Journal of Abnormal Psychology*, *117*, 79–93.

Rash, C. J. & Copeland, A. L. (2008). The Brief Smoking Consequences Questionnaire-Adult (BSCQ-A): Development of a short form of the SCQ-A. *Nicotine & Tobacco Research*, *10*, 1633–1643.

Rotter, J. B. (1954). *Social Learning and Clinical Psychology*. Englewood Cliffs, NJ: Prentice Hall.

Webb, M. S., Hendricks, P. S. & Brandon, T. H. (2007). Expectancy priming of smoking cessation messages enhances the placebo effect of tailored interventions. *Health Psychology*, *26*, 598–609.

Webb, M. S., Simmons, V. N. & Brandon, T. H. (2005). Tailored interventions for motivating smoking cessation: Using placebo-tailoring to examine the influence of personalization and expectancies. *Health Psychology*, *24*, 179–188.

Wetter, D. W., Smith, S. S., Kenford, S. L. Jorenby, D. E., Fiore, M. C., Hurt, R. D., Offord, K. P. & Baker, T. B. (1994). Smoking outcome expectancies: Factor structure, predictive validity, and discriminant validity. *Journal of Abnormal Psyhology*, 103, 801–811.

8

RESPONSE EXPECTANCY AND CANCER CARE

Madalina Sucala, Julie Schnur and Guy H. Montgomery

The beginnings

Response expectancies have been defined as the anticipation of automatic, non-volitional outcomes, such as emotional or physiological responses, as a function of particular situational cues (Kirsch, 1985). According to response expectancy theory, experience is influenced by expectation; response expectancies function as self-fulfilling prophecies. For example, an individual holding expectations about becoming alert after having a caffeinated coffee will report feelings of enhanced alertness, even after drinking decaffeinated coffee (Kirsch, 1997).

Since the seminal article on response expectancies was published by Kirsch in 1985, researchers have investigated the concept of response expectancies across various domains.

Our own program of response expectancy research had the goal to advance the understanding of the role of response expectancies in placebo effects, psychosocial interventions which alter response expectancies (i.e. hypnosis), and side effects and symptoms associated with cancer treatments.

This chapter will present our program of response expectancy research, starting with the state of the art and presenting our early foundational research on the role of response expectancies in the production of placebo effects, and continuing with applied research on the role of response expectancies in patients' experiences of cancer treatment-related side effects, and in psychosocial interventions in cancer care to reduce such side effects. The chapter will conclude with a discussion of future research directions.

The current state of the art

Response expectancies and placebo effects

Placebos have been shown to produce changes in pain, anxiety, depression, alertness, tension, sexual arousal, alcohol craving and consumption, drug withdrawal symptoms, aggression, inhibition of voluntary movements, temporary amnesia, analgesia, and hallucinations (Kirsch, 1997). Although by the mid-1990s, placebo effects had been demonstrated in numerous studies across a range of treatments for a diversity of symptoms and disorders, the mechanisms underlying placebo effects were still unclear. Multiple and varied theories were proposed to explain the mechanisms underlying placebo effects. These included classical conditioning, endogenous opioid release, anxiety reduction, desire, and response expectancies.

Our group conducted a series of experimental studies, testing these hypothesized mechanisms in the context of placebo analgesia, and clarifying the role of response expectancies in the production of placebo effects. In brief, we determined that a theory claiming to explain placebo analgesic mechanisms had to be able to (at a minimum) account for: 1) localized placebo effects (e.g. placebo pain reduction in your right hand but not your left hand (Montgomery & Kirsch, 1996); 2) the influence of verbal information; and 3) the influence of past experience (e.g. classical conditioning). Response expectancy theory met all three criteria. In fact, our research revealed that response expectancies accounted for 49 percent of the variance in placebo analgesic effects (Montgomery & Kirsch, 1997). These results were confirmed in subsequent placebo studies (Price *et al.*, 1999), further supporting the role of response expectancies in placebo pain reduction.

Response expectancies in cancer care

Following these empirical studies advancing the theoretical understanding of response expectancies and their role in placebo effects in healthy populations, we began to investigate the role of response expectancies in: 1) cancer patients' experiences of treatment-related side effects; and 2) psychosocial interventions in cancer care.

Response expectancies effects in the experience of cancer treatment-related side effects

Empirical studies

Nausea. Building on previous research on placebo effects, classical conditioning, and response expectancies, our team has investigated response expectancies' role in the development and experience of anticipatory nausea (AN) in chemotherapy patients. AN had previously been considered a conditioned, learned response to chemotherapy, as during chemotherapy, patients are repeatedly exposed to pairings of chemotherapy infusions and subsequent nausea (Mustian *et al.*, 2008; Roscoe *et al.*, 2011). In one of Montgomery's first studies on this topic (Montgomery & Bovbjerg, 2001), breast cancer patients undergoing chemotherapy ($n = 60$) were asked to rate their expectations of chemotherapy-related nausea prior to the beginning of their treatment. The results indicated that pre-treatment patient expectations of AN made a unique contribution to the experience of AN prior to

Response expectancy and cancer care **71**

the third infusion ($d = 1.18$, a large effect size) in that analysis. These results were confirmed in subsequent studies (Montgomery & Bovbjerg, 1997, 2000; Montgomery et al., 1998) in which the authors replicated the findings that patient expectations make a strong contribution to the development of chemotherapy-related nausea. In other words, patients were experiencing what they expected to experience in regard to their cancer treatment, even controlling for treatment-related variables (chemotherapy regimen, number of prior infusions).

In addition to clarifying the mechanisms of AN in the chemotherapy setting, the team also investigated the relationship between response expectancies and nausea as a breast cancer surgery-related side effect. Montgomery and colleagues conducted a study (Montgomery et al., 2010; $n = 101$ patients undergoing breast cancer surgery) investigating the contribution of pre-surgery response expectancies to common post-surgery side effects such as nausea. Results indicated that response expectancies uniquely contributed to nausea one week after surgery ($d = 0.65$, a medium effect size). Response expectancies also mediated the effects of age on nausea.

Fatigue. Our research has also contributed to the understanding of response expectancies' role in the experience of fatigue as a cancer treatment side effect. To test the contribution of expectancies to common post-surgery fatigue, the team conducted a study (Montgomery & Bovbjerg, 2004) of 63 patients undergoing breast cancer surgery. Results indicated that specific response expectancies about feeling fatigued contributed to patients' experience of post-surgery fatigue ($d = 0.95$, a large side effect), along with pre-surgery emotional distress. The results were confirmed in a larger ($n = 101$) subsequent study (Montgomery et al., 2010), indicating that the experience of cancer treatment-related fatigue is also affected by patients' expectancies.

Pain. Our team also investigated the relationship between response expectancies and pain as a side effect of cancer treatments. Our studies on breast cancer patients undergoing surgery demonstrated that pre-surgery expectancies have a significant contribution to the experience of post-surgery pain intensity ($d = 1.21$, a large effect size; Montgomery & Bovbjerg, 2004), pain severity ($d = 1.07$, a large effect size; Montgomery et al., 2010), and pain unpleasantness ($d = .89$, a large effect size) (Montgomery & Bovbjerg, 2004). These results provide strong evidence for the role of pre-surgery pain expectancies in predicting different dimensions of postsurgical pain experiences.

Emotional distress. Our team also investigated the role of response expectancies in emotional well-being and distress during cancer treatment, specifically radiotherapy. In a study of 104 patients scheduled for radiotherapy (Sohl et al., 2012), the team assessed patients' response expectancies through visual analog scales asking how emotionally upset, depressed, stressed, or relaxed they expected to be while undergoing radiotherapy. The results indicated that specific response expectancies for how emotional upset, depressed mood, stress, and relaxation predicted emotional well-being and distress during radiotherapy, even when controlling for pessimism (all ps <.05).

In sum, the results of the team's empirical studies support the view that response expectancies play a significant role in the experience of nausea, fatigue, pain, and emotional distress in cancer patients.

Meta-analytic studies

In addition to the empirical studies investigating patients' experiences of side effects and symptoms associated with cancer treatments, Montgomery and his collaborators conducted a meta-analysis (Sohl et al., 2009), aiming to clarify the overall magnitude of the relationship between response expectancies and the side effects of cancer treatment.

The meta-analysis included 14 studies and 1,445 total participants. Most of the studies ($k = 12$) included cancer patients undergoing chemotherapy, whereas two studies focused on surgical cancer patients. There was a significant medium overall effect size for the relationship between response expectancies and side effect outcomes, $r = 0.36$, 95 percent confidence interval (CI) 0.26, 0.45, $Z = 6.58$, $P < 0.001$. Fail-safe analyses indicated that it would take 120 studies reporting null results (no effects of response expectancies) to reduce the reported effect size of $r = 0.36$ to $r = 0.05$. The meta-analyses established that there is a significant, positive, medium-sized effect of response expectancies on the experience of cancer treatment-related side effects.

To summarize, Montgomery and his team's empirical and meta-analytic studies support the position that response expectancies lead to a number of cancer treatments-related side effects including nausea, fatigue, pain, and emotional distress, controlling for treatment-related factors.

Hypnosis to manage the side effects of cancer treatments: the role of response expectancies

Once the team's research had indicated that response expectancies predict a variety of cancer treatment-related side effects, they then investigated an intervention known to alter responses expectancies with the hope of improving patients' quality of life – hypnosis (Montgomery et al., 2002, 2007, 2013, 2014; Schnur et al., 2008, 2009). Their work demonstrated that hypnosis is an effective intervention for decreasing nausea, fatigue, pain, and emotional distress during breast cancer treatments. The mediational role of response expectancies was also investigated.

The team conducted a preliminary study (Montgomery et al., 2002; $n = 20$ breast cancer surgical patients) in which they examined response expectancies as a mediator of hypnotic effects in a breast cancer surgical setting. In this small study, response expectancies were found to mediate the effects of hypnosis on postsurgical pain. However, due to the small sample size, the results needed to be replicated. A larger study ($n = 200$; Montgomery *et al.*, 2010) confirmed the positive clinical effects of hypnosis (e.g. hypnosis reduced postsurgical side effects relative to an attention control condition), and also tested the hypothesis that response expectancies mediated the effects of hypnosis on postsurgical side effects (e.g. pain, fatigue) in women undergoing breast conserving surgery. Structural equation modeling revealed that hypnotic effects on postsurgical pain were partially mediated by pain expectancy and that hypnotic effects on postsurgical fatigue were partially mediated by fatigue expectancy.

The applications of research results

Response expectancies have been shown to impact patients' experience of cancer treatment-related side effects (e.g. nausea, fatigue, pain, emotional distress) and interventions which alter response expectancies have also been shown to be effective for managing such treatment-related side effects. This literature suggests that applying interventions which can effectively change patients' response expectancies might greatly benefit patients undergoing cancer treatments. Hypnosis is one such intervention proven to change response expectancies and, in turn, to help cancer patients manage their treatment side effects. Our research results indicate that using hypnosis is an effective intervention for changing breast cancer patients' response expectancies and, in turn, decreasing nausea, fatigue, pain, and emotional distress during their cancer treatments.

Future directions of research

Our foundational and applied research results add to the understanding of the underlying mechanisms responsible for hypnotic phenomena in the surgical setting, and suggest that future hypnotic interventions target patient expectancies to improve postsurgical recovery. The results also suggest that it would be beneficial to continue to develop, test and employ interventions, such as hypnosis, that change patients' expectancies of cancer treatments side-effects, which in turn could reduce their symptoms and improve their quality of life.

References

Kirsch, I. (1985). Response expectancy as a determinant of experience and behavior. *American Psychologist, 40*, 1189–1202.

Kirsch, I. (1997). Response expectancy theory and application: A decennial review. *Applied & Preventive Psychology, 6*, 69–79.

Montgomery, G. & Kirsch, I. (1996). Mechanisms of placebo pain reduction: An empirical investigation. *Psychological Science, 7*, 174–176.

Montgomery, G. H. & Bovbjerg, D. H. (1997). The development of anticipatory nausea in patients receiving adjuvant chemotherapy for breast cancer. *Physiology and Behavior, 61*, 737–741.

Montgomery, G. H. & Bovbjerg, D. H. (2000). Pre-infusion expectations predict post-treatment nausea during repeated adjuvant chemotherapy infusions for breast cancer. *British Journal of Health Psychology*, *5*, 105–119.

Montgomery, G. H. & Bovbjerg, D. H. (2001). Specific response expectancies predict anticipatory nausea during chemotherapy for breast cancer. *Journal of Consulting and Clinical Psychology*, *69*, 831–835.

Montgomery, G. H. & Bovbjerg, D. H. (2004). Presurgery distress and specific response expectancies predict postsurgery outcomes in surgery patients confronting breast cancer. *Health Psychology*, *23*, 381–387.

Montgomery, G. H. & Kirsch, I. (1997). Classical conditioning and the placebo effect. *Pain*, *72*, 107–113.

Montgomery, G. H., Schnur, J. B. & Kravits, K. (2013). Hypnosis for cancer care: over 200 years young. *CA: A Cancer Journal for Clinicians*, *63*, 31–44.

Montgomery, G. H., Weltz, C. R., Seltz, G. & Bovbjerg, D. H. (2002). Brief pre-surgery hypnosis reduces distress and pain in excisional breast biopsy patients. *International Journal of Clinical and Experimental Hypnosis*, *50*, 17–32.

Montgomery, G. H., David, D., Winkel, G., Silverstein, J. H. & Bovbjerg, D. H. (2002). The effectiveness of adjunctive hypnosis with surgical patients: A meta-analysis. *Anesthesia and Analgesia*, *94*, 1639–1645.

Montgomery, G. H., Schnur, J. B., Erblich, J., Diefenbach, M. A. & Bovbjerg, D. H. (2010). Presurgery psychological factors predict pain, nausea, and fatigue one week after breast cancer surgery. *Journal of Pain and Symptom Management*, *39*, 1043–1052.

Montgomery, G. H., Hallquist, M. N., Schnur, J. B., David, D., Silverstein, J. H. & Bovbjerg, D. H. (2010). Mediators of a brief hypnosis intervention to control side effects in breast surgery patients: Response expectancies and emotional distress. *Journal of Consulting and Clinical Psychology*, *78*, 80–88.

Montgomery, G. H., Bovbjerg, D. H., Schnur, J. B., David, D., Goldfarb, A., Weltz, C. R., & Silverstein, J. H. (2007). A randomized clinical trial of a brief hypnosis intervention to control side effects in breast surgery patients. *Journal of the National Cancer Institute*, *99*, 1304–1312.

Montgomery, G. H., David, D., Kangas, M., Green, S., Sucala, M., Bovbjerg, D. H., & Schnur, J. B. (2014). Randomized controlled trial of a cognitive-behavioral therapy plus hypnosis intervention to control fatigue in patients undergoing radiotherapy for breast cancer. *Journal of Clinical Oncology*, *32*, 557–563.

Mustian, K. M., Darling, T. V., Janelsins, M. C., Jean-Pierre, P., Roscoe, J. A. & Morrow, G. R. (2008). Chemotherapy-induced nausea and vomiting. *US Oncology*, *4*, 19–23.

Price, D. D., Milling, L. S., Kirsch, I., Duff, A., Montgomery, G. H. & Nicholls, S. S. (1999). An analysis of factors that contribute to the magnitude of placebo analgesia in an experimental paradigm. *Pain*, *83*, 147–156.

Roscoe, J. A., Morrow, G. R., Aapro, M. S., Molassiotis, A. & Olver, I. (2011). Anticipatory nausea and vomiting. *Support Care Cancer*, *19*, 1533–1538.

Schnur, J. B., Bovbjerg, D. H., David, D., Tatrow, K., Goldfarb, A. B., Silverstein, J. H., . . . Montgomery, G. H. (2008). Hypnosis decreases presurgical distress in excisional breast biopsy patients. *Anesthesia and Analgesia*, *106*, 440–444.

Schnur, J. B., David, D., Kangas, M., Green, S., Bovbjerg, D. H. & Montgomery, G. H. (2009). A randomized trial of a cognitive-behavioral therapy and hypnosis intervention on positive and negative affect during breast cancer radiotherapy. *Journal of Clinical Psychology*, *65*, 443–455.

Sohl, S. J., Schnur, J. B. & Montgomery, G. H. (2009). A meta-analysis of the relationship between response expectancies and cancer treatment-related side effects. *Journal of Pain and Symptom Management*, *38*, 775–784.

Sohl, S. J., Schnur, J. B., Sucala, M., David, D., Winkel, G. & Montgomery, G. H. (2012). Distress and emotional well-being in breast cancer patients prior to radiotherapy: An expectancy-based model. *Psychology and Health*, *27*, 347–361.

9

HOW EXPECTANCIES SHAPE PLACEBO EFFECTS

Zev M. Medoff and Luana Colloca

Introduction

Placebos and placebo effects have been a controversial topic in the medical arena for over two hundred years. In a typical clinical trial, placebos are used as controls to correct for biases and confounding factors. Alone, however, the placebo effect is studied by researching the different components and factors that affect its magnitude. As placebo studies have increased, so has the scientific evidence that the placebo effect represents a complex psychoneurobiological interaction involving previous experience and verbal suggestions that influence pain perception and other symptoms (Benedetti *et al.*, 2005; Colloca & Benedetti, 2005; Colloca *et al.*, 2013; Colloca *et al.*, 2013).

In order to benefit the most from a medicinal treatment, a patient's expectation of the efficacy of their pain management treatment can be as important as his/her actual medicinal pain treatment (Klinger *et al.*, 2014). Through conditioning administering treatment, a placebo given shortly after medicinal painkillers becomes effective, a patient will benefit from future administration of the placebo in the absence of medicine. This benefit comes directly from psychological expectations and physiological changes in the body. Past studies have shown that successful placebos can cause pharmacological release in humans after being repetitively paired with similar-acting pharmacological treatments (Doering & Rief, 2012). Placebos alone have no intrinsic pharmacological properties, so they only trigger release of some neuropeptides due to patients' expectations. Irving Kirsch, author of a theory of expectancy, posited that placebo effects occur solely because a patient expects one. According to this view, Kirsch labeled the beliefs that appear to mediate the placebo effects "response expectancies," defining them as "anticipation of the occurrence of non-volitional responses." Response expectancies can be distinguished from "stimulus expectancies," which "are the anticipation of the occurrence of external consequences" as well as from "anticipation of voluntary response" which have been labeled "intention" (Kirsch, 1985; Kirsch *et al.*, 1999). Reasoning in this way, it is evident that response expectancies would be open to a wide range of variables such as the influence of the therapeutic relationship, sociocultural factors, assumed meaning, modeling, persuasion, etc.

Placebo effects can be due to conscious expectations of pain sensation, which can stem from personal experiences that are recalled through verbal suggestions (Colloca & Miller, 2011b). Expectations occur when experiences are internalized within a person's mind so that when a similar situation presents itself in the future, the individual will recollect the sensation felt in the past and (unconsciously, subconsciously or consciously) attempt to recreate it. As such, verbal instructions that anticipate a benefit will create expectations of analgesia. When previous pain perception is consciously accessible, verbal instructions are a crucial modulator of placebo effects. However, there are also modifications in the body that are not consciously accessible. For example, endocrine placebo responses are not affected by verbal instructions. A strong verbal suggestion that cortisol will change by means of a specific treatment does not produce any effect. As such, an unconscious experience cannot be recreated consciously as Colloca and Miller outlined in their paper entitled "How placebo responses are formed" (Colloca & Miller, 2011a).

A patient can have either conscious, subconscious or unconscious expectancies on pain treatment effectiveness, though these can be difficult to separate in humans. If expectation-induced placebo effects can occur without the patient being fully aware, it is reasonable to assume that these expectations are not totally conscious. However, generally the higher the phylogenetic level, the larger the role of conscious cognition in forming expectations (Colloca & Miller, 2011a, 2011b). As such, it is likely that both types of expectancies overlap and can be built up through learning processes (i.e. verbal instructions, conditioning, and social observation; Colloca & Benedetti, 2009).

Colloca and Miller presented an integrative model that is based on the evidence that verbal instructions, conditioning, and observational learning contribute to create expectations that in turn shape placebo effects (Colloca & Miller, 2011a). If a patient is verbally told that she will experience pain reduction, she will recall a previous experience of analgesia and will experience similar pain relief. Accompanying treatments, such as a cream or a pill, or a specific color, are often paired with verbal suggestions during conditioning trials in which research participants are taught to associate the treatment/color with analgesia. After such trials, verbal suggestions become unnecessary and placebo analgesia can be obtained through the cream or pill alone for a limited time. Conditioned placebo effects cause more enduring analgesic effects compared with verbal suggestions alone.

Humans take advantage of social learning when deciding how to react in different circumstances. As demonstrated in the paragraphs below, observing another person exhibiting either analgesia or hyperalgesia positively correlates with how the participant feels pain in experimental settings. As such, learning and associated mechanisms are key potentil mediators of expectations and placebo responses. Learning processes guide the changes of behaviors and expectations that lead to the formation of placebo effects.

Current state of the art on interpersonal expectancies

Patients who observe pain reduction in other people are more likely to exhibit analgesia themselves (Colloca & Benedetti, 2009; Hunter et al., 2014). Humans naturally learn habits and reactions from others. Past research conducted by Colloca and Benedetti first showed that analgesic effects could be elicited by observing the experience of a demonstrator who was carefully trained to simulate the analgesic experience (Colloca & Benedetti, 2009). In their experiment, two electrodes were attached to the back of the subject's non-dominant hand and a sham electrode was pasted above the subject's middle finger while a set of painful and non-painful stimuli were delivered via electric shock. The demonstrator verbally rated the painful stimuli that were paired to a red light and the non-painful stimuli paired to a green light as depicted in Figure 1 A. The experimental subject was in close proximity to the demonstrator and observed the delivery and subsequent rating of the painful and non-painful stimuli. At the end of this observational phase, the observing subject was asked to undergo a similar procedure. However, the shock intensities were set at the painful level for both the green-paired stimuli and the

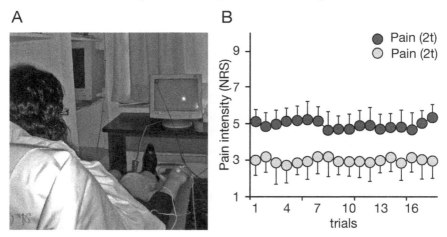

FIGURE 9.1 Socially induced placebo effects. The observer was tested for placebo analgesic effects after having watched a male demonstrator who reported high pain in association with a red cue and hypoalgesia in association with a green cue. However, the testing participant received both red- and green-associated stimulations at the same (high) level of pain (A). Observing pain relief in the demonstrator elicited analgesia as indicated by the difference between red- and green- pain reports shown in the graph during testing phase (B). This effect can be interpreted as a byproduct of expectancies created by the observation and elicited by the green cues that in turn may have led to placebo-induced analgesia.

Adapted from Colloca & Benedetti, 2009.

red-paired stimuli. The testing phase differed from the demonstrator experiment where the shocks associated with the green light were less painful than the shocks associated with the red light.

Results showed that all the green painful stimuli in this experiment were deemed less painful compared to the red stimuli, even though they were all at the same intensity. This suggests that those patients observing a beneficial treatment in another person elicits placebo effects. The observed effects were stable over the entire experimental session, showing no extinction and indicating retention of the acquired behavior (Figure 1B). The magnitude of observationally induced placebo analgesic responses was comparable to those induced by actual experience of analgesia with a conditioning schedule. Observing the demonstrator created a possible outcome in the mind of the subject which drove their expectation of analgesia and dulled their pain perception to high-level shock intensities. The strength of the above placebo effects that resulted from observations correlated with the subjects' personal capacity for empathy. This suggests that patients who have a greater capacity to empathize would benefit most from social observation (Colloca & Benedetti, 2009). Further research has explored components such as live interaction with another person compared to observing a video of someone exhibiting analgesic effects (Hunter et al., 2014). Subjects were randomly selected to watch either a video of a person acting with pain relief or the same live demonstrator exhibiting an analgesic benefit following the presentation of a green light. Afterwards, the subjects received the same set of painful stimuli after the brief presentation of either a red or green light. The live face-to-face observation versus a video replay induced similar placebo analgesic effects in terms of strength, showing that observation activates specific placebo mechanisms independent of social interaction. However, empathy strongly correlated with placebo analgesic responses in the live observation group only, but not in the video replay group (Hunter et al., 2014).

These results suggest that direct in-person observation induces placebo analgesia and that empathy may facilitate these effects when live interactions are involved, but without being the main driving factor. Two recent studies confirming and extending the findings on vicarious learning have been adopted during the observational phase, either a video reply (Vogtle et al., 2013) or live demonstrators (Swider & Babel, 2013). Changes in pain levels due to observation were correlated with the empathy scores only when live demonstrators were involved in the experimental settings, confirming that empathy predicts these effects when interpersonal interactions are involved.

It is worth noting that the effect of observation and modeling applies to the nocebo effect as well, where negative expectations can increase a subject's perceived pain experience.

Vogtle et al. have studied young women, assigning them to a control group, a verbal suggestion group, and an observational learning group (Vogtle et al., 2013). The control group received information that a cream would have no effect on their pain perception. The verbal suggestion group received information that the cream would increase pain sensitivity. The observational learning group was asked to watch a video in which a demonstrator exhibited nocebo effects when cream was applied (Vogtle *et al.*, 2013). All subjects were then exposed to three pressure painful stimuli on their hands. One side was tested before the observational learning and served as control. Pain reports in the control and verbal suggestion groups were at the same level with and without the innocuous cream. However, subjects in the observational group reported higher pain after watching the demonstrator and these responses were higher than in the control group with and without ointment (Vogtle *et al.*, 2013). The nocebo responses induced by observational learning correlated with pain catastrophizing scores, indicating the importance of studying the mechanisms underlying observational learning, psychological traits and nocebo hyperalgesia (Vogtle *et al.*, 2013).

Sex has also been shown to influence the magnitude of nocebo effects induced by observational learning. Subjects (men and women) here were assigned to observational experimental groups in which either a man or a woman was respectively observed. Subjects rated red-light associated stimuli at a higher pain level than control groups who rated pain stimuli who did not observe a demonstrator receive the painful stimuli. Interestingly enough, regardless of the sex of the subject, the nocebo effect was greater after a male demonstrator was observed (Swider & Babel, 2013).

Mechanisms of social learning and expectations: future research directions

One may argue that self-reported ratings of pain levels could create biases generated by the subjects' wishes to please the researcher or fit in a supposed normal range (Hróbjartsson & Gøtzsche, 2001, 2010). However, the experiments described above included control groups that received the same instruction about what to expect, and there were no placebo or nocebo changes in their pain perception, demonstrating that biases are unlikely to account for the difference in the placebo and nocebo effects found in the observational learning groups. Observation of the demonstrator's benefit may have acted as an unconditioned stimulus, indicating possible commonalities between observational learning and classical conditioning. Although future research is needed to understand the neurobiological mechanisms of placebo effects driven by interpersonal expectations and vicarious learning, there have been attempts to analyze observational learning within an associative learning framework for aversive and fear models. Observational aversive learning in rats shows no evidence of blocking, latent inhibition, or overshadowing; three prime characteristics of classical conditioning (Galef & Durlach, 1993). By contrast, studies in humans have found that observational aversive learning is characterized by the aforementioned symptoms of classical conditioning (Lanzetta & Orr, 1980). We can speculate that humans alter and adapt behavior which separates them from the limited stimulus-responses of animals. It is pivotal performing future behavioral and brain-imaging studies to illustrate the mechanisms underlying observationally induced placebo and nocebo phenomena.

Another area of research that deserves further research is represented by the role of expectancies, social learning placebo, and nocebo effects across individuals.

A recent study has demonstrated the far-reaching power of placebo and nocebo effects. Observation has been shown to trigger nocebo effects on mass psychogenic illness (Mazzoni *et al.*, 2010). Healthy subjects were invited to self-administer an intranasal product containing a suspected environmental toxin, which can cause headache, nausea, itchy skin, and drowsiness. Half of the subjects observed an actor who inhaled the product and feigned the four symptoms outlined above. Those who had observed the actor displaying signs of psychogenic illness reported a significant increase of the aforementioned symptoms, suggesting that observational learning is likely involved in mass psychogenic illnesses (Mazzoni *et al.*, 2010).

On a side note, empathic stress responses modulate the hypothalamic–pituitary–adrenal axis activity. Such a modulation is shaped by the familiarity between observer and target, and whether the observation is direct or via video. The observer's exposure to a psychosocial stressor induced physiologically significant cortisol increases. This effect was larger in intimate observer-target dyads (40 percent) and during the real-life representation of the stressor (30 percent; Engert *et al.*, 2014).

A recent study has further demonstrated the effects of interpersonal expectations. Informing a single participant about the possibility to develop hypobaric hypoxia headache in a high-altitude setting produced a propagation of negative information and expectations among several research participants. Under the effect of a sort of "social contagion," those who learnt from a single participant about the possibility of experiencing high-altitude-induced headache actually had headache. The social propagation had an effect not merely at the level of subjective symptoms (e.g. reported headache), but was associated with an increase in cyclooxygenase activity and prostaglandins synthesis (Benedetti *et al.* 2014).

Interpersonal expectancies and implications for patient–clinician interactions

The clinical applications of the placebo effect can be seen in everyday patient–physician relationships. Although interactions between a physician and his/her patient may seem ancillary to the patient's treatment recovery, a recent study has shown that patient–physician interactions are significantly interwoven when it comes to the placebo effect (Jensen *et al.*, 2014). In this study, the physicians were given painful stimuli in order to experience a subsequent placebo and trust its efficacy. The physician then interacted with the patient (an actress) during a routine clinical examination, and sat in on their subsequent painful stimuli treatment with the placebo. Functional magnetic resonance image scans were completed in each of the above three steps. The fMRI scans show that physicians activated brain regions previously implicated in expectancy for pain relief and increased attention during treatment of patients, including the right ventrolateral and dorsolateral prefrontal cortices (Jensen *et al.*, 2014). The physician's ability to empathize with the patient correlated with increased brain activations in the rostral anterior cingulate cortex.

In a similar study, health professionals treating patients with motor disorders were studied and their brain area activations were observed (Fiorio *et al.*, 2010).

Patients with movement disorders typically display hyperkinetic action patterns characterized by an overflow of muscle co-contractions. To investigate whether medical knowledge about atypical movement kinematics affects the viewer's motor system, transcranial magnetic stimulation was applied to clinicians and to naive subjects. The clinicians observed handwriting actions performed by the subjects with two different kinematics: fluent and non-fluent (Fiorio *et al.*, 2010). Non-fluent writing was easily recognized by the clinicians as a typical expression of writer's cramp, whereas it was unknown to the naive subjects. Results showed that clinicians had similar corticospinal activation during observation of dystonic and healthy writings, but subjects were hyper-activated during observation of dystonic movements only. Hyper-activation was selective for the muscles directly involved in the dystonic co-contractions and inversely correlated with subjective movement fluency scores, hinting at a fine-tuned association between the breakdown of observed movement fluency and corticospinal activation (Fiorio *et al.*, 2010). These results indicate that, depending on medical knowledge, observation of unusual pathological actions modulates the viewer's motor system.

By concluding, there are many factors that come together to create the whole placebo effect. Placebo effects can be especially effective, and the relationship and interactions between clinicians and patients contribute significantly to their overall impact. Understanding the neural processes of clinician brain responses is important for the improvement of treatments by exploiting socially induced placebo effects. Understanding the patient's state, close monitoring and feedback of the patient's expectancies, and the physician's own expectations of relief may be a way of promoting successful treatment interactions (Benedetti, 2013). Previous studies have shown that physicians' expectancies can indeed affect patient treatment response and clinical outcomes (Gracely *et al.*, 1985). Additional research is needed to confirm whether physician activations of expectancy brain regions are related to the resulting clinical outcomes involving their patients, but there is great promise for the continued use of the placebo neuropsychosocial mechanisms in limiting pain and improving patient recovery.

Acknowledgement

This research is supported by the National Institute of Dental and Craniofacial Research (1R01DE025946-01, LC).

References

Benedetti, F. (2013). Placebo and the new physiology of the doctor–patient relationship. *Physiological Reviews, 93*, 1207–1246.

Benedetti, F., Durando, J. & Vighetti, S.(2014) Nocebo and placebo modulation of hypobaric hypoxia headache involves the cyclooxygenase-prostaglandins pathway: Pain. *155*(5): 921–928 (May).

Benedetti, F., Mayberg, H. S., Wager, T. D., Stohler, C. S., Zubieta, J. K. (2005). Neuro-biological mechanisms of the placebo effect. *The Journal of Neuroscience, 25*, 10390–10402.

Colloca, L. & Benedetti, F. (2005). Placebos and painkillers: Is mind as real as matter? *Nature Reviews Neuroscience*, *6*, 545–552.

Colloca, L. & Benedetti, F. (2009). Placebo analgesia induced by social observational learning. *Pain*, *144*, 28–34.

Colloca, L. & Miller, F. G. (2011a). How placebo responses are formed: A learning perspective. *Philosophical Transactions of the Royal Society*, *366*, 1859–1869.

Colloca, L. & Miller, F. G. (2011b). Role of expectations in health. *Current Opinion in Psychiatry*, *24*, 149–155.

Colloca, L., Flaten, M. A. & Meissner, K. (2013). *Placebo and Pain: From Bench to Bedside*. Oxford: Elsevier.

Colloca, L., Klinger, R., Flor, H. & Bingel, U. (2013). Placebo analgesia: Psychological and neurobiological mechanisms. *Pain*, *154*, 511–514.

Doering, B. K. & Rief, W. (2012). Utilizing placebo mechanisms for dose reduction in pharmacotherapy. *Trends in Pharmacological Sciences*, *33*, 165–172.

Engert, V., Plessow, F., Miller, R., Kirschbaum, C. & Singer, T. (2014). Cortisol increase in empathic stress is modulated by emotional closeness and observation modality. *Psychoneuroendocrinology*, *45*, 192–201.

Fiorio, M., Zhang, W., Bresciani, M. C., Rodi, G., Bertolasi, L., Gambarin, M. & Tinazzi, M. (2010). Corticospinal excitability during action observation in task-specific dystonia: A transcranial magnetic stimulation study. *Neuroscience*, *171*, 117–124.

Galef, J. B. & Durlach, P. J. (1993). Absence of blocking, overshadowing. And latent inhibition in social enhancement of food preferences. *Animal Learning & Behavior*, *21*, 214–220.

Gracely, R. H., Dubner, R., Deeter, W. R. & Wolskee, P. J. (1985). Clinicians' expectations influence placebo analgesia. *Lancet*, *8419*, 43.

Hróbjartsson, A. & Gøtzsche, P. C. (2001). Is the placebo powerless? An analysis of clinical trials comparing placebo with no treatment. *The New England Journal of Medicine*, *344*, 1594–1602.

Hróbjartsson, A. & Gøtzsche, P. C. (2010). Placebo interventions for all clinical conditions. *Cochrane Database of Systematic Reviews*, *1*, CD003974.

Hunter, T., Siess, F. & Colloca, L. (2014). Socially induced placebo analgesia: A comparison of a pre-recorded versus live face-to-face observation. *European Journal of Pain*, *18*, 914–922.

Jensen, K. B., Petrovic, P., Kerr, C. E., Kirsch, I., Raicek, J., Cheetham, A., Spaeth, R., Cook, A., Gollub, R.L., Kong, J. & Kaptchuk, T. J. (2014). Sharing pain and relief: Neural correlates of physicians during treatment of patients. *Molecular Psychiatry*, *19*, 392–398.

Kirsch, I. (1985). Response expectancy as a determinant of experience and behavior. *American Psychologist*, *40*, 1189–1202.

Kirsch, I., Wickless, C. & Moffitt, K. H. (1999). Expectancy and suggestibility: Are the effects of environmental enhancement due to detection? *International Journal of Clinical and Experimental Hypnosis*, *47*, 40–45.

Klinger, R., Colloca, L., Bingel, U. & Flor, H. (2014). Placebo analgesia: Clinical applications. *Pain*, *155*, 1055–1058.

Lanzetta, J. T. & Orr, S. P. (1980). Influence of facial expressions on the classical conditioning of fear. *Journal of Personality and Social Psychology*, *39*, 1081–1087.

Mazzoni, G., Foan, L., Hyland, M. E. & Kirsch, I. (2010). The effects of observation and gender on psychogenic symptoms. *Health Psychology*, *29*, 181–185.

Swider, K. & Babel, P. (2013). The effect of the sex of a model on nocebo hyperalgesia induced by social observational learning. *Pain*, *154*, 1312–1317.

Vogtle, E., Barke, A. & Kroner-Herwig, B. (2013). Nocebo hyperalgesia induced by social observational learning. *Pain*, *154*, 1427–1433.

PART 2
Interpersonal expectancies

PREFACE

Expectancy about others

Lee Jussim

I have been doing research on both interpersonal and self-expectancies for over thirty years. I cannot say I know every piece of scholarship that has ever been conducted in this area, but I know the literatures pretty well. This is the most comprehensive, balanced, and readable scientific volume on expectancies that has yet been written.

Many terrific and seminal works, books, edited books, reviews, and empirical studies have preceded this – Merton's classic treatise on self-fulfilling prophecies, Rosenthal's many contributions (starting with the classic *Pygmalion in the Classroom*), Brophy & Good's book on teacher–student relationships (and their various collaborative and independent reviews). My own recent, book, *Social Perception and Social Reality*, aspires to join such giants. In addition, there have been edited books on teacher expectations, social stereotypes, and various aspects of self and identity. There have been many influential review articles and chapters.

However, there has never been a book like this. It brings together many of the researchers who have made some of the most influential and important contributions to research on expectancies. This book is organized in a simple and clear manner. There are two sections, one on expectancies for the self, the other on expectancies for others. The editors have insured that the contributions are short and readable. As such, the contributions provide easily accessible reviews of their specific topics – each one perfect for anything from introducing advanced undergraduates or graduate students to research in an area to informing more senior scientists of the state of knowledge in almost any aspect of self- or interpersonal expectancies.

So, even though I was asked to write the Preface for the section on interpersonal expectancies, I want to call your attention to the first section, on self-expectancies, on the chance that you have gotten here without reading it. The first section focuses on self-expectations, which are inherently intertwined with interpersonal expectations. Want to know about self-efficacy? Hypnosis? Placebo effects? Expectations for one's health? It is in the first section of this volume.

But back to the next section, on interpersonal expectancies. The contributors are essentially a Hall of Fame of scholars who have studied interpersonal expectancies. At the same time, the individual chapters are simultaneously the most readable, most comprehensive, and most balanced collection of readings on interpersonal expectancies that I have yet seen. In a mere 91 short pages, one can get a clear understanding of what is known about how and when expectancies, especially stereotype-based expectancies, create social reality; how perceivers and targets implicitly negotiate a shared reality; the role of motivation in expectancy effects; how accuracy and inaccuracy in expectations respectively limit and create self-fulfilling prophecies; and the role of characteristics of teachers and students in self-fulfilling prophecies. Furthermore, the chapters not only provide a review, but historical context, directions for future research, and discussion of how to apply the findings in that area to real-world issues and contexts. This is an extraordinary accomplishment for such short and readable chapters, which is what makes this volume a must-have resource for anyone doing research in these areas or otherwise interested in the distilled wisdom of fifty years of research on interpersonal expectations.

I was flattered when Sławomir Trusz invited me to contribute a Preface to this. I feel honored to have been included in what is simultaneously the most comprehensive and readable volume ever to appear on expectancies.

10

WHEN AND WHY DO EXPECTATIONS CREATE REALITY?

Reflections on behavioral confirmation in social interaction[1]

Mark Snyder

For many years, my colleagues and I have investigated the ways that expectations influence the course of social interaction. In the procedural paradigm that we have used in our research, two people who have never met before have a brief getting-acquainted conversation, with one member of the pair (the "perceiver") being given an expectation about the other person (the "target"). Typically, in these interactions, perceivers act as if their expectations were true, and targets come to behave as if the expectations were in fact true. For example, in an early, paradigmatic demonstration of behavioral confirmation, perceivers had a telephone conversation with targets they believed to be physically attractive (as a result of seeing a photo ostensibly of the target, but actually chosen by random assignment). Over the course of the conversation, those targets came to behave in more friendly, outgoing, and sociable ways than targets interacting with perceivers who believed them to be physically unattractive, with these differences in behavior being readily apparent to raters who listened only to the target's contributions to the conversations and know nothing about the perceiver's expectations (Snyder *et al.*, 1977).

In the beginning: documenting the phenomenon

This "behavioral confirmation" scenario (so named because the target's behavior comes to confirm the perceiver's expectations in the course of their social interaction) has been demonstrated for a wide range of expectations (including beliefs about personality, ability, gender, and race) and a variety of interaction contexts (including relatively unstructured interactions such as initial getting-acquainted conversations between strangers, as well as relatively structured interactions such

90 M. Snyder

as those between teachers and students, supervisors and workers, counselors and clients); for reviews of the diverse contexts in which behavioral confirmation has been documented, see Jussim (1986), Klein and Snyder (2003), Miller and Turnbull (1986), and Snyder and Stukas (1999).

On first consideration, the "formula" for behavioral confirmation seems to be a straightforward one: perceiver + expectation + target = behavioral confirmation. Behavioral confirmation, it appears, can be readily observed in social interaction as seemingly simple as a brief, unstructured telephone conversation, with perceivers and targets not being required to do anything other than get acquainted with each other. Accordingly, it is tempting to view behavioral confirmation as the "natural" and "automatic" consequence of people interacting in the context of expectations, something that "just happens" when people meet others about whom they have expectations.

Yet, as much as the facts of the behavioral confirmation scenario may seem to be straightforward, it has turned out that it's not quite that simple. To the contrary, it appears that there is a much more complicated dynamic in play when expectations create reality.

The state of knowledge: dynamics of the phenomenon

Research on the necessary and sufficient conditions for behavioral confirmation to occur, as well as research on its underlying mechanisms, tells us that the behavioral confirmation scenario requires a fairly elaborate coordination of the motivational agendas of perceiver and target, with both parties to the interaction actively involved in pursuing quite different approaches to pursuing the goal of getting acquainted with each other. The *perceiver*, the evidence tells us, views interaction as an opportunity to "*get to know*" the target, and is motivated to find out if the expectation fits and whether it serves well to predict what the target will be like and as a useful guide to handling the interaction (e.g. Snyder & Haugen, 1994). The way the perceiver pursues that agenda for action is a "confirmatory" one of giving targets opportunities to behave in accordance with expectations more so than opportunities to contradict it (e.g. Snyder & Swann, 1978). The *target*, on the other hand, views interaction as an opportunity to "*get along*" with the perceiver, to find a way to ensure a smooth and pleasing flow of interaction; accordingly, the target uses the perceiver's overtures as cues to handling the interaction and thus goes along with the perceiver's overtures, which has the effect of confirming the perceiver's expectations (e.g. Copeland & Snyder, 1995).

Further indications of the complexity of the behavioral confirmation scenario come from the way that it is embedded in the ongoing flow of social interaction. To be sure, much research on behavioral confirmation has occurred in experimental analogs of first encounters between strangers, encounters that have neither a past nor a future. Although atypical of interactions as they naturally occur, the fact of the matter is that such laboratory studies may be an *under*-estimate of the impact of behavioral confirmation, for, when initial encounters include the prospect of future interaction, the likelihood of confirmation may be enhanced. Thus, when Haugen and Snyder (1995) told participants that their getting-acquainted conversations were the prelude to further interactions, behavioral confirmation effects were greater than when it was made absolutely clear that there would be no further interactions. Moreover, when perceivers interact with the targets of positive expectations, even the possibility of future interaction increases their sociability, which in turn elicits increased sociability from their interaction partners; however, in interactions with the targets of negative expectations, the possibility of future interaction has no comparable effect on perceivers and targets (Stukas and Snyder, 2003). Finally, studies that move beyond first encounters have identified circumstances in which targets demonstrate "carry over" effects such that they continue to confirm perceivers' expectations in subsequent interactions (Smith *et al.*, 1997; Snyder & Swann, 1978; Stukas & Snyder, 2002). Conversely, over the course of multiple encounters, perceivers become more confident in their beliefs, even if these beliefs are initially inaccurate (Gill *et al.*, 1998), making it more likely that they will keep engaging in behaviors that facilitate the persistence of behavioral confirmation.

Adding even greater nuance to the behavioral confirmation scenario, it appears that the contrasting, but interlocking, agendas of perceivers and targets can be (and often are) exacerbated by power differences. Often, it is persons in positions of power who hold expectations (teachers hold expectations of their students, employers hold expectations of their workers, and therapists hold expectations of their clients) and who have the power of their roles to pursue an agenda that involves acting on expectations about the target and leading the target to provide behavioral confirmation. By contrast, targets of expectations, especially those related to stereotyped beliefs and prejudicial attitudes, are often members of disadvantaged and powerless stigmatized groups, having little option other than to go along with the overtures of those in power and confirm their expectations. In fact, research has indicated that a power differential, with the perceiver holding more power than the target, is necessary for behavioral confirmation (e.g. Copeland, 1994), a power differential that can come from the roles and positions that perceivers and targets occupy (e.g. Snyder & Klein, 2005) and that can emerge from the very holding of expectations and the perceiver's inherent advantage of knowing more about the target than the target knows about the perceiver (e.g. Baldwin *et al.*, 2009).

A persistent, and continuing, question in the study of behavioral confirmation is why targets do not resist the pressure to confirm erroneous expectations, particularly those that are rooted in potentially injurious negative stereotypes about them. To be sure, in laboratory experiments, the target is typically unaware of the perceiver's expectation. And there is evidence that, at times, targets will actively disconfirm negative expectations when they are made aware of them (e.g. Hilton & Darley, 1985). However, the "typical" case may be one in which targets are not aware of negative expectations; for a variety of reasons relating to social etiquette and norms of politeness, perceivers may be less likely to reveal negative expectations than positive ones. Accordingly, to the extent that they are unaware of negative expectations, targets may have little opportunity to actively disconfirm them. Moreover, even targets who are aware of negative expectations may confirm these expectations, especially when these expectations are held by powerful perceivers who might retaliate against anyone who challenges their views. Finally, targets may be motivated to confirm negative expectations that are consistent with their own self-concepts, as research on self-verification processes (e.g. Swann, 2012) has demonstrated.

Much of the intrigue of the behavioral confirmation scenario comes from the self-fulfilling impact of *erroneous* beliefs, such as those stemming from widely shared, but not necessarily valid stereotypes (indeed, laboratory experiments, with their defining features of random assignment and experimental manipulation, provide a powerful methodology for creating situations where perceivers hold erroneous beliefs about targets). However, not all beliefs are inaccurate, and accurate beliefs may be powerful predictors of future behavior, not because of behavioral confirmation, but because the perceiver's beliefs and the target's behaviors may both be reflections of the target's prior behaviors. Indeed, in naturalistic studies of teachers and students, Jussim (1993) has documented that "expectation" effects (i.e. associations between teachers' expectations and students' performance) are smaller than "accuracy" effects (i.e. associations between students' prior performance and current performance). However, it is important to note that the predictors of the size of expectation effects in naturalistic settings are quite consistent with known moderators of expectation effects in the laboratory. Thus, in naturalistic studies, the effects of teachers' expectations are larger for students who are low in status, power, and advantage relative to their teachers (Madon *et al.*, 1997). Such findings are clearly convergent with those of laboratory experiments in which behavioral confirmation is particularly evident when targets have less power and status than perceivers (Copeland, 1994; Virdin & Neuberg, 1990).

Looking to the future: new directions for theory and research

Although forecasting the future can be a risky business, it is possible to nominate several possible items for the agenda for the next generations of theory and research relevant to behavioral confirmation. Among these are the need to address the conditions under which social interaction will lead to the *disconfirmation* of beliefs and expectations, to discover when and why perceivers will treat targets in ways that lead them to disconfirm their expectations as well as to discover when and why targets will find ways to avoid confirming and even actively disconfirm the expectations of perceivers.

In addition, and reflecting the fact that much of the interest in behavioral confirmation stems from its possible role in the maintenance of social and cultural stereotypes, and in defining the relations between groups in society, there is a clear need to delineate the similarities and differences between behavioral confirmation as it is typically studied at the "micro" level of individual encounters between individual perceivers and individual targets, and how it may operate at the "macro" level of relations between groups, classes, and collectives in society.

The potential for practical application

These possible future directions for the study of behavioral confirmation also serve to underscore the potential for practical applications of theory and research that can help to understand the involvement of stereotypes in society and the lives of its citizens. The fact that individuals' behaviors can be shaped by the expectations that others hold of them, and the fact that these expectations may be rooted in stereotypes about the groups to which they belong (including race, ethnicity, gender, social class, etc.), has the potential to sensitize members of society to the possibility that life opportunities can be constrained by treatment based on often-erroneous stereotypes about individuals and groups within society. Moreover, and also reflecting concerns about the role of behavioral confirmation in perpetuating stereotypes, there is a clear need to leverage theory and research to develop interventions to short-circuit the self-fulfilling effects of expectations on behavior, interventions that can be applied to both perceivers' and targets' contributions to their interactions.

Conclusion

The lessons of several decades of research on behavioral confirmation in social interaction are that beliefs and expectations aren't just things that reside in people's minds, confined to the world of thought. Rather, beliefs and expectations affect how people act, how they treat other people, and how other people in turn behave. However, the research also instructs us that behavioral confirmation is not something that "just happens" when perceivers interact with the targets of their expectations, with the reality of expectations somehow "spreading" from the mind of the perceiver to the behavior of the target, for it has become increasingly evident that there is much that can and does go on under the surface when two people, one of whom holds an expectation about what the other person is like, meet and get acquainted.

With the understanding generated by a considerable amount of research, involving carefully designed experimental manipulations that systematically influence the agendas of perceivers and targets, and the ways that these agendas play out in ongoing social interaction, it is possible to delineate successive steps in the chain of events that occur when people bring preconceived beliefs and expectations to their dealings with other people. From that research has come an appreciation of the complex intertwining of belief and reality in social interaction.

Note

1   Research on behavioral confirmation in social interaction has been supported by grants from the National Science Foundation to Mark Snyder.

94 M. Snyder

References

Baldwin, A. S., Kiviniemi, M. T. & Snyder, M. (2009). A subtle source of power: The effect of having an expectation on anticipated interpersonal power. *Journal of Social Psychology, 149*, 82–104.

Copeland, J. T. (1994). Prophecies of power: Motivational implications of social power for behavioral confirmation. *Journal of Personality and Social Psychology, 67*, 264–277.

Copeland, J. T. & Snyder, M. (1995). When counselors confirm: A functional analysis. *Personality and Social Psychology Bulletin, 21*, 1210–1220.

Gill, M. J., Swann, W.B. & Silvera, D. H. (1998). On the genesis of confidence. *Journal of Personality and Social Psychology, 75*, 1101–1114.

Haugen, J. A. & Snyder, M. (1995). Effects of perceiver's beliefs about future interactions on the behavioral confirmation process. Paper presented at the annual meeting of the American Psychological Society.

Hilton, J. L. & Darley, J. M. (1985). Constructing other persons: A limit on the effect. *Journal of Experimental Social Psychology, 21*, 1–18.

Jussim, L. (1986). Self-fulfilling prophecies: A theoretical and integrative review. *Psychological Review, 93*, 429–445.

Jussim, L. (1993). Accuracy in interpersonal expectations: A reflection-construction analysis of current and classic research. *Journal of Personality, 61*, 637–668.

Klein, O. & Snyder, M. (2003). Stereotypes and behavioral confirmation: From interpersonal to intergroup perspectives. In M. P. Zanna (ed.), *Advances in Experimental Social Psychology* (Vol. 35, 153–233). San Diego, CA: Academic Press.

Madon, S., Jussim, L. & Eccles, J. (1997). In search of the powerful self-fulfilling prophecy. *Journal of Personality and Social Psychology, 72*, 791–809.

Miller, D. T. & Turnbull, W. (1986). Expectancies and interpersonal processes. *Annual Review of Psychology, 37*, 233–256.

Smith, D. M., Neuberg, S. L., Judice, T. N. & Biesanz, J. C. (1997). Target complicity in the confirmation and disconfirmation of erroneous perceiver expectations: Immediate and longer term implications. *Journal of Personality and Social Psychology, 73*, 974–991.

Snyder, M. (1992). Motivational foundations of behavioral confirmation. *Advances in Experimental Social Psychology, 25*, 67–114.

Snyder, M. & Haugen, J. A. (1994). Why does behavioral confirmation occur? A functional perspective on the role of the perceiver. *Journal of Experimental Social Psychology, 30*, 218–246.

Snyder, M. & Klein, O. (2005). Construing and constructing others: On the reality and the generality of the behavioral confirmation scenario. *Interaction Studies, 6*, 53–67.

Snyder, M. & Stukas, A. A., Jr (1999). Interpersonal processes: The interplay of cognitive, motivational, and behavioral activities in social interaction. *Annual Review of Psychology, 50*, 273–303.

Snyder, M. & Swann, W. B. (1978a). Behavioral confirmation in social interaction: From social perception to social reality. *Journal of Experimental Social Psychology, 14*, 148–162.

Snyder, M. & Swann, W. B. (1978b). Hypothesis-testing processes in social interaction. *Journal of Personality and Social Psychology, 36*, 1202–1212.

Snyder, M., Tanke, E. D. & Berscheid, E. (1977). Social perception and interpersonal behavior: On the self-fulfilling nature of social stereotypes. *Journal of Personality and Social Psychology, 35*, 656–666.

Stukas, A. A. & Snyder, M. (2002). Targets' awareness of expectations and behavioral confirmation in ongoing interactions. *Journal of Experimental Social Psychology, 38*, 31–40.

Stukas, A. A. & Snyder, M. (2003). The influence of possible future interactions on first encounters. Unpublished manuscript: La Trobe University.

Swann, W. B., Jr (2012). Self-verification theory. In Van Lange, P. A., Kruglanski, A. & Higgins, E. T. (eds), *Handbook of Theories of Social Psychology* (23–42). London: Sage.

Virdin, L. M. & Neuberg, S. L. (1990). Perceived status: a moderator of expectancy confirmation. Manuscript presented at the annual meetings of the American Psychological Association.

11

IDENTITY NEGOTIATION IN SOCIAL INTERACTION

Past, present and future

William B. Swann, Jr and Jennifer K. Bosson

Beginnings

The first author began working on expectancy effects nearly four decades ago. Mark Snyder and I were intrigued with the self-fulfilling prophecy effects that Bob Rosenthal had documented and popularized in his studies of experimenter and teacher expectancies (e.g. Rosenthal & Jacobson, 1968). We wondered if these phenomena would generalize beyond the highly structured settings that Rosenthal so fruitfully investigated to freewheeling, casual interactions between peers. Accordingly, we asked if the expectancies of some individuals (arbitrarily dubbed "perceivers") might channel social interaction so as to cause the behavior of other individuals (arbitrarily dubbed "targets") to confirm perceivers' expectancies. We found clear evidence for these self-fulfilling effects (Snyder & Swann, 1978a; Swann & Snyder, 1980). For example, whereas targets labeled as extroverted became more sociable, those thought to be hostile grew more aggressive. We also explored the cognitive mechanisms underlying these effects, and learned that they were driven, in part, by a very basic cognitive preference for information that confirms prior expectancies (Snyder & Swann, 1978b).

Yet, as evidence of behavioral confirmation poured in, it became increasingly clear that this was not the only process unfolding in our studies. True, most target individuals in our research did indeed behaviorally confirm the expectancies of perceivers. Nevertheless, some targets vehemently resisted the labels with which they were tagged. As we examined this phenomenon more closely, it became apparent that targets had their own ideas about themselves and social reality, and if they noticed that their partners did not share those ideas, they took active steps to correct the error. Clearly, the identities of targets were not simply constructed by perceivers; they were negotiated by targets and perceivers working together. It seemed crucial to learn more about this identity negotiation process in general, and the role of targets in this process in particular.

The first step in explicating the role of targets in the process of identity negotiation was the development of self-verification theory. The central notion of the theory is that targets want perceivers to see them as they see themselves. The theory was designed to identify various strategies of self-verification and how those strategies compete with or complement independent psychological processes (Swann & Read, 1981a, 1981b; Swann, 1983). Not surprisingly, one of the competing processes that we considered first was behavioral confirmation. In an early study, we (Swann & Ely, 1984) encouraged perceivers to develop impressions of targets that clashed with targets' self-views. The experimenter manipulated the certainty of perceivers' impressions and measured the certainty of the self-views of targets.

The conclusion was that in most instances the self-views of targets were a more powerful determinant of their behavior than the impressions of perceivers or, simply put, self-verification generally prevailed over behavioral confirmation. There was one exception to this pattern: perceivers' impressions overrode targets' self-views when perceivers were certain of their impressions and targets were uncertain of their self-views. This makes sense, as targets presumably possess a lifetime of support for their self-views while perceivers base their impressions of targets on a brief statement offered by the experimenter. The more general conclusion, however, is that under specifiable circumstances, both self-verification and behavioral confirmation are influential determinants of identity negotiation outcomes (for a recent overview, see Swann, 2012).

State of the art

A later field study reinforced the conclusions from Swann and Ely's (1984) laboratory investigation. In two longitudinal studies of college students, we (McNulty & Swann, 1994) measured the self-views of college roommates as well as their impressions of their roommates at the beginning of the semester. We then followed them for the remainder of the semester. We discovered evidence that both perceiver expectancies and target's self-views were influential determinants of identity negotiation outcomes – that is, just as perceivers' initial impressions shaped the later self-views of targets, so too did targets' initial self-views influence the later impressions of perceivers.

Later field investigations (Swann et al., 1994; Swann & Pelham, 2002) added a new twist to the emerging picture of the identity negotiation process. After assessing the impressions that married people or roommates had of one another and themselves, we assessed the extent to which they were committed to remaining in the relationship. We discovered that people were most interested in remaining with the same partner when the partner perceived them in a self-verifying manner. Furthermore, this pattern emerged even if partners' impressions were negative. In fact, other researchers demonstrated that married couples ran an elevated risk for divorce or separation insofar as partners perceived targets in a non-verifying manner (Cast & Burke, 2002; see also Burke & Stets, 1999; De La Ronde & Swann, 1998).

A final series of studies examined the nature and consequences of identity negotiation in a work group setting. The authors reasoned that self-verification should improve functioning of work groups for at least two reasons. First, feeling known and understood by the group may make members feel more connected to the group and more motivated to immerse themselves in group activities. Second, insofar as group members are convinced that they are embedded in a self-verifying niche, they should feel safe to behave authentically. This may embolden them to advance a wide array of potential solutions for group tasks that will, in turn, maximize creative combinations of ideas and fresh insights.

In a prospective study of four- to six-person study groups of MBA students, the researchers (Swann et al., 2000) assessed the relation between self-verification and creativity. As hypothesized, perceived self-verification at nine weeks predicted targets' feelings of connection to their groups as well as group performance on creative tasks at the end of the semester. A follow-up study (Polzer et al., 2002) extended this line of inquiry by asking if the cultural diversity of study group members interacted with self-verification in determining performance. They reasoned that self-verification encourages diverse group members to apply the differences in knowledge, experiences, and perspectives associated with their cultural identities and categorical differences to the tasks at hand (Ely & Thomas, 2001), thereby facilitating performance. The results supported these ideas. Specifically, among groups that achieved high levels of self-verification, within-group diversity facilitated creative task performance at the end of the semester. In contrast, among groups that failed to achieve substantial self-verification, diversity undermined creative task performance (for a discussion, see Swann et al., 2004).

Future directions

The distinction between personal self-views and social self-views poses a potential problem for identity negotiations. Whereas personal identities refer to traits and qualities that distinguish individuals from one another (e.g. moody, trustworthy), social identities consist of the roles and group memberships that connect people to similar others (e.g. woman, New Yorker; Turner et al., 1987). In principle, personal and social identities are independent. Thus, for example, a woman may view herself as unassertive on a personal level yet link herself to a feminist organization that is renowned for its assertiveness. One challenge for future researchers will be to identify the conditions under which people's personal versus social identities drive identity negotiation processes, especially when the two types of identities are in conflict.

One potentially important variable here may be the certainty of people's self-views. For example, when people are highly certain of their social identities, they seek verification for these identities even if they view them as non-descriptive on a personal level (Gómez et al., 2009). This indicates that people will negotiate highly certain identities associated with valued social groups regardless of the personal relevance of the identities.

Another possibility is that the desirability of social groups plays an important role in identity negotiations. Some groups hold more sociopolitical clout than others, and membership in these groups affords individuals access to power and resources (Pratto *et al.*, 1994). People might therefore negotiate social identities that bolster and affirm their connections to desirable, high-status social groups even when such identities are inconsistent with their personal views. In one set of studies, the researchers found that men – i.e. members of a relatively high-status social group – eschewed feminine traits from their social identities but not from their personal identities, whereas women were much less likely to eschew masculinity (Bosson & Michniewicz, 2013). Future work could thus examine whether men work vociferously to negotiate social identities that strengthen their links to their gender group, while distancing them from other, lower status groups. This phenomenon becomes especially relevant when considering that manhood in general is a more elusive and tenuous social status than womanhood (e.g. Vandello *et al.*, 2008). Given men's chronic concerns about proving their manhood to others, combined with the relative status and power associated with membership in the male gender, men may routinely negotiate social identities intended to prove their masculinity to others despite devaluing masculine traits at the level of their personal identities.

Applications

The average full-time employed American spends close to 2,000 hours per year at work (US Department of Labor, 2014). For many adults, the work environment thus provides the context for numerous identity negotiations. In the set of studies summarized above, work groups produced more creative products to the extent that individual group members succeeded in eliciting self-verifying appraisals from fellow group members. At the same time, participants performed most effectively on non-creative, computational tasks to the extent that group members changed their self-views to match other group members' initial appraisals of them (Swann *et al.*, 2000). One potential application of identity negotiation principles thus lies in the interaction between work group composition and dynamics on one hand and the nature of work tasks on the other hand. The manner in which group members negotiate their self-views over time will have implications for the quality of their work outputs, and managers and organizations who understand these processes will more effectively structure work environments that promote and sustain fruitful identity negotiations.

On an even more basic level, people may be less inclined to stay with organizations that do not foster satisfying identity negotiations. Thus, worker turnover is an area to which identity negotiation research can be usefully applied. Although people typically demonstrate flexibility in their self-views, and are skilled at activating identities that allow them to achieve situation-specific goals (e.g. Swann *et al.*, 2002), environments that regularly force people to enact inauthentic identities can undermine workers' feelings of commitment and connection (Swann *et al.*, 2000). The results may include emotional exhaustion, withdrawal of effort, absenteeism, and turnover (Wiesenfeld *et al.*, 2007). Organizations that hope to cultivate a satisfied and committed workforce will benefit from understanding the importance of identity negotiation processes to people's well-being.

References

Bosson, J. K. & Michniewicz, K. S. (2013). Gender dichotomization at the level of ingroup identity: What it is, and why men use it more than women. *Journal of Personality and Social Psychology*, *105*, 425–442.

Burke, P. J. & Stets, J. E. (2009). *Identity Theory*. Oxford: Oxford University Press.

Cast, A. D. & Burke, P. J. (2002). A theory of self-esteem. *Social Forces*, *80*, 1041–1068.

De La Ronde, C. & Swann, W. B., Jr (1998). Partner verification: Restoring shattered images of our intimates. *Journal of Personality and Social Psychology*, *75*, 374–382.

Ely, R. J. & Thomas, D. A. (2001). Cultural diversity at work: The effects of diversity perspectives on work group processes and outcomes. *Administrative Science Quarterly*, *46*, 229–273.

Gómez, Á., Seyle, C. D., Huici, C. & Swann, W. B., Jr (2009). Can self-verification strivings fully transcend the self-other barrier? Seeking verification of ingroup identities. *Journal of Personality and Social Psychology*, *97*, 1021–1044.

McNulty, S. E. & Swann, W. B., Jr (1994). Identity negotiation in roommate relationships: The self as architect and consequence of social reality. *Journal of Personality and Social Psychology*, *67*, 1012–1023.

Polzer, J. T., Milton, L. P. & Swann, W. B., Jr (2002). Capitalizing on diversity: Interpersonal congruence in small work groups. *Administrative Science Quarterly*, *47*, 296–324.

Pratto, F., Sidanius, J., Stallworth, L. M., & Malle, B. F. (1994). Social dominance orientation: A personality variable predicting social and political attitudes. *Journal of Personality and Social Psychology*, *67*, 741–763.

Rosenthal, R. & Jacobson, L. (1968). *Pygmalion in the Classroom: Teacher Expectation and Pupils' Intellectual Development*. New York: Rinehart & Winston.

Snyder, M. & Swann, W. B., Jr (1978a). Behavioral confirmation in social interaction: From social perception to social reality. *Journal of Experimental Social Psychology*, *14*, 148–162.

Snyder, M. & Swann, W. B., Jr (1978b). Hypothesis testing processes in social interaction. *Journal of Personality and Social Psychology*, *36*, 1202–1212.

Swann, W. B., Jr (1983). Self-verification: Bringing social reality into harmony with the self. In J. Suls & A. G. Greenwald (eds), *Psychological Perspectives on the Self* (Vol. 2, 33–66). Hillsdale, NJ: Erlbaum.

Swann, W. B., Jr (2012). Self-verification theory. In P. Van Lang, A. Kruglanski & E. T. Higgins (eds), *Handbook of Theories of Social Psychology* (23–42). London: Sage.

Swann, W. B., Jr & Ely, R. J. (1984). A battle of wills: Self-verification versus behavioral confirmation. *Journal of Personality and Social Psychology*, *46*, 1287–1302.

Swann, W. B., Jr & Pelham, B. W. (2002). Who wants out when the going gets good? Psychological investment and preference for self-verifying college roommates. *Self and Identity*, *1*, 219–233.

Swann, W. B., Jr & Read, S. J. (1981a). Self-verification processes: How we sustain our self-conceptions. *Journal of Experimental Social Psychology*, *17*, 351–372.

Swann, W. B., Jr & Read, S. J. (1981b). Acquiring self-knowledge: The search for feedback that fits. *Journal of Personality and Social Psychology*, *41*, 1119–1128.

Swann, W. B., Jr & Snyder, M. (1980). On translating beliefs into action: Theories of ability and their application in an instructional setting. *Journal of Personality and Social Psychology*, *38*, 879–888.

Swann, W. B., Jr, Bosson, J. K. & Pelham, B. W. (2002). Different partners, different selves: Strategic verification of circumscribed identities. *Personality and Social Psychology Bulletin, 28*, 1215–1228.

Swann, W. B., Jr, De La Ronde, C. & Hixon, J. G. (1994). Authenticity and positivity strivings in marriage and courtship. *Journal of Personality and Social Psychology, 66*, 857–869.

Swann, W. B., Jr, Milton, L. P. & Polzer, J. T. (2000). Should we create a niche or fall in line? Identity negotiation and small group effectiveness. *Journal of Personality and Social Psychology, 79*, 238–250.

Swann, W. B. Jr, Polzer, J. T., Seyle, C. & Ko, S. (2004). Finding value in diversity: Verification of personal and social self-views in diverse groups. *Academy of Management Review, 29*, 9–27.

Turner, J. C., Hogg, M. A., Oakes, P. J., Reicher, S. D. & Wetherell, M. S. (1987). *Rediscovering the Social Group: A Self-categorization Theory.* Oxford: Basil Blackwell.

US Department of Labor, Bureau of Labor Statistics. (2014). *American Time Use Survey Summary.* Retrieved from: www.bls.gov/news.release/atus.nr0.htm

Vandello, J. A., Bosson, J. K., Cohen, D., Burnaford, R. M. & Weaver, J. R. (2008). Precarious manhood. *Journal of Personality and Social Psychology, 95*, 1325–1339.

Wiesenfeld, B. M., Swann, W.B., Jr, Brockner, J. & Bartel, C. (2007). Is more fairness always preferred? Self-esteem moderates reactions to procedural justice. *Academy of Management Journal, 50*, 1235–1253.

12

MOTIVATION MATTERS

The functional context of expectation confirmation processes

Steven L. Neuberg

People typically enter social encounters with expectations for what the others are going to be like. These expectations may be based on stereotypes, third-party hearsay, or previous encounters with the individual. There is often a substantial kernel of truth to the interpersonal expectations we carry (Jussim, 2012), but this is not always the case. Moreover, even expectations that are somewhat accurate— for example, sex stereotypes when averaging across the broad set of women (Swim, 1994)—almost never perfectly represent any particular individual we encounter. Although erroneous expectations are often corrected during the social interaction process, sometimes they are not. This is because inaccurate expectations can lead to perceptual confirmation, in which we view others' behaviors as consistent with our expectations (whether they are expectation-consistent or not), and behavioral confirmation (or self-fulfilling prophecies), in which we act toward others in ways that cause them to confirm our expectations with their behaviors (for reviews, see Fiske & Neuberg, 1990; Darley & Fazio, 1980; Jussim, 1986; Snyder, 1984).

Genesis

Not all social encounters are heavily biased towards expectation confirmation, however. The aim of my research program was to begin explicating the circumstances under which behavioral confirmation, in particular, does and does not occur. Not only do such investigations provide a deeper, more nuanced understanding of the complex dynamics of interpersonal interaction, but they are also potentially useful for designing interventions to limit the impact of inaccurate expectations in important real-life domains, such as education and employment.

To identify factors that moderate, or alter, the effects of any one variable on another, one needs first to understand the mechanisms that mediate between the

Expectation confirmation processes **103**

causal and outcome variables. Three mechanisms, in particular, stand out as enabling the self-fulfilling prophecy—that is, as mediating between the inaccurate expectations held by a perceiver and the behavioral confirmation of those expectations by a target: biased perceiver information gathering, biased perceiver expressions of warmth and liking, and target deference to perceiver biases. We reasoned that certain goals held by perceivers and targets might alter those mediating mechanisms, and thereby alter the likelihood that targets would behaviorally confirm perceiver expectation.

Current state of the art

I briefly summarize a line of research that has explored these hypotheses (Neuberg, 1994, 1996).

Perceiver accuracy motivation alters target behavioral confirmation by altering perceiver information-gathering behaviors

Perceivers may gather information from targets in ways that encourage them to respond consistently with perceiver expectations and that discourage them from responding inconsistently with perceiver expectations (Snyder *et al.*, 1982; Snyder & Swann, 1978; Swann & Ely, 1984; Trope & Thompson, 1997). Consider a personnel officer interviewing an applicant for a job—an applicant for whom the interviewer holds negative expectations. The interviewer may ask questions that are leading and negatively biased—for example, "Tell me, Ms. Wosinska, about a time you didn't get along with a co-worker." Even the most agreeable applicant is likely to have experienced at least one co-worker conflict in a previous job, and so will be able to discuss that conflict. Note that if the interviewer doesn't also ask about a time the applicant got along wonderfully with a co-worker, then Ms. Wosinska's discussion of co-worker relations will consist only of information suggesting that she may be a difficult employee. Moreover, if this interviewer conducts a short interview, spending little time interacting with and listening to the applicant, he will have even less information available with which to counter his initially unflattering expectations (e.g. Word *et al.*, 1974).

If self-fulfilling prophecies are enabled by expectation-biased information gathering by perceivers, then one would predict that any factors that interrupt this biased information gathering, or make it less biased, would also reduce the likelihood of the self-fulfilling prophecy. One motivational factor, in particular, might play such a role—the extent to which perceivers are motivated to form accurate impressions of their targets. To form an accurate impression of another, one must gather a lot of information about that person and gather it in an unbiased manner. If so, motivating a perceiver holding negative expectations to form an accurate impression of their target should reduce the impact of these negative expectations on the target's behavior. One would, metaphorically, be cutting out

104 S. L. Neuberg

a critical link (biased information gathering) in the chain that connects a perceiver's negative expectations to the target's behavioral confirmation of these expectations. When the link is removed, the chain separates and no longer leads from one point to the other.

I first tested this hypothesis in a laboratory experiment, in which participants were assigned either to interview another person for a job or to be the applicant attempting to win the job (Neuberg, 1989). Interviewers were provided with either negative expectations or no expectations about the applicants (manipulated via personality inventories the applicants had supposedly completed earlier), and were also either encouraged to form accurate impressions of the applicants or were given no specific goal. We then allowed the interviews to proceed, unobtrusively audio-recording them so that outside judges—unaware of the perceivers' expectations and goals—could assess both interviewer behavior and applicant performance. As predicted, non-motivated interviewers engaged in information-gathering behaviors biased against the applicants for whom they held negative expectations; they asked them fewer questions and biased their questions toward the negative. Consequently, their negative-expectation applicants performed more poorly. In contrast, accuracy-motivated interviewers showed no such information-gathering biases, and their negative-expectation applicants performed quite well. Further analyses revealed that it was the shift in interviewer goal to accuracy motivation that worked to break the self-fulfilling chain of negative interviewer expectations.

Follow-up experiments replicated these findings (Biesanz et al., 1999; Biesanz et al., 2001; Judice & Neuberg, 1998) and also revealed some interesting nuances. For example, when we instead motivated interviewers to confirm their erroneous negative expectations—flipping the accuracy motivation on its head—we found that they were more likely to create negative self-fulfilling prophecies; this isn't surprising. More interesting, however, was that these interviewers conveyed to these negatively performing applicants that they had instead done quite well; they were warm and friendly to these applicants (Judice & Neuberg, 1998). The implications of this could be quite problematic. It suggests that those victimized by another's erroneous negative expectations may find themselves unable to avoid the same outcome in the future because they will not have had the opportunity to recognize that victimization.

In sum, perceiver impression formation goals alter the likelihood of the self-fulfilling prophecy by regulating the influences that expectations have on how perceivers gather information about targets.

Perceiver self-presentational goals alter target behavioral confirmation by altering perceiver expressive behaviors

People sometimes create self-fulfilling prophecies because they "leak" their expectations of others in their verbal and nonverbal expressive behaviors (e.g. Harris & Rosenthal, 1985; Ickes et al., 1982; Snyder et al., 1977; Word et al., 1974). Let's return to our interviewer and applicant. If the interviewer holds negative

Expectation confirmation processes **105**

expectations for the applicant, he may verbalize his lack of enthusiasm or, more likely, nonverbally behave in a somewhat colder manner. In return, the applicant may respond with social distance of her own, thereby confirming the interviewer's negative expectations that this applicant is just not that friendly.

Consider, though, how people behave when it's very important to get others to like them. Do they express dislike or disrespect for the other—even if they do indeed dislike or disrespect them—or do they adopt a friendly demeanor and express liking and other favorable sentiments? They do the latter. Just as we've seen that perceivers motivated to be accurate break the negative self-fulfilling chain by adopting unbiased information-gathering behaviors, we hypothesized that perceivers motivated to ingratiate themselves to their targets may break the negative self-fulfilling chain by adopting more favorable expressive behaviors—by greeting them warmly, by using their name, and so on. As a consequence, these targets might behave quite favorably, despite the negative expectations held of them.

We tested this hypothesis in an interview setting like the one described above, and manipulated interviewers' expectations and interaction goals (Neuberg *et al.*, 1993). As anticipated, the "no goal" interviewers were relatively cold and challenging toward their negative-expectation applicants, leading them to perform somewhat less favorably, consistent with their interviewers' expectations. In contrast, the interviewers motivated to get the applicants to like them were relatively warm and unthreatening toward their negative-expectation applicants; as a result, these applicants performed relatively favorably, thereby disconfirming their interviewers' expectations. By regulating how expectations shape perceiver expressive behaviors, perceiver self-presentational goals can alter the likelihood of self-fulfilling prophecies.

Target self-presentational motivation alters the likelihood of behavioral confirmation by altering the extent to which targets defer to constraints imposed by perceivers

We have seen that, in the absence of special perceiver motivation—for example, the desires to form accurate impressions or to get their targets to like them—inaccurate negative perceiver expectations can create self-fulfilling prophecies by constraining the personal information targets provide and the expressions they display. These findings showcase the power of perceiver expectations to shape the actions of the target and, thereby, the target's outcomes.

Note, however, that these perceiver-initiated mechanisms logically require the (usually unintentional) complicity of the target. For example, an applicant could choose to respond to a negatively constraining question with a positive answer, thereby not acceding to the interactional script initiated by the interviewer (e.g. "Well, yes, I did have a short-term conflict with one co-worker, but we worked it out. More generally, though, I get along great with my co-workers. Let me tell you, for instance, about my interactions with Slawomir . . ."). An applicant could also choose to respond to nonverbal expressions of coldness and distance with smiles

106 S. L. Neuberg

and engagement. Such actions break down the negative self-fulfilling prophecy. We see, then, that targets may sometimes be complicit in the confirmation of inaccurate perceiver expectations, via their inclinations or decisions to defer to the constraints imposed by their perceivers. It's thus not surprising that some of the most compelling demonstrations of negative self-fulfilling prophecies take place in settings in which the perceiver has power or status over the target, thereby increasing the target's inclination to defer to the perceiver's constraints (e.g. teachers–students, clinicians–patients, interviewer–applicants, etc.).

To test these ideas, we again used an experimental interview setting in which we manipulated interviewer expectations (Smith *et al.*, 1997). This time, however, instead of manipulating interviewer goals we manipulated the applicants' goals, motivating some to approach the interview with a deferential mindset (which we suggest is the default mindset that enables self-fulfilling prophecies) or a challenging mindset (which we suggest should break down the self-fulfilling prophecy). As predicted, applicants encouraged to be deferential inadvertently succumbed to their interviewers' expectations; applicants encouraged to advance their own agenda, to be "challenging," did not. The applicants motivated to be challenging successfully disconfirmed the interviewers' negative expectations because they presented favorable information about themselves even when confronting negatively biased interviewer questions. By reducing their willingness to defer to the constraints imposed by perceiver behavior, people targeted by others' unflattering expectations can avoid falling prey to them.

In sum, it's clear that the motivational context—the social and information processing goals that perceivers and targets bring to their encounters—plays a very large role in determining the impact of negative expectations. Such findings may not only help explain why there is much variability in the incidence of expectation confirmation (Jussim, 2012), but may also point to ways to reduce the incidence of expectation confirmation in real-world settings.

Future directions

Two issues stand out in terms of further theory development within this motivational approach. First, we know that motivated debiasing of expectation effects is cognitively effortful; it requires attentional resources. Accuracy-motivated perceivers need additional cognitive resources to engage in more thorough and comprehensive information gathering, to debias and balance the questions they ask of others, etc. Targets hoping to challenge the negative expectations of their perceivers need additional cognitive resources to side-step social norms and modify the interactional script created by their perceivers, to provide answers that go beyond the circumscribed aims of the questions they're asked, etc.

Indeed, in the absence of sufficient available cognitive resources, motivated debiasing of the effects of negative expectations is difficult. For example, whereas accuracy-motivated interviewers are often able to overcome their negative expectations by debiasing their information-gathering behaviors, as reviewed above, they are not able to do so if their cognitive resources are simultaneously being taxed by a difficult task (Biesanz *et al.*, 2001). More research is needed to determine whether such attentional constraints apply to the implementation of other goals, whether there are people who are especially susceptible, or not, to cognitive resource constraints in these contexts, whether perceivers and targets can be taught to automatize debiasing strategies, so that the presence of high cognitive load will have minimal effects on motivated debiasing, etc.

Second, research on the motivational moderators of expectation confirmation effects has focused primarily on two classes of goals—information processing goals (e.g. accuracy) and self-presentational goals (e.g. ingratiation, self-promotion). Yet the motivational context for social interaction is much richer than this. Some have argued, for example, that there exist a set of "fundamental" goals—resource acquisition, self-protection, disease avoidance, social affiliation, status-seeking, mate acquisition, mate retention, and kin care—that shape much of everyday social thought and behavior (Kenrick *et al.*, 2010; Neuberg & Schaller, 2014). How do these goals shape expectation-tinged social encounters? Do expectations based on goal-related information people want to know about in much of everyday life— for example, information about whether others will be good mates, parents, or cooperators—work in similar ways and with similar effects as the kinds of expectations studied thus far in the literature? Do different kinds of expectations and different fundamental goals interact in specific ways to shape expectation confirmation? The motivational milieu is much richer than the set of perceiver and target goals explored to this point, and broadening the theoretical scope will be useful.

Applications

Our motivational framework likely has significant real-world applications. A typical approach to reducing the effects of inaccurate perceiver expectations has been to attempt to change the perceiver's expectations. This is an obvious first step, and has been especially prominent in the literature exploring stereotypic and prejudicial expectations. A distinction should be made, however, between changing a perceiver's stereotypic expectations and changing the likelihood that a perceiver applies those expectations to a particular target in a particular situation. Acknow-ledging the difficulty of changing stereotypes and prejudices, and recognizing that one can reduce the application of a belief without changing the belief itself, the current framework suggests an alternative strategy: alter the goals of perceivers and targets within the specific social interaction context. After all, we know that perceivers who hold negative expectations for targets can put aside those expec-tations if their current situation calls for accuracy or ingratiation. We know that targets who face others' negative expectations can choose not to defer to the constraints placed upon them but instead to challenge these constraints.

There are many ways, in circumscribed settings, to motivate someone toward accuracy—for example, via direct instruction, by making perceivers' outcomes dependent on target performances, by making perceivers accountable to third parties who define impression accuracy as the criterion for perceiver success (e.g. Fiske & Neuberg, 1990; Neuberg, 1989; Neuberg & Fiske, 1987). Similarly, there will be many ways to motivate perceivers to want their applicants to like them, and many ways to motivate targets of negative expectations to actively pursue their own self-interests. The motivational framework overviewed here should thus be useful in aiding policy makers, administrators, and interventionists working in schools and workplaces and clinics, to generate creative and workable solutions to the sometimes pernicious effects of inaccurate negative expectations.

References

Biesanz, J. C., Neuberg, S. L., Judice, T. N. & Smith, D. M. (1999). When interviewers desire accurate impressions: The effects of note taking on the influence of expectations. *Journal of Applied Social Psychology, 29*, 2529–2549.

Biesanz, J. C., Neuberg, S. L., Smith, D. M., Asher, T., & Judice, T. N. (2001). When accuracy-motivated perceivers fail: Limited attentional capacity and the reemerging self-fulfilling prophecy. *Personality and Social Psychology Bulletin, 27*, 621–629.

Darley, J. M. & Fazio, R. H. (1980). Expectancy confirmation processes arising in the social interaction sequence. *American Psychologist, 35*, 867–881.

Fiske, S. T. & Neuberg, S. L. (1990). A continuum of impression formation, from category-based to individuating processes: Influences of information and motivation on attention and interpretation. In M. P. Zanna (ed.), *Advances in Experimental Social Psychology* (Vol. 23, 1–74). New York: Academic Press.

Harris, M. J. & Rosenthal, R. (1985). Mediation of interpersonal expectancy effects: 31 meta-analyses. *Psychological Bulletin, 97*, 363–386.

Ickes, W., Patterson, M. L., Rajecki, D. W. & Tanford, S. (1982). Behavioral and cognitive consequences of reciprocal versus compensatory responses to pre-interaction expectancies. *Social Cognition, 1*, 160–190.

Judice, T. N. & Neuberg, S. L. (1998). When interviewers desire to confirm negative expectations: Self-fulfilling prophecies and inflated applicant self-perceptions. *Basic and Applied Social Psychology, 20*, 175–190.

Jussim, L. (1986). Self-fulfilling prophecies: A theoretical and integrative review. *Psychological Review, 93*, 429–445.

Jussim, L. (2012). *Social Perception and Social Reality: Why Accuracy Dominates Bias and Self-fulfilling Prophecy*. New York: Oxford University Press.

Kenrick, D. T., Griskevicius, V., Neuberg, S. L. & Schaller, M. (2010). Renovating the pyramid of needs: Contemporary extensions built upon ancient foundations. *Perspectives on Psychological Science, 5*, 291–314.

Neuberg, S. L. (1989). The goal of forming accurate impressions during social interactions: Attenuating the impact of negative expectancies. *Journal of Personality and Social Psychology, 56*, 374–386.

Neuberg, S. L. (1994). Expectancy-confirmation processes in stereotype-tinged social encounters: The moderating role of social goals. In M. P. Zanna & J. M. Olson (eds), *The Psychology of Prejudice: The Ontario Symposium* (Vol. 7, 103–130). Hillsdale, NJ: Lawrence Erlbaum.

Neuberg, S. L. (1996). Social motives and expectancy-tinged social interactions. In R. M. Sorrentino & E. T. Higgins (eds), *Handbook of Motivation and Cognition: The Interpersonal Context* (Vol. 3, 225–261). New York: The Guilford Press.

Neuberg, S. L. & Fiske, S. T. (1987). Motivational influences on impression formation: Outcome dependency, accuracy-driven attention, and individuating processes. *Journal of Personality and Social Psychology*, *53*, 431–444.

Neuberg, S. L. & Schaller, M. (2014). Evolutionary social cognition. In M. Mikulincer & P. R. Shaver (eds), *APA Handbook of Personality and Social Psychology* (Vol. 1, Attitudes and social cognition, 3–45, E. Borgida & J. A. Bargh (assoc. eds)). Washington, DC: American Psychological Association.

Neuberg, S. L., Judice, T. N., Virdin, L. M. & Carrillo, M. A. (1993). Perceiver self-presentational goals as moderators of expectancy influences: Ingratiation and the disconfirmation of negative expectancies. *Journal of Personality and Social Psychology*, *64*, 409–420.

Smith, D. M., Neuberg, S. L., Judice, T. N. & Biesanz, J. C. (1997). Target complicity in the confirmation and disconfirmation of erroneous perceiver expectations: Immediate and longer term implications. *Journal of Personality and Social Psychology*, *73*, 974–991.

Snyder, M. (1984). When belief creates reality. In L. Berkowitz (ed.), *Advances in Experimental Social Psychology* (Vol. 18, 248–306). New York: Academic Press.

Snyder, M. & Swann, W. B., Jr (1978). Hypothesis-testing processes in social interaction. *Journal of Personality and Social Psychology*, *36*, 1202–1212.

Snyder, M., Campbell, B. H. & Preston, E. (1982). Testing hypotheses about human nature: Assessing the accuracy of social stereotypes. *Social Cognition*, *1*, 256–272.

Snyder, M., Tanke, E. D. & Berscheid, E. (1977). Social perception and interpersonal behavior: On the self-fulfilling nature of social stereotypes. *Journal of Personality and Social Psychology*, *35*, 656–666.

Swann, W. B., Jr & Ely, R. J. (1984). A battle of wills; self-verification versus behavioral confirmation. *Journal of Personality and Social Psychology*, *46*, 1287–1302.

Swim, J. K. (1994). Perceived versus meta-analytical effect sizes: An assessment of the accuracy of gender stereotypes. *Journal of Personality and Social Psychology*, *66*, 21–36.

Trope, Y. & Thompson, E. P. (1997). Looking for truth in all the wrong places? Asymmetric search of individuating information about stereotyped group members. *Journal of Personality and Social Psychology*, *73*, 229–241.

Word, C. O., Zanna, M. P. & Cooper, J. (1974). The nonverbal mediation of self-fulfilling prophecies in inter-racial interaction. *Journal of Experimental Social Psychology*, *10*, 109–120.

13

WHY ACCURACY DOMINATES SELF-FULFILLING PROPHECIES AND BIAS

Lee Jussim and Sean T. Stevens

Social psychology has a longstanding consensus that social perception is dominated by self-fulfilling prophecy, error and bias (e.g. Darley & Fazio, 1980; Hastorf & Cantril, 1954; Katz & Braly, 1933; Ross *et al.*, 2010; Snyder, 1984). In this short chapter, we explain why this consensus is not justified. Broad and seemingly unrelated literatures converge on three conclusions: 1) Although errors, biases, and self-fulfilling prophecies in person perception are real, reliable, and occasionally quite powerful, on average, they tend to be weak, fragile and fleeting. 2) Perceptions of individuals and groups tend to be at least moderately, and often highly accurate. 3) Common scholarly conclusions routinely overstate the power and pervasiveness of expectancy effects, and consistently ignore evidence of accuracy, agreement, and rationality in social perception. This pattern occurs repeatedly across a wide variety of research areas within social perception. For short, therefore, we simply refer to it as "the tripartite pattern."

The beginnings of expectancy research

Social psychologists have demonstrated an interest in, at minimum, three ways that social beliefs may be related to social reality. Self-fulfilling prophecies occur when initially erroneous beliefs lead to their own fulfillment (Merton, 1948). When a self-fulfilling prophecy occurs, the target person actually behaves in a manner that confirms the originally false expectation. In contrast, expectancy bias refers to social beliefs that influence or distort subjective perceptions and judgments. Expectancy biases change the image of social reality in the perceiver's own mind, without changing the target's actual behavior. Social perceptual accuracy is correspondence between perceivers' beliefs (expectations, perceptions, judgments, etc.) about one or more target people and what those target people are actually like, independent of perceivers' influence on them. More correspondence without influence typically means more accuracy.

The story: the "extraordinary" power of self-fulfilling prophecies and biases to create social reality

The self-fulfilling and biasing effects of expectancies became a major area of research after the publication of the famous and controversial Pygmalion study (Rosenthal & Jacobson, 1968). School teachers were led to believe that a subset of their students (who were actually randomly selected) would show dramatic IQ increases over the course of the year. Confirming the self-fulfilling prophecy hypothesis, on average, those late bloomers did indeed show greater IQ increases than their classmates.

Especially when combined with subsequent research showing e.g. that stereotypes can be self-fulfilling (e.g. Snyder *et al.*, 1977; Word *et al.*, 1974), research on expectancies has been interpreted by many scholars as providing a powerful and profound insight into a major source of social, educational, and economic inequality (e.g. Darley & Fazio, 1980; Gilbert, 1995; Jones, 1990; Ross *et al.*, 2010; Snyder, 1984; Weinstein *et al.*, 2004). Teacher expectations (Rist, 1970; Rosenthal & Jacobson, 1968) seemed to systematically advantage students from already advantaged backgrounds (e.g. Whites, middle-class students, etc.), and disadvantage students from already disadvantaged backgrounds (e.g. ethnic minorities, students from lower social class backgrounds). To the extent that education is a major stepping-stone towards occupational and economic advancement, self-fulfilling prophecies, it would seem, constituted a major social force operating to keep the oppressed in "their place."

On the basis of these types of findings, and especially when combined with the assumption of stereotype inaccuracy, some scholars have concluded that self-fulfilling prophecies are likely to be a powerful and pervasive source of social injustice and group inequalities (e.g. Claire & Fiske, 1998; Jones, 1990; Ross *et al.*, 2010; Weinstein *et al.*, 2004). The narrative of this story contends that stereotypes lead to inaccurate expectations for individuals. Inaccurate expectations are powerfully and pervasively self-fulfilling. Because stereotypes are, the story goes, so widely shared and so widely inaccurate, their powerfully self-fulfilling effects will accumulate over time and across perceivers. Because self-fulfilling prophecies are so consistently harmful, damaging self-fulfilling prophecy on top of damaging self-fulfilling prophecy will be heaped upon the backs of those already most heavily burdened by disadvantage and oppression. Thus, the achievement and advancement of people from socially stigmatized groups will be so repeatedly undermined by self-fulfilling prophecies that self-fulfilling prophecies constitute a major source of social inequalities and social problems.

The current state of research on expectancies

The inadequacy of the "story"

The most benevolent interpretation of this sort of conclusion is that it is woefully incomplete. Cognitive biases do sometimes lead to expectancy confirmation and

112 L. Jussim and S. T. Stevens

expectancies do sometimes lead to self-fulfilling prophecies. But the power of expectations to distort social beliefs through biases, and to create actual social reality through self-fulfilling prophecies is, in general, so small, fragile, and fleeting that it is quite difficult to make a convincing case that such effects likely constitute a major source of inequality.

Even the original Rosenthal and Jacobson (1968) study only found an overall self-fulfilling prophecy effect of r=.15. Statistically significant expectancy effects occurred in only three of eleven grades studied. Furthermore, rather than increasing over time, the effects declined from year one to year two. Thus, even if one takes their results at face value, the effects were generally weak, fragile, and fleeting, and provide little support for the "story." Many, however, do not take the results at face value (e.g. Elashoff & Snow, 1971; Snow, 1994; Wineburg, 1987). Although there are many reasons to doubt the study's conclusions, perhaps the clearest is this: there were five students who showed incredible IQ gains over the first year – 17–110, 18–122, 133–202, 111–208, and 113–211 (Snow, 1995). If one removes these five bizarre outliers, the significant expectancy effect disappears.

The "story," however, is not invalidated merely by limitations to Roesenthal and Jacobson's (1968) study. However, hundreds of studies show that (see Jussim, 2012 for a review addressing each of these points):

1 Replications of some of the most classic studies of self-fulfilling prophecy or expectancy-induced bias have often failed.
2 Many studies routinely interpreted as showing pervasive evidence of bias (e.g. Hastorf & Cantril, 1954; Rosenhan, 1973) actually provide far more evidence of accuracy.
3 The biasing effects of expectations and stereotypes on person perception hover barely above zero, making stereotype and expectancy biases one of the smallest effects in a field characterized by generally modest effects (Richard *et al.*, 2003).
4 Self-fulfilling prophecy effects are often modest, averaging about r=.10 to.20 under naturally occurring conditions.
5 Every study that has examined long-term self-fulfilling prophecy effects in classrooms has found that, rather than accumulating over time, they dissipate (Rist, 1970; Rosenthal & Jacobson, 1968; Smith *et al.*, 1999; West & Anderson, 1976).
6 Some of the largest self-fulfilling prophecy effects ever obtained increased rather than decreased the performance of low-achieving students (Madon *et al.*, 1997).

When considered together, these findings suggest that the "story" is at best incomplete.

Future directions of research on expectancies

The tripartite pattern characterizes not just individual studies, but whole areas of research. For example, social psychologists have been declaring stereotypes to be "inaccurate" for over half a century (e.g. Allport, 1954/1979; Bargh & Chartrand, 1999; Jones, 1986; Miller & Turnbull, 1986). Defining stereotypes as inaccurate turns out to be logically incoherent, because it can mean only one of two things: 1) all beliefs about groups are inaccurate, or 2) stereotypes are the subset of beliefs about groups that are inaccurate. Both are incoherent, for different reasons. This is explained briefly below (see Jussim, 2012 for a full exposition).

Any claim that all beliefs about groups are inaccurate means both that believing two groups differ is inaccurate, and believing they do not differ is inaccurate. This is logically impossible. If, instead, stereotypes are the subset of beliefs about groups that are inaccurate, then one must first demonstrate inaccuracy in a belief about a group before it can be known to be a stereotype. If inaccuracy is not demonstrated a priori, the beliefs under investigation cannot be known to be stereotypes. This has never been done in any study purporting to study a "stereotype" (see Jussim, 2012 for a review). Therefore, the entire corpus of social psychological literature framed as addressing stereotypes must be rejected – absent first, showing that the belief was inaccurate, none of it can be known to have actually studied a stereotype.

In the context of this sort of incoherence, it should then perhaps be less surprising to discover that not only is there considerable evidence of accuracy in many stereotypes, but that stereotype accuracy is one of the largest and most replicable effects in all of social psychology. Whereas only 5 percent of social psychological effects exceed $r = .50$ (Richard *et al.*, 2003), more than half of all race and gender stereotype accuracy correlations exceed $r = .50$ (Jussim *et al.*, 2016). In contrast to many far more famous – and less replicable – effects in social psychology, this pattern has been obtained by multiple independent researchers. To be sure, there is some evidence of inaccurate stereotypes, especially regarding national stereotypes, and political partisans often exaggerate one another's views (see Jussim *et al.* 2016, for a review). Nonetheless, the big picture remains intact: in sharp contrast to decades of claims about stereotype inaccuracy, the actual data shows that stereotype accuracy is one of the largest and most replicable effects in all of social psychology.

The evidence on stereotype accuracy, therefore, also supports the tripartite conclusion. Social interaction does often confirm people's expectations – mainly because those expectations are often at least moderately accurate. Biases occur, but rather than being powerful and pervasive, are weak, fragile, and fleeting. Abundant evidence attests to the implausibility of "the story"; very little actually supports it. "The story" is maintained primarily by a very selective and uncritical consideration of the evidence.

Why is "the story" so popular?

"The story" seems to be sustained primarily by its political appeal as a basis for fighting oppression (Jussim, 2012; Jussim *et al.*, in press). Fighting oppression is a good thing. But here again, we are faced with an apparent choice between laudatory goals. Sometimes social scientists' desire to contribute to a more fair and just society may appear to conflict with the results of their research. If stereotypes

114 L. Jussim and S. T. Stevens

cannot be credibly condemned as massively invalid distortions, if expectancies do not bias perception, memory, and information-seeking to any great extent, if self-fulfilling prophecies do not accumulate to create ever-increasing differences between demographic groups, we would lose some valuable rhetorical tools for fighting oppression. But the research on self-fulfilling prophecies, person perception biases, and stereotypes raises the following questions: do social psychologists really want to continue promoting false ("stereotypes are inaccurate") or misleading ("self-fulfilling prophecies are powerful and pervasive") conclusions, even if they are in the service of laudatory political goals?

Applications of results from research on expectancies

The main reason social beliefs correspond to social reality is not self-fulfilling prophecy, it is not judgmental bias, it is accuracy. Nonetheless, except to be dismissed as uninteresting or unimportant, it remains largely ignored when articles discuss the role of stereotypes or self-fulfilling prophecies in social problems. Despite the fact that stereotype accuracy is one of the largest effects in all social psychology (Jussim, 2012; Jussim *et al.*, 2009; Jussim *et al.* in press), social psychology textbooks spend pages and pages on bias and rarely mention accuracy (Clark & Clark-Polner, 2012). Indeed, some of the most classic demonstrations of "bias" actually provide far more evidence of accuracy. For example, in the aftermath of a hotly contested (American) football game between Dartmouth and Princeton, Hastorf & Cantril (1954) showed a film of the game to 48 Dartmouth students and 49 Princeton students, and had them rate the total number of infractions by each team. Dartmouth students saw both the Dartmouth and Princeton teams as committing slightly over four (on average) infractions. The Princeton students also saw the Princeton team as committing slightly over four infractions, but they also saw the Dartmouth team as committing nearly ten infractions.

Because the Dartmouth and Princeton students diverged in the number of infractions they claimed were committed by Dartmouth, Hastorf & Cantril (1954) concluded that Princeton and Dartmouth students seemed to be actually seeing different games. The study has long been cited as a demonstration of how motivations and beliefs color social perception (e.g. Ross *et al.*, 2010; Schneider *et al.*, 1979; Sedikedes & Skowronski, 1991). As Ross *et al.* (2010, p. 23) put it: "The early classic study by Hastorf and Cantril (1954) . . . reflected a radical view of the 'constructive' nature of perception that anticipated later discussions of naïve realism."

And yet, the actual study provided far more evidence of agreement than bias. First, there was no bias in perceptions of infractions committed by Princeton. Thus, for half the game, bias, subjectivity, and constructivism were essentially nonexistent. What about the other half? With respect to perceptions of infractions committed by Dartmouth, subjectivity and bias occurred for a grand total of six plays (the ten Dartmouth infractions seen by the Princeton students versus the four Dartmouth infractions seen by the Dartmouth students. There are typically 80–100 plays in a football game. Even if one assumes only 60 plays, bias of six means that 10 percent of judgments were biased – which means the same thing as 90 percent unbiased. Unbiased responding massively dominated over bias and constructivism. A similar pattern characterizes other "classics" of bias, such as Rosenhan (1973). The manner in which such studies have been almost universally interpreted reflects the tripartite pattern:

1 Bias is real, but modest.
2 Accuracy dominates over bias.
3 Conclusions routinely overstate the power and pervasiveness of expectancy effects, and consistently ignore evidence of accuracy, agreement, and rationality in social perception.

Conclusion

Accuracy dominates bias and self-fulfilling prophecy

Social perceptions can construct social realities. People are indeed subject to all sorts of imperfections, errors, and biases. Occasionally, such effects are quite large. Sometimes, such effects can have important effects on targets' lives. In general, however, the evidence to date supports the tripartite pattern:

1 Biases and self-fulfilling prophecies, though real, are generally weak, fragile, and fleeting.
2 Many social perceptions, including social stereotypes, are often more heavily based on social reality than they distort or create such realities.
3 Social psychological conclusions routinely overstate the power of expectancy effects, and consistently ignore evidence of accuracy in social perception.

References

Allport, G. W. (1954/1979). *The Nature of Prejudice* (2nd edn). Cambridge, MA: Perseus Books.

Bargh, J. A. & Chartrand, T. L. (1999). The unbearable automaticity of being. *American Psychologist*, *54*, 462–479.

Claire, T. & Fiske, S. (1998). A systemic view of behavioral confirmation: Counterpoint to the individualist view. In C. Sedikedes, J. Schopler, C. A. Insko (eds), *Intergroup Cognition and Intergroup Behavior* (pp. 205–231). Mahwah, NJ: Erlbaum.

Clark, M. S. & Clark-Polner, E. (2012). Thinking critically about research on accuracy and bias in social perception. *PsycCRITIQUES*, *57*. Available at: http://psycnet.apa.org/doi/10.1037/a0030346

Darley, J. M. & Fazio, R. H. (1980). Expectancy-confirmation processes arising in the social interaction sequence. *American Psychologist*, *35*, 867–881.

Elashoff, J. D. & Snow, R. E. (1971). *Pygmalion Reconsidered*. Worthington, OH: Charles A. Jones.

Gilbert, D. T. (1995). Attribution and interpersonal perception. In A. Tesser (ed.), *Advanced Social Psychology* (pp. 99–147). New York: McGraw-Hill.

Hastorf, A. H. & Cantril, H. (1954). They saw a game: A case study. *Journal of Abnormal and Social Psychology*, *47*, 129–143.

Jones, E. E. (1986). Interpreting interpersonal behavior: The effects of expectancies. *Science*, *234*, 41–46.

Jones, E. E. (1990). *Interpersonal Perception*. New York: W.H. Freeman.

Jussim, L. (2012). *Social Perception and Social Reality: Why Accuracy Dominates Bias and Self-fulfilling Prophecy*. New York: Oxford University Press.

Jussim, L., Cain, T., Crawford, J., Harber, K. & Cohen, F. (2009). The unbearable accuracy of stereotypes. In T. Nelson (ed.), *Handbook of Prejudice, Stereotyping, and Discrimination* (pp.199–227). Hillsdale, NJ: Erlbaum.

Jussim, L., Crawford, J. T., Anglin, S. M., Chambers, J. R., Stevens, S. T. & Cohen, F. (2016). Stereotype accuracy: One of the largest and most replicable effects in all of social psychology. In T. Nelson (ed.), *Handbook of Prejudice, Stereotyping, and Discrimination*. (2nd edn)(pp. 31–63). Hillsdale, NJ: Erlbaum.

Katz, D. & Braly, K. (1933). Racial stereotypes of one hundred college students. *Journal of Abnormal and Social Psychology*, *28*, 280–290.

Madon, S. J., Jussim, L. & Eccles, J. (1997). In search of the powerful self-fulfilling prophecy. *Journal of Personality and Social Psychology*, *72*, 791–809.

Merton, R. K. (1948). The self-fulfilling prophecy. *Antioch Review*, *8*, 193–210.

Miller, D. T. & Turnbull, W. (1986). Expectancies and interpersonal processes. *Annual Review of Psychology*, *37*, 233–256.

Richard, F. D., Bond, C. F., Jr & Stokes-Zoota, J. J. (2003). One hundred years of social psychology quantitatively described. *Review of General Psychology*, *7*, 331–363.

Rist, R. (1970). Student social class and teacher expectations: The self-fulfilling prophecy in ghetto education. *Harvard Educational Review*, 40, 411– 451.

Rosenhan, D. L. (1973). On being sane in insane places. *Science*, *179*, 250–258.

Rosenthal, R. & Jacobson, L. (1968). *Pygmalion in the Classroom: Teacher Expectations and Student Intellectual Development*. New York: Holt, Rinehart & Winston.

Ross, L. D., Lepper, M. & Ward, A. (2010). History of social psychology: Insights, challenges, and contributions to theory and application. *Handbook of Social Psychology* (Vol. 1, 5th edn). Hoboken, NJ: Wiley.

Schneider, D. J., Hastorf, H. & Ellsworth, P. C. (1979). *Person Perception* (2nd edn). Reading, MA: Addison-Wesley.

Sedikides, C. & Skowronski, J. (1991). On the law of cognitive structure activation: Reply to commentaries. *Psychological Inquiry*, *2*, 211–219.

Smith, A., Jussim, L., Eccles, J., Van Noy, M., Madon, S.J. & Palumbo, P. (1998). Self-fulfilling prophecies, perceptual biases, and accuracy at the individual and group level. *Journal of Experimental Social Psychology*, *34*, 530–561.

Snow, R. E. (1995). Pygmalion and intelligence? *Current Directions in Psychological Science*, *4*, 169–171.

Snyder, M. (1984). When belief creates reality. *Advances in Experimental Social Psychology*, *18*, 247–305.

Snyder, M., Tanke, E. D.& Berscheid, E. (1977). Social perception and interpersonal behavior: On the self–fulfilling nature of social stereotypes. *Journal of Personality and Social Psychology*, *35*, 656–666.

Weinstein, R. S., Gregory, A. & Strambler, M. J. (2004). Intractable self-fulfilling prophecies: Fifty years after Brown v. Board of Education. *American Psychologist*, *59*, 511–520.

West, C. & Anderson, T. (1976). The question of preponderant causation in teacher expectancy research. *Review of Educational Research*, *46*, 613–630.

Wineburg, S. S. (1987). The self-fulfillment of the self-fulfilling prophecy: A critical appraisal. Educational Researcher, 16, 28–40.

Word, C. O., Zanna, M. P. & Cooper, J. (1974). The nonverbal mediation of self-fulfilling prophecies in interracial interaction. *Journal of Experimental Social Psychology*, *10*, 109–120.

14

UNDERSTANDING THE CONNECTIONS BETWEEN SELF-FULFILLING PROPHECIES AND SOCIAL PROBLEMS

Jennifer Willard and Stephanie Madon

Genesis: are self-fulfilling prophecies powerful enough to contribute to social problems?

A prevailing theme in the psychological literature is that perceivers' false beliefs can shape the future behavior of targets – a process referred to as a self-fulfilling prophecy (Merton, 1948). The term self-fulfilling prophecy was first introduced to the social sciences by Robert Merton (1948). A sociologist by training, Merton proposed that self-fulfilling prophecies had the potential to produce profound social problems, including economic downturns, unfair labor practices, and discriminatory policies. Research bearing on Merton's analysis clearly supported the existence of self-fulfilling prophecies (Harris & Rosenthal, 1985; Rosenthal & Jacobson, 1968; Rosenthal & Rubin, 1978; Snyder *et al.*, 1977; Swann & Ely, 1984), but did not support his suggestion that self-fulfilling prophecies were powerful sources of social problems (Jussim, 1989, 1991, 2012; Jussim & Eccles, 1992, 1995; Jussim *et al.*, 1996). Both experimental and naturalistic research have converged on the conclusion that self-fulfilling prophecy effects are relatively modest in magnitude.

Our interest in self-fulfilling prophecies emerged out of this observation. We wondered whether Merton's hypothesis that self-fulfilling prophecies contributed to social problems had simply been wrong or whether there might be mechanisms that could render self-fulfilling prophecies powerful enough to produce the kinds of social problems that he had proposed. For nearly twenty years, this question has guided our research. In classrooms, among families, and in the lab, we have searched for mechanisms that have the potential to render even small self-fulfilling prophecy effects powerful. We summarize our main findings in this chapter and then discuss avenues of research that we believe will shed additional light on the link between self-fulfilling prophecies and social problems.

What we discovered

Some people are more susceptible to self-fulfilling prophecies than others

Despite a substantial body of research showing that self-fulfilling prophecies occur in a variety of contexts (e.g. parent–child, teacher–student, experimenter–participant, therapist–client, and interrogator–suspect), the overall magnitude of self-fulfilling prophecy effects is relatively small (Jussim, 1991; Jussim & Eccles, 1992; Rosenthal, 2002; Rosenthal & Rubin, 1978). Nonetheless, there still exists the possibility that self-fulfilling prophecies could exert relatively powerful effects on the behaviors of some individuals. Our research, for example, has shown that self-fulfilling prophecies have powerful effects on the behaviors of individuals who belong to stigmatized social groups or who have personal vulnerabilities, including African American students, girls in math classes, students from lower social class backgrounds, students with histories of poor academic performance, students who belong to more than one stigmatized group, and youth with low self-efficacy (Jussim et al., 1996; Madon et al., 1997; Smith et al., 1998). In fact, the magnitudes of some of these relations represent the most powerful self-fulfilling prophecy effects ever observed in naturalistic settings (Jussim et al., 1996; Madon et al., 1997).

The tendency for stigmatized and vulnerable individuals to be highly susceptible to self-fulfilling prophecy effects appears to provide support for the idea that self-fulfilling prophecies contribute to social problems. However, such an interpretation implies that the effects of self-fulfilling prophecies are primarily harmful, suggesting, for instance, that teachers' self-fulfilling effects tend to undermine the academic achievement of stigmatized students more than they raise their achievement, or that parents' self-fulfilling effects tend to increase the rate of alcohol use among vulnerable youth more than they reduce their rate of alcohol use. The possibility that such patterns of self-fulfilling influence might characterize interpersonal relationships involving stigmatized and vulnerable individuals certainly makes sense. Stigmatized individuals are often viewed unfavorably (Goffman, 1963) and people generally react more strongly to negative information than to positive information (Baumeister et al., 2001; Coleman et al., 1987).

However, the empirical evidence is not so clear. Whereas some studies have found that self-fulfilling prophecies are more harmful than helpful (Alvidrez & Weinstein, 1999; Babad et al., 1982; Sutherland & Goldschmid, 1974), others have found just the opposite – that self-fulfilling prophecies are more helpful than harmful (Madon et al., 1997, 2003, 2004; Willard et al., 2008). For example, we have found that teachers' false beliefs raised students' achievement more than they lowered it (Madon et al., 1997) and that mothers' false beliefs buffered their adolescents against increased alcohol use rather than putting them at greater risk (Madon et al., 2003, 2004; Willard et al., 2008).

Moreover, these disproportionately positive self-fulfilling effects were strongest among stigmatized and vulnerable individuals, including students with a history of poor academic performance (Madon *et al.*, 2003) and youth with low self-efficacy to refuse alcohol from their peers (Willard *et al.*, 2008). Thus, a susceptibility to self-fulfilling prophecy effects can have beneficial consequences. Nevertheless, it is also important to recognize that due to prejudice or stereotypes, stigmatized and vulnerable individuals may be far more likely to encounter unfavorable beliefs from those with whom they interact than they are to encounter favorable beliefs. Accordingly, even though stigmatized and vulnerable individuals have the potential to benefit greatly from self-fulfilling prophecies, they may only rarely have the chance to reap those benefits.

Self-fulfilling prophecy effects can accumulate

Self-fulfilling prophecies can also be rendered powerful through accumulation processes. The potential for self-fulfilling prophecy effects to accumulate has been of particular interest to social scientists because of the possibility that such effects could widen the gap between individuals who are the targets of unfavorable versus favorable false beliefs (Jussim *et al.*, 1996; Klein & Snyder, 2003; Snyder & Stukas, 1999). In fact, the accumulation of self-fulfilling prophecy effects is one of the primary ways that self-fulfilling prophecies have been thought to generate and perpetuate social inequities (see Jussim *et al.*, 1996; Klein & Snyder, 2003; Madon *et al.*, 2004, 2006; Snyder, 1992; Snyder & Stukas, 1999, for reviews). There are two general classes of accumulation that have been distinguished in the literature – accumulation that occurs over time and accumulation that occurs across perceivers.

Accumulation over time

Self-fulfilling prophecies accumulate over time when a self-fulfilling effect becomes successively stronger as time passes, such as across several years. For example, the false belief that a teacher holds about a student at the beginning of the 6th grade may have a stronger self-fulfilling effect on the student's 10th grade achievement than it had on the student's 7th grade achievement. This form of accumulation reflects the single belief model (Madon *et al.*, 2008) because it involves the self-fulfilling effect of a single false belief (e.g. teacher's false belief held at the beginning of the 6th grade) on an outcome that occurs at multiple future points in time (e.g. student's achievement in the 7th and 10th grades). Five studies have tested whether self-fulfilling prophecies accumulate via the single belief model, but only one supported an accumulation effect (Madon *et al.*, 2006; Rist, 1970; Rosenthal & Jacobson, 1968; Smith *et al.*, 1999; West & Anderson, 1976). Rosenthal and Jacobson (1968) found that the self-fulfilling effect of teachers' false beliefs on students' IQs was stronger after eight months (year-end) than after only four months (mid-year). However, the accumulation effect dissipated after students transitioned into the next grade level, thereby suggesting that the effect was short-lived (see Madon *et al.*, 2011 for a review).

Another form of accumulation over time reflects the *repeated belief model* (Madon *et al.*, 2006). This occurs when multiple false beliefs held at different points in time combine to have a stronger self-fulfilling effect on a person's outcome that occurs at a single later point in time. For example, the false beliefs that a mother holds about her adolescent's alcohol use in the 7th and 8th grades may each uniquely contribute to her adolescent's 9th grade alcohol use through each belief's independent self-fulfilling effect. One study has tested whether self-fulfilling prophecies accumulate in this way, and the results supported the hypothesized pattern of accumulation. Madon *et al.* (2006) found that mothers' self-fulfilling effects accumulated over time when their beliefs were similar in terms of favorability, such as when mothers repeatedly held negative beliefs about their adolescents' likelihood of alcohol use across multiple years. Moreover, the accumulation of mothers' self-fulfilling effects over these years exacerbated differences between the alcohol use of adolescents who were exposed to consistent histories of unfavorable versus favorable beliefs.

Accumulation across people

Psychological theory also hypothesizes that self-fulfilling prophecies can accumulate across perceivers (Jussim *et al.*, 1996; Klein & Synder, 2003; Madon *et al.*, 2004; Snyder, 1992; Snyder & Stukas, 1999). According to this idea, small self-fulfilling prophecy effects become powerful when the individual self-fulfilling effects of multiple people combine. For example, in a typical day, a student may interact with several different teachers, each of whom may hold a false belief about the student, and each of whom could have a self-fulfilling effect on the student's achievement as a result. Although each teacher's self-fulfilling effect may be small by itself, together, the teachers' self-fulfilling effects could be quite powerful.

The literature has long recognized the potential for self-fulfilling prophecies to accumulate across people (Jussim *et al.*, 1996; Klein & Snyder, 2003; Merton, 1948), but only one study has tested this idea. Madon *et al.* (2004) examined whether the false beliefs that mothers and fathers held about their adolescents' alcohol use potentiated each other's self-fulfilling effects when their beliefs were similar in terms of favorability (i.e. both unfavorable or both favorable) – a process that they labeled *synergistic accumulation*. Results supported synergistic accumulation for unfavorable beliefs: adolescents' alcohol use was greatest when both mothers and fathers held unfavorable beliefs about their children's alcohol use. Results did not support synergistic accumulation for favorable beliefs: adolescents' alcohol use was similar regardless of whether one parent or both held favorable beliefs about their children's alcohol use. Accordingly, the findings demonstrated an asymmetry in the accumulation of self-fulfilling prophecy effects – that is, the effects caused by unfavorable beliefs accumulated whereas the effects caused by favorable beliefs did not. These results are important because they suggest that the self-fulfilling prophecy effects reported in the literature may underestimate the true extent to which individuals are harmed by others' unfavorable beliefs because that literature has focused exclusively on dyadic relations, largely ignoring the possibility that harmful self-fulfilling prophecy effects may accumulate across people more than do helpful ones.

Future directions in the study of cumulative effects

The self-fulfilling prophecy has a long and rich history in psychology and, we believe, an exciting future. After nearly eighty years of inquiry, many questions about the process have been answered, but these answers have raised new questions. For example, we know that some individuals, because of stigma or personal vulnerabilities, are more susceptible to self-fulfilling prophecies than others, but we do not know why. A host of possibilities exist – negative stereotypes, limited social and psychological resources, and even environmental stressors such as poverty and crime (Jussim *et al.*, 1996) – but there are no clear answers. Of these possibilities, negative stereotypes is the only potential cause that has been tested. Jussim *et al.* (1996) examined whether teachers' racial, social class, and sex stereotypes could explain why stigmatized students were more susceptible to their teachers' self-fulfilling effects than were non-stigmatized students. However, stereotypes did not emerge as a particularly viable explanation. With few exceptions, teachers did not use stereotypes to judge students. Instead, teachers overwhelmingly judged students on the basis of students' personal characteristics, such as their prior achievement and motivation. With so little evidence of stereotype-based bias, Jussim *et al.* concluded that stereotypes were not responsible for the powerful self-fulfilling prophecy effects that emerged among stigmatized students in their data.

However, their study (like nearly all studies on self-fulfilling prophecies) focused exclusively on dyadic relations, examining whether an individual teacher's stereotype was associated with a particular student's subsequent achievement. Although a focus on dyadic relations is often warranted, it also has the potential to obscure the true extent to which false beliefs alter behavior because, as we explained above, such relations cannot account for the possibility that self-fulfilling prophecy effects can accumulate. The potential for accumulation is particularly relevant with respect to stereotype-based beliefs. Because social stereotypes are consensual, individuals who belong to stereotyped groups may repeatedly confront similar stereotypic expectations from many different people, across many different contexts, and over the span of many different years (Madon *et al.*, 2001). If these stereotypic expectations are false and negative (as they often are), then unjust social trajectories may form (see Klein & Snyder, 2003; Jussim *et al.*, 1996; Snyder & Stukas, 1999, for reviews). Although the psychological literature has long recognized the potential for stereotypes to have cumulative self-fulfilling effects on behavior, no prior research has tested this idea. We believe that testing the cumulative self-fulfilling effect of social stereotypes is extremely important. In fact, social stereotypes may be the missing link that explains how self-fulfilling prophecy effects – effects that tend to be small and beneficial at the dyadic level – may be powerful enough to create and perpetuate large-scale social disparities.

Implications: why this research matters

Throughout the chapter we have focused on self-fulfilling prophecies created by teachers and parents. Our interest in their self-fulfilling effects reflects the potential for teachers and parents to influence youth's educational, occupational, and social outcomes. Madon's *et al.*'s (2006) repeated belief model suggests that the tendency for people's self-fulfilling effects to accumulate over time is important to psychological theory because it shows how even small self-fulfilling prophecy effects can widen the gap between advantaged and disadvantaged individuals and groups, thus creating, perpetuating, and exacerbating social inequalities. Furthermore, self-fulfilling prophecy effects can accumulate across perceivers in an asymmetrical pattern, favoring the accumulation of negative self-fulfilling prophecies over positive self-fulfilling prophecies (Madon *et al.*, 2004). Thus, self-fulfilling prophecies can benefit targets in general, while simultaneously harming targets who are disproportionately exposed to unfavorable beliefs from multiple perceivers.

These findings are particularly important to individuals from stigmatized groups or at-risk students who tend to be disproportionately affected, favorably or unfavorably, by their teachers' or parents' self-fulfilling influences (Jussim *et al.*, 1996; Madon *et al.*, 1997, 2003; Willard *et al.*, 2008). One way to increase the chances that stigmatized and vulnerable individuals will benefit from self-fulfilling prophecies is by instituting policy changes that encourage teachers, employers, and parents to hold realistic, but high, expectations for their students, employees, and children (Eden, 1986). Our research suggests that under these conditions stigmatized and vulnerable individuals will be able to benefit considerably from the potentially positive effects of self-fulfilling prophecies.

References

Alvidrez, J. & Weinstein, S. R. (1999). Early teacher perceptions and later student academic achievement. *Journal of Educational Psychology*, *91*, 731–746.

Babad, E. Y., Inbar, J. & Rosenthal, R. (1982). Pygmalion, Galatea, and the Golem: Investigations of biased and unbiased teachers. *Journal of Educational Psychology*, *74*, 459–474.

Baumeister, R. F., Bratslavsky, E., Finkenauer, C. & Vohs, K. D. (2001). Bad is stronger than good. *Review of General Psychology*, *5*, 323–370.

Coleman, L. M., Jussim, L. & Abraham, J. (1987). Students' reactions to teachers' evaluations: The unique impact of negative feedback. *Journal of Applied Social Psychology*, *17*, 1051–1070.

Eden, D. (1986). OD and self-fulfilling prophecy: Boosting productivity by raising expectations. *Journal of Applied Behavioral Science*, *22*, 1–13.

Goffman, E. (1963). *Stigma: Notes on the Management of a Spoiled Identity*. Englewood Cliffs, NJ: Erlbaum.

Harris, M. J. & Rosenthal, R. (1985). Mediation of interpersonal expectancy effects: 31 meta-analyses. *Psychological Bulletin*, *97*, 363–386.

Jussim, L. (1989). Teacher expectations: Self-fulfilling prophecies, perceptual biases, and accuracy. *Journal of Personality and Social Psychology*, *57*, 469–480.

Jussim, L. (1991). Social perception and social reality: A reflection-construction model. *Psychological Review, 98*, 54–73.

Jussim, L. (2012). *Social Perception and Social Reality: Why Accuracy Dominates Bias and Self-fulfilling Prophecy.* New York: Oxford University Press.

Jussim, L. & Eccles, J. S. (1992). Teacher expectations: II. Construction and reflection of student achievement. *Journal of Personality and Social Psychology, 63*, 947–961.

Jussim, L. & Eccles, J. (1995). Naturalistic studies of interpersonal expectancies. *Review of Personality and Social Psychology, 15*, 74–108.

Jussim, L., Eccles, J. & Madon, S. (1996). Social perception, social stereotypes, and teacher expectations: Accuracy and the quest for the powerful self-fulfilling prophecy. In M. P. Zanna (ed.), *Advances in Experimental Social Psychology*, Vol. 28 (281–388). San Diego, CA: Academic Press.

Klein, O. & Snyder, M. (2003). Stereotypes and behavioral confirmation: From interpersonal to intergroup perspectives. In M. P. Zanna (ed.). *Advances in Experimental Social Psychology*, Vol. 35 (153–234). San Diego, CA: Academic Press.

Madon, S., Jussim, L. & Eccles, J. (1997). In search of the powerful self-fulfilling prophecy. *Journal of Personality and Social Psychology, 72*, 791–809.

Madon, S., Guyll, M., Spoth, R. & Willard, J. (2004). Self-fulfilling prophecies: The synergistic accumulative effect of parents' beliefs on children's drinking behavior. *Psychological Science, 15*, 837–845.

Madon, S., Willard, J., Guyll, M. & Scherr, K. C. (2011). Self-fulfilling prophecies: Mechanism, power, and links to social problems. *Social and Personality Psychology Compass, 5*, 578–590.

Madon, S., Willard, J., Guyll, M., Trudeau, L. & Spoth, R. (2006). Self-fulfilling prophecy effects of mothers' beliefs on children's alcohol use: Accumulation, dissipation, and stability over time. *Journal of Personality and Social Psychology, 90*, 911–926.

Madon, S., Guyll, M., Spoth, R. L., Cross, S. E. & Hilbert, S. J. (2003). The self-fulfilling influence of mother expectations on children's underage drinking. *Journal of Personality and Social Psychology, 84*, 1188–1205.

Madon, S., Guyll, M., Buller, A. A., Scherr, K. C., Willard, J. & Spoth, R. (2008). The mediation of mothers' self-fulfilling effects on their children's alcohol use: Self-verification, informational conformity, and modeling processes. *Journal of Personality and Social Psychology, 95*, 369–384.

Madon, S., Guyll, M., Aboufadel, K., Montiel, E., Smith, A., Palumbo, P. & Jussim, J. (2001). Ethnic and national stereotypes: The Princeton trilogy revisited and revised. *Personality and Social Psychology Bulletin, 27*, 996–1010.

Merton, R. K. (1948). The self-fulfilling prophecy. *Antioch Review, 8*, 193–210.

Rist, R. C. (1970). Student social class and teacher expectations: The self-fulfilling prophecy in ghetto education. *Harvard Education Review, 40*, 411–451.

Rosenthal, R. (2002). Covert communication in classrooms, clinics, courtrooms, and cubicles. *American Psychologist, 57*, 839–849.

Rosenthal, R. & Jacobson, L. (1968). *Pygmalion in the Classroom: Teacher Expectation and Pupils' Intellectual Development.* New York: Holt, Rinehart & Winston.

Rosenthal, R. & Rubin, D. B. (1978). Interpersonal expectancy effects: The first 345 studies. *Behavioral and Brain Sciences, 1*, 377–415.

Smith, A. E., Jussim, L. & Eccles, J. (1999). Do self-fulfilling prophecies accumulate, dissipate, or remain stable over time? *Journal of Personality and Social Psychology, 77*, 548–565.

Smith, A. E., Jussim, L., Eccles, J., VanNoy, M., Madon, S. & Palumbo, P. (1998). Self-fulfilling prophecies, perceptual biases, and accuracy at the individual and group levels. *Journal of Experimental Social Psychology, 34*, 530–561.

Snyder, M. (1992). Motivational foundations of behavioral confirmation. In M. P. Zanna (ed.), *Advances in Experimental Social Psychology*, Vol. 25. (67–114). San Diego, CA: Academic Press.

Snyder, M. & Stukas, A. A. (1999). Interpersonal processes: The interplay of cognitive, motivational, and behavioral activities in social interaction. *Annual Review, 50*, 273–303.

Synder, M., Tanke, E. D. & Berscheid, E. (1977). Social perception and interpersonal behavior: On the self-fulfilling nature of social stereotypes. *Journal of Personality and Social Psychology, 35*, 656–666.

Sutherland, A. & Goldschmid, M. L. (1974). Negative teacher expectation and IQ change in children with superior intellectual potential. *Child Development, 45*, 852–856.

Swann, W. B. & Ely, R. J. (1984). A battle of wills: Self-verification versus behavioral confirmation. *Journal of Personality and Social Psychology, 46*, 1287–1302.

West, C. K. & Anderson, T. H. (1976). The question of preponderant causation in teacher expectancy research. *Review of Educational Research, 46*, 613–630.

Willard, J., Madon, S., Guyll, M., Spoth, R. & Jussim, L. (2008). Self-efficacy as a moderator of negative and positive self-fulfilling prophecy effects: Mothers' beliefs and children's alcohol use. *European Journal of Social Psychology, 38*, 499–520.

15

PYGMALION AND THE CLASSROOM AFTER 50 YEARS

Elisha Babad

Genesis

It must have been predestined that teacher expectancies would play a central role in my scientific career. I was sent by the Hebrew University of Jerusalem in 1968 for doctoral studies at Duke University. In my first semester at Duke I took Michael Wallach's course on creativity and intelligence. In the Wallach and Kogan (1965) book I must have been particularly struck by a marginal paragraph that mentioned teacher expectations in the classroom. Two decades later – me being then a social/educational psychology professor at Hebrew University of Jerusalem, deeply involved in teacher expectancy research – I discovered a faint pencil comment on the margin of that 1968 page: "Think about it in a future day in Jerusalem!"

I learned about *Pygmalion in the Classroom* (Rosenthal & Jacobson, 1968) a year later, and met Rosenthal personally for the first time only in 1971, when I spent my post-doctoral year in the Boston area, teaching at Wellesley College. By that time, the controversy over "Rosenthal effects" (on experimenter effects, SFP, Pygmalion and teacher expectancy effects) was fully blown and quite intense (Barber & Silver, 1968; Elashoff & Snow, 1971, and later Rosenthal & Rubin, plus 29 peer reviews, in 1978). I was fascinated by SFP and expectancy phenomena and dedicated most of my scientific career to the educational–psychological investigation of these phenomena in education.

Rosenthal and I became (transatlantic) friends, meeting once or twice a year over the 1970s. We started actual research collaboration in the early 1980s, and published nine joint research papers over the next 25 years in three extensive research projects, one in each decade.

Our work focused on the documentation of teachers' expectancy-related differential verbal and nonverbal behavior toward high- and low-expectancy students in the classroom, and the examination of the social/emotional outcomes of teacher differentiality. My other studies (alone and with various partners) dealt with the entire spectrum of SFP: from the formation of expectancies (teachers'

126 E. Babad

bias research); through the behavioral transmission of expectancies via teachers' differential behavior (TDB); students' perceptions of expectancy-related teacher behavior; all the way to the effects of teacher expectancies on students' scholastic and social outcomes and classroom-wide effects on classroom climate. A number of my studies partitioned teachers according to their relative susceptibility to biasing information and the resultant likelihood of finding SFP effects in their classrooms. Earlier studies involved behavioral observations in classrooms, whereas later studies were based on teachers' NV behavior in very brief exposure.

The current state of the art: major findings

Summarizing across numerous studies, the following list presents the generalized findings on TDB (see Babad, 1993a, 1993b, 1995, 2005, 2007, 2009; Babad *et al.*, 1982, 1989, 2003, 2004:

1   Teachers indeed demonstrate substantial differential behavior in their classrooms. The TDB can be reliably measured through classroom behavioral observations and, alternatively, through judgments of thin slices (10 s) of their NV behavior toward high- and low-expectancy students. (The same pattern is true for TV interviewers in their differential NV behavior toward interviewed politicians that they like or dislike.)
2   TDB is reliably perceived and reported by classroom students.
3   Teachers often compensate low-expectancy students with "Learning Support," but they transmit more negative emotions and lower "Emotional Support" to these students.
4   The negative outcomes of TDB are detected mostly in the affective domain, in more negative classroom climate and more student anger at the teachers. For the entire spectrum from equitable teachers to highly differential teachers, the negative outcomes in the social/affective domain are substantial (up to $r = -.63$).
5   TDB is not limited to situations where fabricated expectations are planted in teachers' minds (as in Pygmalion and SFP studies). Rather, TDB is a wide and general classroom phenomenon, reflecting teachers' difficulties in dealing effectively with the great heterogeneity of their classrooms in the social/emotional/behavioral domain.
6   The teacher's pet phenomenon is a unique manifestation of extreme TDB directed at specially selected individual favorites. This phenomenon characterizes a substantial proportion of teachers and classrooms, and it carries a noticeable potential for negative outcomes under given conditions.

Critical issues

To understand the present status of Pygmalion, teacher expectancies, and TDB, and to predict future trends, several critical issues must be discussed.

1   *Pygmalion in the lab versus Pygmalion in the classroom.* Although the Pygmalion research was conducted in a real school, doubts about its ecological validity have always existed. Classroom teachers never receive information about "potential late bloomers" in a fashion similar to the Pygmalion procedure, and therefore the experimental situation stood out as quite unique and non-characteristic of the ways teachers form expectations about their students. Instead of the fabricated expectations planted in teachers' minds independent of any real characteristic of the relevant student (SFP), teachers' real self-maintaining expectations (SME) are based on real characteristics of every student. Realistic expectations should, in a way, be realized in due course, and thus TDB is (at least partially) justified. Therefore, the Pygmalion study might have indicated what *might* happen under special circumstances, but could not really predict what actually happens in real classrooms.

2   *Magnitude of teacher expectancy effects.* Even in the original 1968 study, SFP effects were recorded only for some teachers in some classrooms. Much of the post-Pygmalion research was aimed at defining the particular conditions, procedures, and teachers' personality attributes that could predict expectancy effects. Brophy (1983, 1985) minimized the probabilities for substantial expectancy effects, claiming (a) that "teacher expectancies are generally accurate, reality-based, and open to corrective feedback" (1985, p. 304); and (b) that only a small fraction of "over-reactive teachers" (1985, p. 314) would be likely (personality wise) to be influenced by biasing information and hamper the performance of their low-achieving students.

3   *Scholastic versus affective outcomes.* The Pygmalion effect was measured by changes in the intellectual domain – in IQ scores in fact. Very few subsequent researchers used IQ as the dependent variable, and the most frequent criterion to measure expectancy effects consisted of students' school achievements. But as research studies accumulated over the years, it became more and more evident that clear teacher expectancy effects on actual achievements are quite minimal (e.g. Jussim & Harber, 2005). Other, stronger variables (such as students' background and ability and the quality of teaching) can have a more substantial effect on students' achievements. I argued almost two decades ago that the crux of the teacher expectancy issue lies in preferential affect, namely, in the social/emotional domain – classroom climate, students' satisfaction and their emotional reactions to the teachers (Babad, 1998; in press). The argument proceeds with two important points: (a) The causal factor is not "teacher expectancies" as claimed in most studies, but rather the more global phenomenon of teachers' differential behavior in the classroom. Of course, TDB reflects teacher expectancies, but most differential behavior cannot be simply considered "expectancy effects." (b) The social/emotional effects to refer to are classroom-wide effects, and not individual outcomes for specific high- and low-expectancy students. In summary, then, teachers' greater overall differential behavior (proven to be perceived and clearly picked up by students) has negative effects on their classrooms' climate and on their students' morale.

128 E. Babad

4   *Galatea versus the Golem.* The legendary sculptor Pygmalion (or the teacher Professor Higgins in the modern version) affected Galatea (or Lisa Doolittle) in a very positive way. In the old Jewish legend, the Golem of Prague was also a sculpture brought to life, but the outcomes were very negative. In *Pygmalion in the Classroom* (1968) Rosenthal truly meant to examine the good effects of positive teacher expectancies on chosen students (and no negative expectancy group existed in that study). However, the controversy soon shifted to focus on presumable negative effects caused by TDB to low-expectancy students, and educators wondered to what extent teachers' negative expectancies can cause damage to underprivileged students. And indeed we (Babad *et al.*, 1982; Rosenthal & Babad, 1985) demonstrated clear and substantial Golem effects. The negative effects of TDB are very disturbing and maybe even threatening to teachers and to prospective teachers, especially if they are deep-rooted and resistant to change. I believe (next section) that this issue is most critical for understanding the current status of Pygmalion and expectancy research in educational psychology.

Pygmalion after 50 years

Pygmalion in the Classroom was a breakthrough research in the 1960s. It led to intense controversy that lasted several decades; it served as impetus for hundreds of empirical studies; and the terms "Pygmalion," SFP, and "expectancy effects" became household words among educated people. The stream of studies focused directly on these phenomena naturally slowed down over the years, in a way that was characteristic of most scientific topics and breakthrough research studies.

Today, in the long perspective of a half-century, we can inquire about the long-term "heritage" of this phenomenon in general psychology and in educational psychology. Some past breakthrough studies seem to be eternal, such as Lewin *et al.*'s (1939) study on three types of leadership, whereas others fade out over time. A useful way for assessing the contemporary impact of a given past phenomenon is to scrutinize current and recent citations in the literature. I considered several options for such examination. One possibility was to check scientific citations in the relevant indexes, which would demonstrate the impact and current interest in the scientific community. In fact, in such examination it is possible to separate instances of "just mentioning" given terms, concepts and studies from actual research investigations within the boundaries of the defined phenomenon. A second option was to focus the examination on the most widely published psychology textbooks. Most college (and probably high school) graduates obtain their systematic "psychological knowledge" from the textbooks in the introductory psychology courses that almost everybody enrolls in. It can be assumed that most students do not participate in additional psychology courses. Therefore, the current status of a past phenomenon can be deducted from its weight and volume in the contemporary textbooks. The same holds true for prospective teachers in teacher-training programs, where the most widely used textbooks in educational psychology represent the range of the knowledge provided to them about educational psychology and about specific phenomena and fields of research.

I applied these three strategies in my scrutiny of citations about *Pygmalion, expectancy effects, SFP, and Robert Rosenthal* in recent years in the SSCI, in introductory textbooks in general psychology, and in introductory textbooks in educational psychology. The comparison between these three types of search yielded a very interesting (even fascinating) trend, from steady stream of citations at one end of the continuum to almost total absence of citations at the other end:

1   In the SSCI, the most widely used citation index in the social sciences, I found a steady and unchanging stream of citations of the above terms. Several dozen scientific citations can be found for each year since the turn of the century. Most of them "mention" the relevant name and terms, and only a few papers can be said to actually report new relevant research studies. Thus, *Pygmalion, expectancy effects, SFP and Robert Rosenthal* are well known and recognized by fellow scientists even 50 years after the Pygmalion research.

2   I scrutinized about two dozen recent introductory textbooks in general psychology. Rosenthal and the three terms were indexed in some of these books, and not mentioned at all in the majority of the textbooks. Content-wise, the coverage of these terms was typically quite short, used mainly as demonstrations of stereotyping. A more thorough discussion of SFP studies and of expectancy phenomena was largely nonexistent.

3   In a recent large AERA national annual convention, I examined all intro-ductory textbooks in educational psychology presented by the various publishers. In these books, *Pygmalion, SFP, expectancy effects and Robert Rosenthal* did not exist! Very few citations were made at all, and these were mostly found in textbooks that had been published in multiple editions over the years, with minor changes from edition to edition. The unavoidable conclusion was that Pygmalion does not exist in the classroom anymore, and future teachers will not learn to know about these phenomena at all. Of course, there might be some exceptions to this overall conclusion, but it seems that the various book publishers (and the various authors, of course) have implicitly decided that the inclusion of teacher expectancy phenomena in new educational psychology textbooks is not worthwhile and not recommended.

To understand this historical turn, we must include in this discussion the meteoric development of Classroom Management (CM) in the literature on the psychology of the classroom. In the last decades CM has become one of the trendy and popular topics in educational psychology, occupying a central position in the various introductory textbooks, in addition to the publication of numerous books, classroom manuals, and research publications focusing exclusively on CM.

In the grand picture of "psychology-at-large," we have witnessed over the last few decades a paradigm shift to Positive Psychology (Seligman & Csikszentmihalyi, 2000). Instead of focusing on human failings of all kinds (psychodynamic,

130 E. Babad

motivational, cognitive, and/or behavioral) and attempting "to correct" them, the new psychology is focused on positive and healthy inner forces, and attempts are made in a humanistic way to develop these resources into personal growth, well-being and self-efficacy. This shift has clearly affected the applied practice of psychology (in clinical psychology and psychotherapy, and no less in industrial/organizational psychology and counseling), but its impact is also very noticeable in rigorous experimental research areas such as cognition and decision making.

An excellent example of this paradigm shift can be demonstrated through the work of Daniel Kahneman, the Nobel prize-winner of 2002. Kahneman and Tversky (Kahneman *et al.*, 1982; Tversky & Kahneman, 1974) presented over three decades ago a set of "heuristics," which were biased and mistaken common ways of thinking that lead people to deviate from rational thinking. This image – that people are biased, wrong, and can almost never process information correctly – dominated cognitive social psychology for decades. These very same mechanisms are now viewed as representing positive forces and adaptive ways of thinking. Kahneman now exalts the extraordinary capabilities of fast thinking, praises the pervasive influence of intuition, and encourages people to trust their intuition (Kahneman, 2011). He wrote in recent years about well-being (Kahneman & Diener, 2003) and about "happiness by design" (Dolan & Kahneman, 2014).

The future directions of the research

Education and educational research did not lag behind this historical trend, and contemporary CM actually represents an application of positive psychology to the classroom. In the authoritative *Handbook of Classroom Management* (Everston & Weinstein, 2006, with 1,346 pages and 47 chapters by 91 authors), the editors summarized the common themes and consensus among most writers in contemporary CM:

1   Positive teacher–student relationships are at the very core of effective CM.
2   CM is seen as a social and moral curriculum for fostering students' social, emotional, and moral development, not only as a method for controlling the classroom.
3   Strategies based on external punishment and rewards are not desirable.
4   Teachers must take into account students' characteristics and differences among students, and the variation among students must mediate their managerial decisions.

To return to our topic of teacher expectancies, nobody would argue at all that all relevant expectancy phenomena clearly belong within the scope of CM. Although the original Pygmalion research examined the effects of teachers' *positive* expectancies, the main thrust of subsequent expectancy research dealt mostly with the *negative* and potentially damaging potential of teachers' expectancy-related differential behavior. Therefore, expectancy research does not represent the ideology of positive psychology. Therefore, it should come as no surprise that *Pygmalion, expectancy effects, SFP and Robert Rosenthal* are not cited at all nor discussed in any manner in the comprehensive 2006 CM handbook.

The conclusion that the omission of expectancy research from the CM literature is ideologically rooted rather than an accidental fluke is further confirmed by the examination of Brophy's (2006) chapter in the CM handbook. Brophy wrote a comprehensive chapter on the history of classroom management research, reviewing research since the beginning of the twentieth century. The terms *Pygmalion, expectancy effects, SFP and Robert Rosenthal* were not mentioned at all in this chapter. Brophy also failed to mention or even hint that he, himself, was a salient researcher of teacher expectancies until the mid-1980s, and made no reference to any of his numerous publications on the topic. He must have thought that it would be better that future teachers and educators would not be informed at all about this entire domain.

Applications of the results

The guidelines sent by the editors of this book to the prospective authors of chapters included: (a) the current state of the art; (b) the future directions of the research; and (c) the applications of the results. In the present chapter, this section can be rather short. It seems that, after 50 years, Pygmalion is *not* in the classroom any more. The grave implications of the potentially negative effects of teachers' differential behavior do not fit the reigning vision of positive emotional relationships between teachers and students.

I think that the only type of expectancy research that has a chance to survive, and perhaps to flourish in the current Zeitgeist is the positively tuned research on "Pygmalion managers" (Eden, 1990, 1992) and "Pygmalion teachers" (Rubie-Davies, 2014; Rubie-Davies *et al.*, in press). This type of research focuses exclusively on positive expectations of managers and teachers toward *all* their workers and students. Eden and Rubie-Davies developed training methods to foster positive beliefs and expectations toward all workers and students. This promising direction is harmonious with the philosophy of positive psychology and fits with the conceptual framework of contemporary CM.

References

Babad, E. (1993a). Teachers' differential behavior. *Educational Psychology Review*, 5, 347–376.

Babad, E. (1993b). Pygmalion – 25 years after: Interpersonal expectations in the classroom. In P. D. Blanck (ed.), *Interpersonal expectations: Theory, Research, and Application* (pp. 125–153). London: Cambridge University Press.

Babad, E. (1995). The "teacher's pet" phenomenon, teachers' differential behavior, and students' morale. *Journal of Educational Psychology*, 87, 361–374.

Babad, E. (1998). Preferential affect: The crux of the teacher expectancy issue. In J. Brophy (ed.). *Advances in Research on Teaching: Expectations in the Classroom*, Vol. 7 (183–214). Greenwich, CT: JAI Press.

Babad, E. (2005). The psychological price of media bias. *Journal of Experimental Psychology: Applied, 11*, 245–255.

Babad, E. (2007). Teachers' nonverbal behavior and its effects on students. In R. Perry & J. Smart (eds), *The Scholarship of Teaching and Learning: An Evidence-based Perspective* (201–261). Holland: Springer Publications. Also in J. Smart (ed.), *Higher Education: Handbook of Theory and Research*, Vol. 22 (219–279). Holland: Springer.

Babad, E. (2009). Teaching and nonverbal behavior in the classroom. In L. Saha & A. Dworkin (eds), *International Handbook of Research on Teachers and Teaching* (797–807). Holland: Springer Science/Business Media LLC.

Babad, E. (in press). The social psychology of the classroom: Reflections about past, present and future. In C. Rubie-Davies, J. Stephens & P. Watson, (eds), *The Routledge International Handbook of Social Psychology of the Classroom*. London: Routledge.

Babad, E., Inbar, J. & Rosenthal, R. (1982). Pygmalion, Galatea, and the Golem: Investigations of biased and unbiased teachers. *Journal of Educational Psychology, 74*, 459–474.

Babad, E., Bernieri, F. & Rosenthal, R. (1989). When less information is more informative: Diagnosing teacher expectancies from brief samples of behaviour. *British Journal of Educational Psychology, 59*, 281–295.

Babad, E., Avni-Babad, D. & Rosenthal, R. (2003). Teachers' brief nonverbal behaviors can predict certain aspects of students' evaluations. *Journal of Educational Psychology, 95*, 553–562.

Babad, E., Avni-Babad, D. & Rosenthal, R. (2004). Prediction of students' evaluations from brief instances of professors' nonverbal behavior in defined instructional situations. *Social Psychology of Education, 7*, 3–33.

Barber, T. & Silver, M. (1968). Fact, fiction and the experimenter bias effect. *Psychological Bulletin Monographs Supplement, 70*, 1–29.

Brophy, J. (1983). Research on the self-fulfilling prophecy and teacher expectations. *Journal of Educational Psychology, 75*, 631–661.

Brophy, J. (1985). Teacher-student interaction. In J. Dusek (ed.), *Teacher Expectancies* (303–328). Hillsdale, NJ: Erlbaum.

Brophy, J. (2006). History of research on classroom management. In C. Everston & C. Weinstein (eds), *Handbook of Classroom Management: Research, Practice and Contemporary Issues* (17–43). Mahwah, NJ: Erlbaum.

Dolan, P. & Kahneman, D. (2014). *Happiness by Design: Change What You Do, Not How You Think*. London: Penguin.

Eden, D. (1990). *Pygmalion in Management: Productivity as a Self-fulfilling Prophecy*. Lexington, MA: Lexington Books.

Eden, D. (1992). Self-fulfilling prophecy as a management tool: Harnessing Pygmalion. *Academy of Management Review, 9*, 64–73.

Elashoff, J. & Snow, R. (eds). (1971). *Pygmalion Reconsidered*. Worthington, OH: Charles A. Jones.

Everston, C. & Weinstein, C. (eds). (2006). *Handbook of Classroom Management: Research, Practice and Contemporary Issues*. Mahwah, NJ: Erlbaum.

Jussim, L. & Harber, K. (2005). Teacher expectations and self-fulfilling prophecies: Known and unknowns, resolved and unresolved controversies. *Personality and Social Psychology Review, 9*, 131–155.

Kahneman, D. (2011). *Thinking Fast and Slow*. New York: Farrar, Straus, & Giroux.

Kahneman, D. & Diener, E. (eds). (2003). *Well-being: Foundations of Hedonic Psychology*. New York: Russell Sage Foundation.

Kahneman, D., Slovic, P. & Tversky, A. (eds). (1982). *Judgment under Uncertainty: Heuristics and Biases*. New York and Cambridge: Cambridge University Press.

Lewin, K., Lippitt, R. & White, R. (1939). Patterns of aggressive behavior in experimentally created social climates. *Journal of Social Psychology*, *10*, 271–299.

Rosenthal, R. & Babad, E. (1985). Pygmalion in the gymnasium. *Educational Leadership* (September), 36–39.

Rosenthal, R. & Jacobson, L. (1968). *Pygmalion in the Classroom*. New York: Holt, Rinehart & Winston.

Rosenthal, R. & Rubin, D. (1978). Interpersonal expectancy effects: The first 345 studies. *The Behavioral and Brain Studies*, *3*, 377–415.

Rubie-Davies, C. M. (2014). *Becoming a High Expectation Teacher: Raising the Bar*. London: Routledge.

Rubie-Davies, C. M., Peterson, E. R., Sibley, C. G. & Rosenthal, R. (in press). A teacher expectation intervention: Modeling the practices of high expectation teachers. *Contemporary Educational Psychology*.

Seligman, M. & Csikszentmihalyi, M. (2000). Positive psychology: An introduction. *American Psychologist*, *55*, 5–14.

Tversky, A. & Kahneman, D. (1974). Judgment under uncertainty: Heuristics and biases. *Science*, *185*, 1124–1130.

Wallach, M. & Kogan, N. (1965). *Modes of Thinking in Young Children: A Study of the Creativity-Intelligence Distinction*. New York: Holt, Rinehart & Winston.

16

CHILDREN'S AWARENESS OF DIFFERENTIAL TREATMENT

Toward a *contextual* understanding of teacher expectancy effects

Rhona S. Weinstein

Beginnings

I first thought seriously about the role of expectations and how such beliefs might become self-fulfilling prophecies in the context of a case I was assigned while training as a clinical and community psychologist at the Yale University Psycho-Educational Clinic. I was referred a ten-year-old boy who could not read. My classroom observations revealed his placement in the lowest reading group, a setting where the school work was remedial, repetitive, and dull. And not surprisingly, classroom peer relationships mirrored the hierarchy of reading group membership. My efforts to move this child into a higher reading group were resisted. School staff argued that I must prove he was capable of work *at that level* and I responded, in turn, that until we believed in his ability, he likely would not learn. The school finally agreed to his promotion, with seemingly miraculous results to follow. Placed in a higher reading group, the child learned to read, making enormous progress both academically and socially within the school year. This case was pivotal in shifting my interests away from clinical toward community psychology, where I could take a systemic (e.g. ability-based reading groups), population-based, and preventive, rather than treatment, perspective in addressing child maladjustment problems. Since that time, my curiosity about the social phenomenon of expectancy effects has never abated.

I puzzled over what elements might have caused the behavioral changes – the belief that he was capable, more challenging lessons, positive reinforcement from the teacher, the opportunity to belong to a more popular group of peers or all of the above? This question sent me scurrying to the research literature where I discovered the emerging field of teacher expectancy effects and four seminal scientific contributions. These included Robert J. Merton's (1948) conceptualization of the self-fulfilling prophecy, Robert Rosenthal and Lenore Jacobson's (1968) experimental evidence for expectancy effects (the induction of high expectations in teachers for randomly selected students), Jere Brophy and Tom Good's (1970) empirical demonstration of differential treatment within classrooms (a pathway that might mediate between expectations and outcomes), and Ray Rist's (1970) identification of reading groups as an institutional context for expectancy effects.

Blending insights from practice and science, my doctoral dissertation explored the evolution of reading group membership in first-grade classrooms across one school year, quantitatively tracking expectancy formation, communication, and outcomes (Weinstein, 1976). I examined group assignment and group change as well as *within-group* teacher–student interaction, peer relationships, and student achievement. As predicted, given equal student achievement at entry, higher reading group membership was associated with higher achievement as well as peer popularity. However, the direction of *observed* differential treatment by teachers, the hypothesized mediating pathway, did not confirm our hypotheses. Instead, teachers favored lower achievers with more praise and less criticism. It was an astute undergraduate research assistant who raised the issue of interpretation. She suggested that the praise allocated to lows was not authentic and the criticism given highs could be understood as constructive.

I realized then how *rarely* we ask children about *their* experiences of schooling (Weinstein, 1982). Listening to children might enable new understandings about teacher expectations, differential treatment, and their effects. Boldly at the time, we embraced a student, rather than observer, point of view in building our research program. We have progressively addressed three domains of questions. First, are children aware of teacher expectations, in what ways, and with what effects? Second, what conditions magnify or diminish the power of teacher expectancy effects? And third, can this knowledge be applied to prevent negative prophecies and promote positive ones in schooling, especially to address inequity in educational opportunity?

What is known

A child-mediated model of teacher expectancy effects

One can think about teacher expectations as shaping opportunities to learn, which would have a direct impact on student achievement, regardless of student awareness. One can also imagine that differential treatment might communicate clues to students about their achievement status – indirectly shaping learning through motivation or self-image. Our goal was to study this *indirect* route of influence, and we began with instrument development.

We created the Teacher Treatment Inventory (TTI), an instrument which was factored into three scales. Elementary school-aged children provided *independent* ratings of the frequency of differential behaviors by teachers toward an imaginary high- or low-expectation student, with the difference score reflecting the degree of differential treatment perceived (Weinstein & Middlestadt, 1979; Weinstein

136 R. S. Weinstein

et al., 1987). Numerous studies utilizing the TTI have shown that children as young as first graders are aware that high achievers are favored by their teachers (e.g. Brattesani *et al.*, 1984). For example, highs as compared to lows were accorded higher expectations ("The teacher is interested in him"), more opportunity ("The teacher asks him to lead activities"), and more choice ("The teacher lets him make up his own projects") in the classroom.

A second instrument, the "Learning about smartness" interview, allowed us to move beyond the awareness question to interpretation, where, in children's own words, we could capture qualities of the expectancy climate and inferences drawn about ability differences (Weinstein, 2002). Not only could children read the expectations of teachers in remarkably sophisticated ways, but beyond discrete and differentially accorded teacher behaviors, they could identify teachers' choices of curriculum allocation and grouping, evaluation and motivational strategies, student agency, and climate as critical clues about expectations. The aligned synergy between these instructional elements created equitable and talent-development cultures ("all children can learn") or differentiated and talent-selection cultures ("not much they [low achievers] can do"). These systemic choices, identified by children, have also been replicated in classroom observational studies (Bohlmann & Weinstein, 2013; Marshall & Weinstein, 1986) and form the road map for our efforts to create positive expectancy environments.

Contextual factors that moderate teacher expectancy effects

Our studies have documented differences in teachers (degree of differential treatment, stratified-ability beliefs), students (age, stereotyped ethnic minorities), and time period (longitudinal effects of the expectations of single or multiple teachers) that have startling implications for the magnitude of expectancy effects across a range of outcomes. Beginning with a study by Brattesani *et al.* (1984), we have found consistent variation in the degree of differential treatment between classrooms: the more differential teacher treatment that favors highs (perceived or observed), the larger the gap in outcomes between high- and low-expectation students. For example, despite equal student achievement at entry, teacher expectations explained more of the year-end achievement gap between stereotyped and non-stereotyped groups in high bias classrooms (mean effect size of $d = .29$) than in low bias classrooms (mean effect size of $d=.003$). Bias was measured by child-perceived differential treatment (McKown & Weinstein, 2008).

Our studies have also uncovered differences in children's vulnerability, either as the target of low expectations or as susceptible to confirming the expectations of another. There are important developmental differences to track. For example, a study by Kuklinski and Weinstein (2001) documented, first, stronger expectancy confirmation in high differential treatment classrooms at third and fifth but not first grade, and second, mediation through children's self-expectations only at fifth grade and only in classrooms where ability cues were evident. Minority group status also plays a critical role. As one example, ethnic minority children who are

Children's awareness of differential treatment **137**

stigmatized in the US context – that is, believed to be less intelligent – have been found to be more vulnerable to confirming teacher-underestimates of ability, whereas Caucasian children proved more vulnerable to overestimates of ability, perhaps a contributing factor to the achievement gap (McKown & Weinstein, 2002).

Finally, an examination of teacher expectancy effects across school years has also identified contextual factors, such as the home environment and successive teachers that interact with expectancy effects. Alvidrez and Weinstein (1999) found that children, who at age four were seen by teachers as less intelligent that their IQ scores suggested, did in fact earn lower grade point averages at the end of high school, fourteen years later, and were less likely to take the tests required for college admission. Importantly, this predictive relationship did not hold for children from more achievement-oriented homes. Our recent investigation of the relationship between the expectations of multiple teachers, from preschool through fourth grade, showed the additive results of expectancy effects from successive teachers but also demonstrated disruptions in the expectation trajectory, where successive teachers perceived students differently (Rubie-Davies *et al.*, 2014).

Applications of expectancy effects knowledge to teaching practices and school design

A talent-development culture in classrooms and schools can be taught or created. We have applied what we learned from students and teachers about equitable classroom environments, with high expectations for all, to intervention studies. In a two-year project at the high school level, we worked with teachers and administrators to detrack their high school curriculum, moving two cohorts of 9th grade students out of remedial classes into a college preparatory program. We used a school-based participatory process (reading research, observing, innovating, and evaluating) to teach positive expectancy practices. These included access to a rigorous curriculum, the development of an inclusive class climate, and motivational strategies that prioritized the process of learning, evaluation of improvement, cooperative methods, and student agency. The results were promising. Using an archival cohort design, intervention students, as compared to similar students from previous years, demonstrated higher grades at the end of 9th grade and less attrition into 10th grade, but not higher grades, likely because of the increasingly challenging curriculum (Weinstein *et al.*, 1991; Weinstein, 2008). Application continues in a university-charter district partnership to create a new early-college secondary school for "first in the family to attend college" youth, where we interweave a rigorous curriculum and robust supports (Weinstein & Worrell, 2016).

Future directions

Revitalizing the field of teacher expectancy research is critical – hence, the importance of this book. From the time of the Rosenthal and Jacobson *Pygmalion* study (1968), now more than-forty five years ago, critics have been harsh about

138 R. S. Weinstein

the state of the evidence – noting limitations in methods, failed replications, small effects, and dissipation of effects over time. Progress has stalled and interest stifled in the continued exploration of this important social phenomenon and in the application of knowledge to practice. Much of the criticism stems from a world-view of a *universal* rather than a *contextualized* or *conditional* psychology. Expectancy effects are not found everywhere. Rather, individual and group differences, organizational and societal policies, and culture interact to create conditions that magnify or minimize such effects. Our research task is to clarify those conditions, demonstrate how they operate, and create interventions to disrupt the impact of negative self-fulfilling prophecies. Our studies provide consistent evidence for a *contextual* model of teacher expectancy effects, and we are not alone.

Further, while researchers have balked, the educational policy world, at least in the US, has embraced the importance of *high expectations* in promoting student achievement. Unfortunately, expectations have been narrowly conceived (as curricular standards) and negatively implemented (with sanctions), and important mediating mechanisms have been ignored. Again, our knowledge base has much to offer the policy world but the teacher expectancy field also has critical steps to bridge. The majority of the research on teacher expectancy effects, with some exceptions, has been (a) conducted in elementary school classrooms, (b) focused on differential treatment *within* classrooms, and (c) narrowly framed (teacher behaviors, achievement gains, single teachers).

Here are some thoughts to guide future research. Researchers need to investigate the more complex settings of middle and high school – with multiple teachers for each student (see Gregory & Huang, 2013). We need to learn more about the interactive expectations at a classroom, school, and district level, about complex links between learning opportunities and messages about competence, about the discipline gap, and about indices of attainment, not only achievement gains, such as course placement, attrition, high school graduation, and college-going rates. Small effects accumulated over a school career can make a significant difference to educational attainment. We need a developmental map of children's awareness of teacher expectations for other and self *in context* and when such expectations become internalized – that is, when an interpersonal process becomes an intrapersonal process. We need to study the relationship between students placed at risk (e.g. stereotyped minorities) and the expectations of successive teachers, taking into account teachers' differential susceptibility to bias. We need to understand why some children accept the expectations of others and some children show resilience in the face of negative messages about ability. Finally, we need to seriously invest in application of this knowledge to improved teaching practices and schools (see Rubie-Davies *et al.*, 2015).

Applications

My work has always been grounded in classrooms and schools, as I have moved back and forth between basic research and application. As I look at where I began and what I have learned since that time, I share two observations that have implications for the application of our findings to educational practice. First, elementary school children are deeply sensitive observers of their school reality, in ways that I had underestimated. This fact provides us both an opportunity and a warning. Our capacity to assess children's awareness of academic expectations and differential treatment provides a wonderful research tool to test interventions and to improve practice. But if children know what we think of them and are not fooled by, for example, inauthentic praise, we must be careful about what we communicate. If education is intended to help *all* exceed their grasp, we need to learn to believe in capability of each child and to provide every opportunity to reach higher. The term *accuracy* of expectations, where teacher expectations match current levels of achievement, has limited usefulness if we take seriously the purpose of schooling to promote growth.

Second, when I began this research, a behavioral perspective dominated the field. We looked to identify discrete teaching behaviors that communicated differential expectations and we taught teachers to equalize their treatment of students. It is, of course, much more complicated. The very systems (for curriculum allocation, for evaluation and so on) that we set up in schools and classrooms can create equitable or differentiated environments that greatly shape opportunities to learn as well as messages about capability. For example, Claude Steele's (2010) stereotype threat conditions reflect practices which make ability salient (as does differential treatment) whereas the non-threat conditions promote mastery learning or a focus on process not ability. While teachers might hold certain beliefs about student ability and chose certain practices, they are also situated within a set of organizational and societal constraints that shape actions. So as we think of applying this knowledge of teacher expectancy effects to practice, we need to adopt a social-cognitive perspective, emphasizing a conceptual road map for teacher expectancy effects and the meaning to and for children. We also need to think systemically, searching for the ways in which we institutionalize differential opportunity – for example, in how we group children for instruction – thus coming full circle to where my own work began.

References

Alvidrez, J. & Weinstein, R. S. (1999). Early teacher perceptions and later academic achievement. *Journal of Educational Psychology, 91*, 731–746.

Bohlmann, N. L. & Weinstein, R. S. (2013). Classroom context, teacher expectations, and cognitive development: Predicting young children's self-judgments of mathematics ability. *Journal of Applied Developmental Psychology, 34*, 288–298.

Brattesani, K. A., Weinstein, R. S. & Marshall, H. H. (1984). Student perceptions of differential teacher treatment as moderators of teacher expectation effects. *Journal of Educational Psychology, 76*, 236–247.

Brophy, J. E. & Good, T. L. (1970). Teachers' communication of differential expectations for children's classroom performance: Some behavioral data. *Journal of Educational Psychology, 61*, 365–374.

Gregory, A. & Huang, F. (2013). It takes a village: The effects of 10th grade college-going expectations of students, parents, and teachers: Four years later. *American Journal of Community Psychology, 52*, 41–55.

Kuklinski, M. R. & Weinstein, R. S. (2001). Classroom and developmental differences in a path model of teacher expectancy effects. *Child Development, 72*, 1554–1578.

McKown, C. & Weinstein, R. S. (2002). Modeling the role of child ethnicity and gender in children's differential response to teacher expectations. *Journal of Applied Social Psychology, 32*, 159–184.

McKown, C. & Weinstein, R. S. (2008). Teacher expectations, classroom context, and the achievement gap. *Journal of School Psychology, 46*, 235–261.

Marshall, H. H. & Weinstein, R. S. (1986). The classroom context of student-perceived differential teacher treatment. *Journal of Educational Psychology, 78*, 441–453.

Merton, R. K. (1948). The self-fulfilling prophecy. *Antioch Review, 8*, 193–210.

Rist, R. C. (1970). Student social class and teacher expectations: The self-fulfilling prophecy in ghetto education. *Harvard Educational Review, 40*, 411–451.

Rosenthal, R. & Jacobson, L. (1968). *Pygmalion in the Classroom: Teacher Expectation and Pupils' Intellectual Development*. New York: Holt, Rinehart, & Winston.

Rubie-Davies, C. M., *Peterson*, E., Sibley, C. G. & Rosenthal, R. (2015). A teacher expectancy intervention: Modeling the practices of high expectation teachers. *Contemporary Educational Psychology, 40*, 72–85.

Rubie-Davies, C. M., Weinstein, R. S., Huang, F., Gregory, A., Cowan, P. & Cowan, C. (2014). Successive teacher expectancy effects across the early school years. *Journal of Applied Developmental Psychology, 35*, 181–191.

Steele, C. M. (2010). *Whistling Vivaldi: How Stereotypes Affect Us and What We Can Do*. New York: W.W. Norton.

Weinstein, R. S. (1976). Reading group membership in first grade: Teacher behaviors and pupil experience over time. *Journal of Educational Psychology, 68*, 103–116.

Weinstein, R. S. (ed.) (1982). Students in classrooms (special issue). The *Elementary School Journal, 82*, 397–540.

Weinstein, R. S. (2002). *Reaching Higher: The Power of Expectations in Schooling*. Cambridge, MA: Harvard University Press.

Weinstein, R. S. (2008). Schools that actualize high expectations for all youth: Theory for setting change and setting creation. In B. Shinn & H. Yoshikawa (eds), *Toward Positive Youth Development: Transforming Schools and Community Programs*. New York: Oxford University Press.

Weinstein, R. S. & Middlestadt, S. E. (1979). Student perceptions of teacher interactions with male high and low achievers. *Journal of Educational Psychology, 71*, 421–431.

Weinstein, R. S. & Worrell, F. C. (eds) (2016). *Achieving College Dreams: How a University – Charter District Partnership Created an Early College High School*. New York: Oxford University Press.

Weinstein, R. S., Marshall, H. H., Sharp, L. & Botkin, M. (1987). Pygmalion and the student: Age and classroom differences in children's awareness of teacher expectations. *Child Development, 58*, 1079–1093.

Weinstein, R. S., Soule, C. R., Collins, F., Cone, J., Mehlhorn, M. & Simontacchi, K. (1991). Expectations and high school change: Teacher-researcher collaboration to prevent school failure. *American Journal of Community Psychology, 19*, 333–363.

17

INDIVIDUAL DIFFERENCES IN RESPONSE TO EXPECTATIONS

Charles K. West

The beginnings of the research

The late Lloyd Humphries of the University of Illinois reanalyzed the same data that we used in our paper (West & Anderson, 1976).[1] Professor Humphries used what was at the time a new statistic called cross-lagged panel analysis. This statistic allows an analysis of data where two variables are measured at two different times. It presumably allows the inference of preponderant causation, a response to the "chicken-egg" issue. In the data we had used, both student achievement and teacher expectation were measured repeatedly over several years.

Professor Humphries' analyses confirmed our findings that student's achievements determined the formation of later teacher's expectations rather than the reverse. More specifically, using factor analysis we demonstrated that student achievement in one year was a more robust predictor the next year of expectation than the reverse.

Oddly enough, several of the more notable expectation research efforts had the data sufficient to analyze achievement effects on expectation yet chose to only examine expectation on achievement. Since the two variables are highly correlated, one could easily predict and observe some kind of an effect on either chosen variable. Professor Anderson and I were aware of the cross-lagged panel analysis technique but we felt that it was new at the time and that factor analysis was a proven technique and that more researchers were familiar with it.

The only further research on teacher expectation since our review that I have done was a qualitative piece that I presented at the Midwestern Educational Research Association (West, Fisher & Cuttill, 1987) and I no longer have access to the original document or the data. It seems not to be in my career files, so I can only provide the gist of it. It was done before I had access to a personal computer.

This piece would not be widely known, given the source of presentation and even I do not have a copy of the data or the presentation. Beginning in the 1980s

142 C. K. West

or 1990s, a substantial shift from quantitative to qualitative research occurred in the United States, however. Perhaps his piece would create more interest today than it did then. The most basic thesis driving this effort was an abiding belief in individual differences, even in response to expectations by others. In most variables in human characteristics and behavior, individual differences abide. Why not reactions to expectations by others?

In his doctoral dissertation, Professor Anderson noted that high expectation students seemed to dislike being expected to do well. I think that his observation set me thinking of individual differences in the area of teacher expectation along with the famous line from the song in Shaw's *Pygmalion*, "Just you wait, Henry Higgins, just you wait!" Recall that Professor Higgins had communicated a prediction to Liza that she would not do well. She seemed determined to "Prove him wrong!" I like to think of this as the "Liza" effect.

The current state of the art

In our individual differences effort (West *et al.*, 1987) we surveyed several hundred undergraduate students asking them several questions about teacher's expectations for them. I asked them what they would feel and what they would do under two conditions. The first question was "What you would do and how would you feel if a professor told you that there would be a test soon and that he did not expect you to do well on that test?"

Student's responses clearly varied considerably with no clear consensus. Some simply questioned the professor's motives or his knowledge about him or her. Some were angry. Some claimed that they would simply ignore the statement. Some reflected, "Who cares?" Others thought they would try harder so as to prove the professor wrong: the "Liza effect." Others felt that more effort would be futile.

The "Liza effect" clearly flies in the face of the idea that low expectancy uniformly causes low achievement. All of these responses should engender a strong commitment to individual differences in this area of human affairs. Under the condition "What would you do and how would you feel if a professor told you that there would be a test soon and that he expected you to do well on that test?" individual differences were also paramount.

Many reflected that they were very busy and had to carefully husband their time so they could ignore the area of the test and use the time on another upcoming test. This is directly counter to the belief that high expectation always results in more effort. As was the case in the low expectation treatment, some simply questioned the professor's motives or his knowledge about him or her. This was an oddity, to have the same response under both conditions. One critic to my paper at the conference was that my subjects were high-achieving students – and they were. My response to this is that the criticism might be valid. However, are we to infer that while high-achieving students display individual differences, lower achieving students do not? I do not think so. It may be that individual differences

Individual differences in response to expectations **143**

are high in one area (academic achievement) but attenuated in another (height, weight, response to expectations).

The future directions of the research

In any case, my observation of individual differences could be a fruitful area of further research. I also think that individual differences of teachers in responding to their judgments about students' future progress are a related area for future research. For example, some teachers may try harder when they fear a student is expected not to do well. Another teacher may consciously refrain from formulating an expectation or communicating an expectation.

I am not convinced that teachers formulate expectations of many of their students, particularly in the absence of someone requesting those expectations. Remember that the researcher's queries may induce an expectation that may or may not have existed prior to the query. Thus, a query would be obtrusive. Without a query the researcher must rely on inference. I would predict individual differences on this issue also.

There are several questions that deserve research. First, what are the bases of teacher expectations, if any, other than prior and current achievement? Some possibilities are gender, ethnicity, and family social status. What are the possible effects of any of these? What role do individual differences among teachers play on these issues? Another set of questions might involve differential effects, if any, of induced expectations, those supposedly communicated by experimenters. Do teachers pay much attention to what others claim about their students? Then there are likely individual differences among teachers on these issues also. I do not mean to claim that some research does not exist on these issues of which we are not aware. We have been inactive for several decades in the area of expectation research and have been retired for about a decade.

The applications of the results

My field was applied learning and instructional design. I was drawn to the findings of Bob Rosenthal primarily because I knew that academic achievement was determined by numerous complex variables and was stunned by the possibility that a single variable could have a powerful effect on academic achievement as claimed by some researchers. Years ago in a letter in reply to a request for our findings from Bob Rosenthal, I wrote that while my research findings contrasted with his, he had initiated a very interesting area of research for me and I thanked him for that. It surely was, even though my basic interests lay outside it. In that same letter I sent, at his request, a copy of West and Anderson (1976), but he did not respond to me about it. Someone, perhaps a reviewer, must have privately informed him of my research. Oddly enough, his request for a copy arrived about the same time as the notification of acceptance of the 1976 paper by the Review of Educational Research.

Note

Because I am no longer active at the University I cannot provide references to the work of others. I apologize.

References

West, C. K. & Anderson, T. H. (1976). The question of preponderant causation in teacher expectancy research. *Review of Educational Research, 46,* 613–630.

West, C. K., Fisher, A. T. & Cuttill, C. (1987, 15 October). Student cognitions, feelings, and reactions to teacher expectations: Individual differences. Paper presented at the Mid-Western Educational Research Association Annual Meeting, Chicago.

18

HIGH AND LOW EXPECTATION TEACHERS

The importance of the teacher factor

Christine Rubie-Davies

The beginnings of the teacher expectation research

The seminal work in the teacher expectation field was conducted by Rosenthal and Jacobson (1968). Rosenthal had conducted earlier studies (e.g. Rosenthal, 1963, 1964, 1966) which had shown that experimenters could inadvertently influence the results of experiments. He contemplated whether, if teachers were given false information about their students, this could lead to them influencing student achievement. In what has become a classic study, *Pygmalion*, Rosenthal and Jacobson showed that by experimentally inducing false expectations in teachers, students made intellectual gains. Thus, when teachers were led to believe that some of their students would suddenly blossom, indeed across one year, they did improve. While there was controversy about this study at the time with some making exaggerated claims and others questioning the results, nevertheless even the most avid critics (e.g. Snow, 1969) accepted the existence of teacher expectations and the possibility that they might influence student academic results.

The development of the teacher expectation field

The initial work left many unanswered questions which became the directions that researchers took during the 1970s and 1980s. It was accepted that for teacher expectations to have an effect on students, teachers must interact differently with students for whom they had high expectations (high expectation students) compared with how they interacted with students for whom they had low expectations (low expectation students). Researchers such as Brophy and Good (1970) conducted observations in classrooms with the objective of ascertaining how behaviors towards high and low expectation students might differ. Indeed, from a synthesis of studies conducted at the time Brophy (1983) identified seventeen teacher behaviors

146 C. Rubie-Davies

that differed depending on whether teachers were interacting with high or low expectation students. For example, teachers paid less attention to low expectation students and interacted with them less frequently. However, while behaviors could be identified that differed depending on whether teacher interactions were with high versus low expectation students, at the time the effect size of these behaviors on student outcomes were not measured. A little later, Harris and Rosenthal (1985) showed that the behaviors that had most effect on student achievement were first, that teachers created a warmer socioemotional climate for high expectation students and second, that they taught those for whom they had high expectations more concepts and at a faster pace, and they more frequently enabled these students to engage in interactions with the teacher.

Another area that warranted researcher attention was the conception that there may be particular student characteristics that influence teachers' expectations. Those that were most frequently investigated included ethnicity, social class, and gender. However, more latterly diagnostic labels have been found to shape teachers' expectations. Researchers (e.g. Rubie-Davies *et al.*, 2006; Tenenbaum & Ruck, 2007) have shown that teachers tend to have higher expectations for majority rather than for minority group students. Further, expectations for middle-class students tend to be higher than those for students in poorer communities (Jussim *et al.*, 1996; Solomon *et al.*, 1996). The research related to gender has been less conclusive, although it is mostly argued that teacher expectations are higher for girls in the language arts (Cloer & Dalton, 2001; Page & Rosenthal, 1990) and higher for boys in mathematics and the sciences (Hatchell, 1998; Li, 1999; Robinson *et al.*, 2011). In terms of diagnostic labels, it has been shown that when students are labeled, teachers' expectations for the students become lowered. For example, in a recent experimental study (Batzle *et al.*, 2010), teachers were read a description of a hypothetical student. If the student had no label, teachers' expectations for the student were higher than if the teacher was labeled either ADHD or ADHD and on stimulant medication. These findings were similar to the results of an earlier study with pre-service teachers (Stinnett *et al.*, 2001).

Of course, in order for teacher expectations to have an effect on student outcomes, students need to recognize and comply with their teachers' expectations. Hence, another group of researchers (Babad, 2009; Cooper & Good, 1983; Weinstein, 2002) investigated how students know whether their teachers have high or low expectations for them. Weinstein (2002) in particular has led this field. Her work provides poignant details of critical incidents which students were able to explicitly describe that provided salient evidence of their teachers' expectations for them. In particular, students described teachers as providing challenging work for only high achievers. Students described high expectation students as being trusted by the teacher and as being provided with opportunities that low expectation students were not given, such as leadership positions. Conversely, low expectation students were viewed as being frequently admonished, as being constantly monitored, and as being provided with frequent help with academic tasks. From the student perspective, these teacher behaviors reveal their status in the classroom

– that is, students perceive that teachers like and favor high achievers more than they do low achievers.

Teacher individuality

The work above examines student differences as influencing teachers' expectations. The idea that teachers are likely to vary in their beliefs, and that the beliefs of specific teachers might moderate the expectation effects, has been less often studied. Researchers in this area show that some teachers have substantial expectation effects on their students while others do not. This means that when data for all teachers are aggregated, overall the effects of teachers' expectations on student achievement appear relatively small (Brophy, 1983). Babad (Babad *et al.*, 1989a, 1989b, 1991; Babad & Taylor, 1992) has identified biased versus unbiased teachers. He has shown that biased teachers are easily influenced by false and stereotypical information about students. On the other hand, unbiased teachers judge students objectively and when given false information about their students, they ignore the information and use their own professional judgment in interacting with students. In one experiment (Babad, 1998), teachers and university students were given two drawings of a person which had been taken from a test manual and which showed equivalent capability. However, in Babad's experiment, one drawing was attributed to a high status student (majority group and middle class) while the other was attributed to a low status student. Biased teachers assigned very different scores to the drawings dependent on the demographic information provided whereas there was no difference in the scores for the unbiased teachers. Babad and his colleagues (Babad *et al.*, 1982) conducted another experiment in which teachers were given false information about the potential of their students. The highly biased teachers were swayed by what they were told by the experimenters and showed substantial expectancy effects on their students. On the other hand, unbiased teachers disregarded the information and no expectancy effects were found for these teachers.

Weinstein (2002) has also examined teacher difference as moderating expectation effects. In particular, she and her colleagues (Kuklinski & Weinstein, 2000; McKown & Weinstein, 2008; Weinstein, 1993; Weinstein *et al.*, 1982) have identified high and low differentiating teachers. High differentiating teachers treat very differently students for whom they have high versus low expectations. Low differentiating teachers treat all students similarly. Weinstein (2002) has shown that these differences between high and low differentiating teachers can be identified in six specific areas: the ways that teachers group students, how they motivate and evaluate students, the degree to which the curriculum delivered is differentiated, the degree of autonomy that students are given, and the types of relationships that are fostered in the classroom. High differentiating teachers assign students to ability groups in which they sit and work, whereas low differentiating teachers have students working in family groupings in which they are encouraged to support each other. High differentiating teachers use extrinsic motivation and public declaration of marks on tests, whereas low differentiating teachers place the emphasis on intrinsic

148 C. Rubie-Davies

motivation and student evaluations are based on student progress rather than grades. High differentiating teachers take charge of student learning and ask students to seek teacher assistance when they need help. Low differentiating teachers, on the other hand, encourage student independence and support from their peers. Finally, high differentiating teachers create a tense and negative climate for most students such that high expectation students are clearly favored over low expectation students. Low differentiating teachers create a classroom community in which students are encouraged to work together and support each other. There is no distinction in the ways in which low differentiation teachers interact with high versus low expectation students. Perhaps not surprisingly, high differentiating teachers exacerbate student differences and have large expectation effects on student outcomes, whereas low differentiating teachers reduce the achievement gap between high and low expectation students and there are minimal expectation effects (McKown & Weinstein, 2008).

The current state of the art: high and low expectation teachers

Rubie-Davies (2006, 2007, 2008, 2010) has identified what she calls high and low expectation teachers. High expectation teachers are those who have high expectations for all their students relative to achievement whereas low expectation teachers have low expectations for all their students. Students with high expectation teachers make large academic gains across one year (their teachers have large, positive expectation effects on their achievement), whereas students with low expectation teachers make very few gains (Rubie-Davies et al., 2007). Rubie-Davies (2006) has also shown that there are implications for student self-beliefs as well, depending on the classroom in which students are placed. Across one year, the study showed that whereas the self-beliefs of students with high expectation teachers remained positive, those of students with low expectation teachers declined markedly. Further, the students seemed aware of their teachers' expectations since perceptions that teachers had high expectations for them remained high for students with high expectation teachers but deteriorated significantly for students with low expectation teachers. Rubie-Davies also interviewed high and low expectation teachers (2008) and had independent observers who were unaware of the teachers' classifications or the purpose of the study record the teaching behaviors of the participants (2007). These studies suggested that differences in teacher instructional practices and beliefs were found in three main areas: grouping and learning activities, class climate, and student motivation, evaluation, and autonomy and teacher evaluation and feedback – which were all related to goal-setting.

High expectation teachers did not maintain within-class ability grouping as is common in New Zealand (Wagemaker, 1993) where the studies cited above took place. Instead, high expectation teachers used a variety of methods that meant that students worked with their peers across the classroom. Students were given choices of the activities they could complete and either chose the peers they would work with or the teacher assigned them to complete tasks in mixed ability groupings. Low expectation teachers placed students in within-class ability groups and the students completed activities in those groups. The class climate of high expectation teachers was positive, warm, caring, and supportive (Rubie-Davies & Peterson, 2011). Further, the teachers fostered a classroom community, changing seating groups regularly, and frequently engaging students in cooperative and collaborative tasks. The class climate of low expectation teachers was far less engaging and supportive. Teachers frequently reacted negatively to any student infractions and mostly set learning tasks for students that were to be completed independently. Student friendships were based on the within-class ability groups to which students had been assigned. High expectation teachers set individual learning goals with their students. They were continuously challenging all students. Students were given choices in the activities they completed, in the goals for their learning, and often in who they worked with on tasks. Further, student interests were often incorporated into learning activities. All these organizational and instructional decisions by high expectation teachers meant that students were motivated and engaged. Teachers monitored student progress regularly and moved students to higher levels individually as they were ready. They gave students regular feedback on their learning based on their learning goals and assimilation of concepts. In contrast, low expectation teachers did not set learning goals with their students. Students were given no choices in their learning activities nor in whom they would work with. Motivation and engagement was lower in the classes of low expectation teachers. They taught and monitored the students as groups. Monitoring was infrequent and when it occurred it was based on whole groups being tested at a particular level and the whole group being moved to more difficult material when the teacher deemed them ready. Feedback was infrequent in the classes of low expectation teachers and when it did occur was often based on surface features of tasks, for example, the neatness of the work completed or how quickly students had completed activities.

The Teacher Expectation Project

It seemed that the beliefs and practices of high expectation teachers could be taught to other teachers such that all teachers could become high expectation teachers leading to accelerated achievement for their students and positive self-beliefs. The three core groups of practices: grouping and learning experiences, class climate, and goal-setting (incorporating student motivation, engagement, autonomy and teacher evaluation and feedback) became the basis for the Teacher Expectation Project (www.education.auckland.ac.nz/uoa/teacher-expectation; TEP), a three-year project. Primary school teachers ($N = 83$) whose students were aged 8–12 years were randomly assigned to either the intervention or the control group. The control group took part in their school's regular professional development during the year of the intervention but did not participate in the workshops or other activities of the intervention teachers described below. In the second year of the project, control group teachers were also taught the practices of the high expectation teachers and the final year of the project involved monitoring the teachers and students to determine whether or not the practices teachers had been taught were sustained. Full details about the project can be found in a recently published book (Rubie-Davies, 2015).

Both teacher and student measures were included in the project. All teachers completed their expectations of their students twice each year. They also completed a questionnaire that measured their motivation, teaching efficacy, and performance and mastery goal orientation. Those involved in the intervention (only intervention teachers in the first year of the project, all teachers in the subsequent years) indicated each year the degree to which they had implemented the core practices of the TEP and made comments on their success and any difficulties. Further, intervention teachers were videoed teaching twice in the first year of the project (before and after the intervention) and once in each subsequent year. Student achievement in reading and mathematics was measured three times in the first year of the project, and twice in each subsequent year. Students also completed a self-report questionnaire twice a year which measured their self-concept, self-efficacy, perceived competence, performance and mastery goal orientation, beliefs about intelligence, intrinsic and utility value, self-expectations and perceptions of teachers' expectations, and perceptions of the class climate. Students in the classes of intervention teachers were tracked throughout the project.

Intervention teachers took part in a series of four full-day workshops designed to teach them the practices of high expectation teachers. The first workshop was a general introduction to the teacher expectation field and to the work related to high and low expectation teachers. In all subsequent workshops, teachers were introduced successively in each workshop, to one of the three core areas. They were shown the beliefs and practices of high expectation teachers and the core theoretical understandings were presented. For example, in the workshop related to grouping and learning experiences, research related to the divisive effects of ability grouping was presented as was research showing the positive effects on student learning of mixed ability and flexible grouping. Teachers then spent time working collaboratively to plan how they would implement more flexible forms of grouping into their classrooms and planned the types of activities that they could use in their classes, activities that would be available for all students. The researchers visited schools three times during the year following the workshops so that teachers could share successes and ideas with each other, and gain peer and researcher support. During the first workshop, the intervention teachers were also introduced to Babad's work (Babad, 2009; Babad et al., 2003, 1987, 1989a) related to teacher non-verbal behavior and leakage – the idea that what teachers say is not necessarily what is portrayed by their body language. The videos were then used by teachers to self-analyze their own non-verbal behavior throughout the project. These videos will form the basis for future academic papers.

The TEP is relatively recent (it began at the beginning of the academic year in 2011) and so preliminary analyses have only been conducted for the first-year results.

It is anticipated that many academic articles will result from the project. Changes in student achievement in mathematics and reading in the first year of the project have been analyzed, however, using Bayesian latent growth curve modeling (Rubie-Davies *et al.*, 2015). The results showed that students in the classes of intervention teachers gained more marks on their standardized tests by the end of the year than did students in the classes of control teachers. Indeed, they gained the equivalent of 28 percent more marks than students in the control group, or almost three additional months of learning compared to the control group. However, statistically significant differences between intervention and control groups were not found for students in reading. It is surmised that this was because more teachers, and to a greater extent, introduced flexible grouping into their classes in mathematics rather than in reading. However, it is interesting that the original *Pygmalion* data (Rosenthal & Jacobson, 1968) also showed gains for students in the experimental group in reasoning IQ but not in verbal IQ. It will be interesting to see whether the gains from the first year of the project in mathematics extend to reading in subsequent years.

There were some interesting changes in both teacher and student beliefs during the first year of the project. In terms of teacher expectations, in the first year of the project these were measured at the beginning of the academic year and then again four months later when the intervention teachers had only just begun grappling with the quite substantial changes to their instructional practices. Despite that, the expectations of the intervention teachers showed no change four months later whereas the expectations of the control group teachers had dropped significantly. However, by the end of the year, the intervention teachers were reporting more positive teaching efficacy than were the control group teachers. Further areas where the intervention teachers showed gains on their questionnaires were that by the end of the year they reported less anxiety than the control group but greater perceptions of being in control than did the control group teachers. Control group teachers showed no gains in comparison with intervention teachers.

It was thought-provoking to find that intervention students' self-esteem in mathematics but not in reading increased significantly over the year considering that mathematics was the curriculum area in which students made substantial learning gains. These students also showed increases in their perceptions that mathematics was useful outside of school (utility value). This was in comparison with control group students whose self-beliefs did not change over the year. A further area in which there were changes for students with intervention teachers but not control was in student perceptions of teachers' expectations. Students with intervention teachers significantly more than control group students came to believe that their teachers had high expectations for their achievement. Again, there were no areas of the student questionnaire in which control group students made gains on the intervention students.

A further area in which the preliminary analyses showed some differences was in parallels in changes in the beliefs of the intervention teachers and their students. Performance and mastery goal orientation of both teachers and students was

152 C. Rubie-Davies

measured. Over the first year of the TEP, beliefs in performance goals declined for both intervention teachers and their students. This meant that both teachers and students came to believe less that motivation was dependent on outperforming peers. Instead, while not statistically significant, there was a trend for intervention teachers and their students (when compared with the intervention group) to come to believe more that their motivation for learning was in acquiring and learning new skills.

The teacher qualitative data from the TEP evaluations were overwhelmingly positive, with teachers strongly endorsing the effectiveness of the practices and the positive benefits they had noticed for their classes. However, apart from the comparisons of achievement data between students of teachers in the intervention and control groups which have been analyzed using sophisticated statistical methods, the remaining findings reported above have involved only preliminary repeated measures analyses of variance using no control variables such as socioeconomic indicators – hence the findings should be interpreted with some caution.

Future directions of the research

The work of Rubie-Davies in relation to class-level expectations is worth pursuing as a direction for future research projects because first, teachers who have high expectations for all their students can be identified (so there are measurable class-level differences in teachers' expectations) and their students make well above average learning gains. Hence, further research delving more deeply into the beliefs and practices of high expectation teachers is warranted. Second, the primary focus of expectation research has been on expectations for individual students rather than expectations at the class level, yet students spend far more of their time in school as part of the class and in interactions with the teacher directed at the class than they do in interactions as an individual with teachers (Pellegrini & Blatchford, 2000). Moreover, students are directly affected by teacher class-level expectations through opportunity to learn. Teachers generally plan learning experiences at the group and class level and so, depending on their expectations for the class, the learning experiences can constrain or increase opportunities to learn. Further, the class climate is also a class-level variable and is something that all students experience every day in the classroom. The class climate can be very different in the classes of high and low expectation teachers and therefore can have effects on all students (the socioemotional factor which Harris and Rosenthal (1985) identified as having the largest effect on student achievement). Even if students favor one group over another, this will affect the whole class (Babad, 2009). Third, while expectation effects at the individual level do have measurable effects on learning ($d = 0.43$; Hattie, 2009), the positive expectation effects for students with high expectation teachers are even greater ($d = 1.01$).

Another direction for research in the teacher expectation field is to investigate school-level effects. It is likely that some principals create high expectation schools, places where proportionately more high expectation teachers may be found.

High and low expectation teachers **153**

Similarly, it will be worth exploring if the key practices in the TEP can be taught and applied in high schools.

An aspect of the TEP which was different from many experimental studies was that the intervention targeted teacher practice in the hopes of altering teacher beliefs. The preliminary results suggest that this approach has been successful. Hence, future research projects within broader areas than the teacher expectation field could confirm if the targeting of practice rather than beliefs is indeed more fruitful.

Practical applications of the results

Clearly, the findings from the TEP have practical applications within schools. The changes that teachers made in the three key areas of grouping and learning experiences, class climate, and goal-setting resulted in improved student achievement in mathematics for students in the intervention group even though the practices were new to teachers and took time to introduce into their classes. While the results for the second year of the project are currently unknown, it is anticipated that the positive results from the first year will be even more substantial in subsequent years when teachers have fully incorporated all practices into their teaching. It appears that using professional development to teach teachers the practices of high expectation teachers could be worthwhile.

Within-class ability grouping is entrenched in New Zealand primary schools as well as in other countries and in many other schools streaming or tracking is a feature. These are divisive practices known to exacerbate student differences and to have negligible effects on achievement. On the contrary, there appear to be negative effects of ability grouping on student self-beliefs for the very high as well as the very low achievers (Marsh, 1987; Oakes, 1990) and yet one argument for implementing ability grouping is that there are benefits for high achievers. If the research findings resulted in the elimination of ability grouping in schools, that would be a major contribution to schooling.

The fostering of a warm, caring, positive class climate was also part of the intervention, as was goal-setting. These practices stem from the high expectation teachers' decision not to ability group students. The warm class climate originates from teachers' positive interactions but is also attributable to the teacher practice of encouraging and supporting all students to work together cooperatively and collaboratively such that they form a classroom community. Similarly, goal-setting is the result of high expectation teachers' decision to enable student choice in their learning activities (again, a result of not using within-class ability grouping) and in the next steps in their learning. This cultivated a climate of intrinsic engagement and motivation because all students were challenged and interested in achieving their learning goals. Because the high expectation teachers were not planning specific activities for separate groups, they regularly monitored the achievement of all students through individual formative assessment and provided students with clear feedback about what they had achieved and about the next steps in their learning. This enabled teachers to progress student learning at a faster rate as teachers and

154 C. Rubie-Davies

students set goals together and monitored progress. Students also became very adept at setting and monitoring their own achievement.

Finally, while high expectation teachers make large, positive differences to student learning, high expectation schools are likely to contribute even more. Supporting the inclusion of the practices of high expectation teachers into all schools would be likely to have large benefits for learners. In the same way that high expectation teachers built a classroom community, principals can be encouraged to promote a positive, supportive school community in which teachers as well as students flourish.

References

Babad, E. (1998). Preferential affect: The crux of the teacher expectancy issue. In J. Brophy (ed.), *Advances in Research on Teaching: Expectations in the Classroom* (Vol. 7, 183–214). Greenwich, CT: JAI Press.

Babad, E. (2009). *The Social Psychology of the Classroom*. New York: Routledge.

Babad, E. & Taylor, P. B. (1992). Transparency of teacher expectancies across language, cultural boundaries. *Journal of Educational Research*, 86, 120–125.

Babad, E., Avni-Babad, D. & Rosenthal, R. (2003). Teachers' brief nonverbal behaviors can predict certain aspects of students' evaluations. *Journal of Educational Psychology*, 95, 553–562.

Babad, E., Inbar, J. & Rosenthal, R. (1982). Pygmalion, Galatea and the Golem: Investigations of biased and unbiased teachers. *Journal of Educational Psychology*, 74, 459–474.

Babad, E., Bernieri, F. & Rosenthal, R. (1987). Nonverbal and verbal behavior of preschool, remedial, and elementary school teachers. *American Educational Research Journal*, 24, 405–415.

Babad, E., Bernieri, F. & Rosenthal, R. (1989a). Nonverbal communication and leakage in the behavior of biased and unbiased teachers. *Journal of Personality and Social Psychology*, 56, 89–94.

Babad, E., Bernieri, F. & Rosenthal, R. (1989b). When less information is more informative: Diagnosing teacher expectations from brief samples of behaviour. *British Journal of Educational Psychology*, 59, 281–295.

Babad, E., Bernieri, F. & Rosenthal, R. (1991). Students as judges of teachers' verbal and nonverbal behavior. *American Educational Research Journal*, 28, 211–234.

Batzle, C. S., Weyandt, L. L., Janusis, G. M. & DeVietti, T. L. (2010). Potential impact of ADHD with stimulant medication label on teacher expectations. *Journal of Attention Disorders*, 14(2), 157–166.

Brophy, J. E. (1983). Research on the self-fulfilling prophecy and teacher expectations. *Journal of Educational Psychology*, 75, 631–661.

Brophy, J. E. & Good, T. L. (1970). Teacher–child dyadic interaction system *Mirrors for Behaviour: An Anthology of Observation Instruments continued* (Vol. A.). Philadelphia, PA: Research for Better Schools.

Cloer, T. & Dalton, S. R. (2001). Gender and grade differences in reading achievement and in self-concept as readers. *Journal of Reading Education*, 26(2), 31–36.

Cooper, H. M. & Good, T. L. (1983). *Pygmalion Grows Up: Studies in the Expectation Communication Process*. New York: Longman.

Harris, M. J. & Rosenthal, R. (1985). Mediation of interpersonal expectancy effects: 31 meta-analyses. *Psychological Bulletin*, 97, 363–386.

Hatchell, H. (1998). Girls' entry into higher secondary sciences. *Gender and Education, 10*(4), 375–386.

Hattie, J. (2009). *Visible Learning: A Synthesis of Over 800 Meta-Analyses Relating to Achievement.* London: Routledge.

Jussim, L., Eccles, J. S. & Madon, S. (1996). Social perception, social stereotypes, and teacher expectations: Accuracy and the quest for the powerful self-fulfilling prophecy. In M. P. Zanna (ed.), *Advances in Experimental Social Psychology* (Vol. 28, 281–388). San Diego, CA: Academic Press.

Kuklinski, M. R. & Weinstein, R. S. (2000). Classroom and grade level differences in the stability of teacher expectations and perceived differential treatment. *Learning Environments Research, 3,* 1–34.

Li, Qing. (1999). Teachers' Beliefs and Gender Differences in Mathematics: A Review. *Educational Research, 41*(1), 63–76.

McKown, C. & Weinstein, R. S. (2008). Teacher expectations, classroom context and the achievement gap. *Journal of School Psychology, 46,* 235–261. doi: 10.1016/j.jsp.2007.05.001

Marsh, H. W. (1987). The big-fish-little-pond effect on academic self-concept. *Journal of Educational Psychology, 79,* 280–295.

Oakes, J. (1990). *Multiplying Inequalities: The Effects of Race, Social Class, and Tracking on Opportunities to Learn Mathematics and Sciences.* Santa Monica, CA: Rand Corporation.

Page, S. & Rosenthal, R. (1990). Sex and expectations of teachers and sex and race of students as determinants of teaching behavior and student performance. *Journal of School Psychology, 28,* 119–131.

Pellegrini, A. D. & Blatchford, P. (2000). *The Child at School: Interactions with Peers and Teachers* (90–114). London: Arnold.

Robinson, J. P., Lubienski, S. T. & Copur, Y. (2011). The effects of teachers' gender-stereotypical expectations on the development of the math gender gap. Paper presented at the Society for Research on Educational Effectiveness Fall Conference, Washington, DC.

Rosenthal, R. (1963). On the social psychology of the psychological experiment: The experimenter's hypothesis as unintended determinant of experimental results. *American Scientist, 51,* 268–283.

Rosenthal, R. (1964). The effect of the experimenter on the results of psychological research. In B. A. Maher (ed.), *Progress in Experimental Personality Research* (Vol. 1, 79–114). New York: Academic.

Rosenthal, R. (1966). *Experimenter Effects in Behavioral Research.* New York: Appleton.

Rosenthal, R. & Jacobson, L. (1968). *Pygmalion in the Classroom: Teacher Expectation and Pupils' Intellectual Development.* New York: Holt, Rinehart & Winston.

Rubie-Davies, C. M. (2006). Teacher expectations and student self-perceptions: Exploring relationships. *Psychology in the Schools, 43,* 537–552. doi: 10.1002/pits.20169

Rubie-Davies, C. M. (2007). Classroom interactions: Exploring the practices of high and low expectation teachers. *British Journal of Educational Psychology, 77,* 289–306.

Rubie-Davies, C. M. (2008). Teacher beliefs and expectations: Relationships with student learning. In C. M. Rubie-Davies & C. Rawlinson (eds), *Challenging Thinking about Teaching and Learning* (25–39). Haupaugge, NY: Nova.

Rubie-Davies, C. M. (2010). Teacher expectations and perceptions of student attributes: Is there a relationship? *British Journal of Educational Psychology, 80,* 121–135.

Rubie-Davies, C. M. (2015). *Becoming a High Expectation Teacher: Raising the Bar.* London: Routledge.

Rubie-Davies, C. M. & Peterson, E. R. (2011). Teacher expectations and beliefs: Influences on the socioemotional environment of the classroom. In C. M. Rubie-Davies (ed.), *Educational Psychology: Concepts, Research and Challenges* (134–149). London: Routledge.

Rubie-Davies, C. M., Hattie, J. & Hamilton, R. (2006). Expecting the best for New Zealand students: Teacher expectations and academic outcomes. *British Journal of Educational Psychology, 76,* 429–444.

Rubie-Davies, C. M., Peterson, E. R., Sibley, C. G. & Rosenthal, R. (2015). A teacher expectation intervention: Modelling the practices of high expectation teachers. *Contemporary Educational Psychology, 40,* 72–85.

Rubie-Davies, C. M., Hattie, J., Townsend, M. A. R. & Hamilton, R. J. (2007). Aiming high: Teachers and their students. In V. N. Galwye (ed.), *Progress in Educational Psychology Research* (65–91). Hauppauge, NY: Nova.

Snow, R. E. (1969). Unfinished Pygmalion [Review of Pygmalion in the classroom]. *Contemporary Psychology, 14,* 197–199.

Solomon, D., Battistich, V. & Hom, A. (1996). Teacher beliefs and practices in schools serving communities that differ in socioeconomic level. *The Journal of Experimental Education, 64,* 327–347.

Stinnett, T. A., Crawford, S. A., Gillespie, M. D., Cruce, M. K. & Langford, C. A. (2001). Factors affecting treatment acceptability for psychostimulant medication versus psychoeducational intervention. *Psychology in the Schools, 38,* 585–591.

Tenenbaum, Harriet R. & Ruck, Martin D. (2007). Are teachers' expectations different for racial minority than for European American students? A meta-analysis. *Journal of Educational Psychology, 99*(2), 253–273.

Wagemaker, H. (ed.). (1993). *Achievement in Reading Literacy: New Zealand's Performance in a National and International Context.* Wellington, New Zealand: Ministry of Education.

Weinstein, R. S. (1993). Children's knowledge of differential treatment in school: Implications for motivation. In T. M. Tomlinson (ed.), *Motivating Students to Learn: Overcoming Barriers to High Achievement* (197–224). Berkeley, CA: McCutchan.

Weinstein, R. S. (2002). *Reaching Higher: The Power of Expectations in Schooling.* Cambridge, MA: Harvard University Press.

Weinstein, R. S., Marshall, H. H., Brattesani, K. A. & Middlestadt, S. E. (1982). Student perceptions of differential teacher treatment in open and traditional classrooms. *Journal of Educational Psychology, 74,* 678–692.

19

INACCURATE TEACHER EXPECTATIONS

Relationships with student and class characteristics, and its effect on long-term student performance

Hester de Boer, Anneke C. Timmermans and Margaretha P. C. van der Werf

Genesis

The Dutch secondary school system is, with five levels of education, highly tracked. At the end of primary school, students are recommended by their teacher which track or combination of adjacent tracks of secondary education is the most suitable for them. The track recommendation therefore reflects the teachers' expectation about the students' future academic performance. Almost all students follow this recommendation, and secondary schools attach great value to it, in addition to the students' scores on the standardized Final School Leaving Test. Although there are some possibilities to switch tracks during secondary education, the initial placement has great impact on the educational career of students.

There were indications, however, that some students received a secondary school recommendation that deviated from what one might expect on the basis of their current performance level. When talking with people about their school career, it was not uncommon to hear them saying that they had followed a certain track, but could easily have done a higher track. Furthermore, the scientific and political debate in the Netherlands centered on the possible negative and later positive discrimination of teachers toward minority students. Finally, several Dutch studies suggested there were discrepancies between teacher recommendations and student performance. Therefore, we started to examine whether, how often, and to what extent the teacher expectations deviate from the students' performance level. We also examined whether these deviations in expectations relate to characteristics of the student and the class composition, in order to assess whether teachers have biased expectations.

158 H. de Boer, A. C. Timmermans and M. P. C. van der Werf

Moreover, and most important, we addressed the question whether inaccurate teacher expectations affect students' future academic performance.

Current state of the art

In our research we examined the previous questions by analyzing the data of two large Dutch cohort studies. The database VOCL'99 (Kuyper *et al.*, 2003), analyzed by de Boer *et al.* (2010), included information of about 11,000 students who started secondary school in the year 1999, and who were followed for five consecutive years. The dataset PRIMA (Driessen *et al.*, 2006), analyzed by Timmermans *et al.* (2015), consisted of about 7,500 students who were in the final year of primary school in 2004/2005.

We found that teacher expectations are indeed sometimes inaccurate. For 19 percent of the students, the teacher expectations are at least half a track lower than what could be expected from the students' actual performance level, and for another 19 percent of the students the teacher expectations are at least half a track higher (de Boer *et al.*, 2010). Furthermore, we found indications of bias in the teachers' expectations, as the expectations of teachers for students with equal records of achievement related to several student characteristics, such as gender and socioeconomic status. The teachers' expectations for students with high educated parents are higher than for students with lower educated parents, performance level being equal. Similarly, girls tend to receive higher expectations than boys after controlling for the actual performance level. In the study of de Boer *et al.* (2010), no differences in teacher expectations were found between ethnic groups. In the study of Timmermans *et al.* (2015), however, it was found that Dutch students with low educated parents received lower expectations from their teachers than minority students with low educated parents.

Furthermore, our results suggest that with respect to gender and socioeconomic status, not all teachers have equally biased expectations (Timmermans *et al.*, 2015). The bias related to gender can partly be explained by teachers' perception of the student attributes. Accounting for the perception of students' social behavior in the classroom, work habits and self-confidence reduced the gender difference in teacher expectations significantly (Timmermans *et al.*, 2016).

Two other characteristics that relate to bias in teacher expectations are the parents' educational aspirations for the student (quite strongly), and student achievement motivation. Higher values on these characteristics relate to more positive bias (de Boer *et al.*, 2010). Additional analysis showed that misaligned parents' educational aspirations (it is, aspirations for their child that are higher or lower than the child's prior performance level) strongly relate to inaccurate teacher expectations. It is not clear, however, whether the parents' aspirations affect the teacher expectations, whether it is the other way around, or whether they mutually influence each other (de Boer & van der Werf, 2015).

Besides the relationships with individual student characteristics, bias in teacher expectations is also affected by class composition. All student characteristics being equal, the teachers' expectations are higher for students in high performing classes, and lower in low performing classes. Similarly, expectations are higher in classes consisting of students with at average high educated parents, and lower in classes with a lower education level of parents (Timmermans *et al.*, 2015).

Finally, the results of our studies turned out that inaccurate teacher expectations affect students' long-term performance during secondary education (de Boer *at al.*, 2010). Compared with students whose teacher expectation is accurate, students of whom teachers have too high expectations end up in a higher track of education after four years of secondary school, while students of whom teachers have too low expectations end up in a lower education track. The effects of inaccurate teacher expectations become larger as the inaccuracy increases. The initial (dis)advantage in educational position as a consequence of inaccurate teacher expectation dissipates partly (about the half) in the first two years of secondary school, but then remains quite stable over time. This implies that a teacher expectation that was one track too high or too low results in a half a track difference, on average, after four years of education. Furthermore, evidence was found that the effect of inaccurate teacher expectations on long-term student performance is moderated by several student characteristics, in particular by prior achievement, IQ, and parents' aspirations. The effect of inaccurate teacher expectations is larger for students with a high score on these variables than for students with a low score.

Directions for future research

Similar to many researchers investigating teacher expectations, we have examined differences in expectation among groups of students based on demographic characteristics. However, in the aforementioned studies we were not able to investigate why teachers showed differential expectations towards students. Obtaining more insights into the "why" question may be of particular importance to develop interventions in order to prevent negative effects of inaccurate teacher expectations. Investigating class composition, parental expectations and teacher perceptions of student attributes are first attempts to get more insight in the why questions. Further research may include, for example, characteristics of the student–teacher interactions, characteristics of the teacher, the home situation of the child, parental aspirations, and the students' personality.

Analyzing the relationships between these characteristics and teacher expectations should preferably occur on the basis of longitudinal data, which comprise information of every year's scores on these aspects. In this way, it can be analyzed how these characteristics interact with teacher expectations. Furthermore, research on the accuracy of teacher expectations may benefit from methodological advances such as multilevel modeling. Our previous research provided indications that teachers differ considerably in their bias towards or against groups of students. We therefore argue for a stronger focus on research with respect to differences among teachers instead of general associations between expectations and student characteristics. All in all, multilevel models should not only be applied because of the nested structure of educational data, but also to analyze in more detail the complex nature of between-teacher differences to increase the understanding of why some teachers appear more biased than others, and which circumstances contribute to biased teacher expectations.

A final direction for future research relates to the effects of teacher expectations on the future educational careers of students. In the Dutch context, inaccurate teacher expectations have a large impact on the placement of students in secondary school tracks. However, it might also affect the students' well-being during secondary education. Being placed in a track too high because of the teacher recommendation may lead to feelings of exhaustion, disengagement, and finally inadequacy. Similarly, being placed in a track too low may also lead to feelings of disengagement. Therefore, we would like to argue for the investigation of multiple outcomes, both cognitive and non-cognitive.

Practical relevance of the results

Our results showed that teacher expectations are not always accurate, and that some students are subject to inaccurate expectations. Too high teacher expectations have a positive effect on student performance, whereas too low expectations affect it negatively, and these effects are substantial. Negative effects of too low teacher expectations not only happen at the allocation of students to one of the secondary school tracks, but they can occur during the entire educational career of students. For example, when teachers use ability grouping to differentiate their instruction along to the (perceived) performance level of the students, or in their general approach to students (asking less challenging questions, creating a less ambitious learning environment with less opportunities to learn).

It is therefore in particular important to early identify the students of whom teacher expectations are too low, or may become too low. Especially the teachers and the school should be aware of the negative effects of too low expectations, and act upon it. But not only the teachers and the schools can do something to prevent negative effects to occur. In the Dutch context, currently interventions are implemented to prevent negative effects of low teacher expectations, by enhancing student performance and raising the ambitions of schools, teachers, and parents. Also, a new instrument has been developed for the allocation of students to secondary school tracks.

References

de Boer, H. & van der Werf, M. P. C. (2015). Influence of misaligned parents' aspirations on long-term student academic performance. *Educational Research and Evaluation: An International Journal on Theory and Practice, 21*, 232–257.

de Boer, H., Bosker, R. J. & van der Werf, M. P. C. (2010). Sustainability of teacher expectation bias effects on long-term student performance. *Journal of Educational Psychology, 102*, 168–179.

Driessen, G., Langen, A. van & Vierke, H. (2006). *Basisonderwijs: Veldwerkverslag, leerlinggegevens en oudervragenlijsten. Basisrapportage PRIMA-cohortonderzoek. Zesde meting 2004/05 [Primary school: Field research report, student data and parent questionnaires. Sixth measurement 2004/05].* Nijmegen: ITS.

Kuyper, H., Lubbers, M. J. & van der Werf, M. P. C. (2003). *VOCL'99–1: Technisch rapport [VOCL'99–1: Technical report.]* Groningen: GION.

Timmermans, A. C., De Boer, H. & Van der Werf, M. P. C. (2016). An investigation of the relationship between teachers' expectations and teachers' perceptions of student attributes. *Social Psychology of Education.*

Timmermans, A. C., Kuyper, H. & Van der Werf, M. P. C. (2015). Accurate, inaccurate or biased teacher expectations: Do Dutch teachers differ in their expectations at the end of primary education? *British Journal of Educational Psychology. 85*, 459–478.

20

EXPECTANCY EFFECTS

An attempt to integrate intra- and interpersonal perspectives[1]

Przemysław Bąbel and Sławomir Trusz

As we noted in the first chapter of the book, although a long tradition of research and theoretical accounts on both intrapersonal and interpersonal expectancies exists, these two perspectives on expectancy effects have been developing independently. Even if some attempts to integrate both domains have been already made (e.g., Harris, 1993; Jussim, 1986, 2012; Neuberg, 1994; Olson *et al.*, 1996; Roese & Sherman, 2007), so far attempts to integrate the intrapersonal and interpersonal perspectives in the analysis of the expectancy effects have mostly come down to distinguishing the mediator and/or moderator variables – i.e. the factors influencing the strength and/or direction of the process of confirming hypotheses about one's own responses or interaction partners' behavior. These factors, according to the most popular models of interpersonal expectancy effects or self-fulfilling prophecy (Cooper & Good, 1983; Darley & Fazio, 1980; Jussim, 1986; Rosenthal, 1981), can be treated either as correlates of intrapersonal expectancies (e.g. perceived control over reinforcements, self-schemas) or as variables that interact with them (e.g. emotions, attributions, objectives and motives), and thus determining, on one hand, observers' susceptibility to create expectations about themselves (the intra-perspective) or about their interaction partner (the inter-perspective), as well as their communication, whereas, on the other hand, the objects' susceptibility to behavioral or perceptual confirmation of these expectancies (DiMatteo, 1993; Hilton & Darley, 1985, 1991; Harris, 1993; Neuberg, 1994; Olson *et al.*, 1996; Roese & Sherman, 2007). In other words, what has been done so far are attempts to incorporate some constructs of intrapersonal expectancies to the models of interpersonal expectancies rather than to integrate both domains.

Although the main aim of our book is to open a discussion between researchers and theoreticians representing intra- and interpersonal expectancies' perspectives, we would also like to make an attempt to integrate both domains. However, as most of the models of intrapersonal expectancies deal with the placebo and nocebo effects, and most of the models of interpersonal expectancies deal with the Golem and Galatea effects, we will focus on these specific examples of the effects of both intra- and interpersonal expectancies.

The similarities between intrapersonal and interpersonal expectancies

It is worth starting an attempt to integrate the intra- and interpersonal perspectives on expectancies by posing a fundamental question about the scope of content and formal similarity of working and effects of both types of expectancies. First, the intrapersonal and interpersonal expectancy effects have their positive and negative varieties – a kind of obverse and reverse. Second, the intrapersonal and interpersonal expectancy effects have similar formal characteristics.

Content characteristics

Intrapersonal expectancies may produce both positive and negative effects. The best examples of both outcomes are placebo and nocebo effects. Although many different definitions of placebo and nocebo effects have been proposed so far, there is no agreement on the definitions. Hahn (1985, 1997) distinguishes between both effects on the basis of an expectancy (positive or negative) and an outcome (positive or negative). As a result, the placebo effect is the positive outcome of having positive expectations. Thus, we can talk about the placebo effect, when an objectively neutral substance – e.g. a red pill containing sugar – or a procedure – e.g. a simulated operation on the ankle – together with positive expectancis, brings about positive results in the form of health improvement – normalization of blood pressure, reduction of the pain, increase of one's physical efficiency, and the like. On the other hand, the nocebo effect is the negative outcome of negative expectations (Hahn, 1985, 1997). We can talk about the nocebo effect when taking an objectively neutral substance or submitting oneself to a simulated medical procedure together with negative expectancies, brings about negative effects in the form of health deterioration – an unfavorable increase of blood pressure, greater sensitivity to pain, decrease in one's physical efficiency, etc.

Similarly, within the interpersonal expectancy process one can distinguish the Galatea effect that occurs when positive assumptions by an observer (a parent, teacher, therapist, employer, etc.) concerning personal qualities, intelligence, motivation, educational achievements, or behavior of an object (a child, student, client, employee) are transformed in interaction into actually existing (or perceived) achievements and behaviors, testifying to a favorable arrangement of personal qualities and motivation – e.g. high empathy, openness and diligence, high level of intelligence, and special abilities (Babad, 2009; Babad et al., 1982; Blanck, 1993; Jussim et al., 1996; Rosenthal & Jacobson, 1968; Rubie-Davies, 2015). At the other extreme of the dimension, there is the Golem effect, which occurs when an observer's initially negative hypotheses concerning qualities of an object over time induce the object to present behaviors indicating an unfavorable arrangement of

164 Przemysław Bąbel and Sławomir Trusz

personal qualities, motivation, intelligence, and achievements (e.g. in education) below the objective level of the object's cognitive abilities (Babad, 2009; Babad *et al.*, 1982; Jussim *et al.*, 1996; Snyder *et al.*, 1977; Sutherland & Goldschmid, 1974; Word *et al.*, 1974).

If the cited analogy is not accidental, then it seems reasonable to hypothesize that at the root of both types of expectancy effects there are similar (or even identical) cognitive, emotional, and behavioral mechanisms and processes. For example, both in the case of intra- and interpersonal expectancies, their falsification should evoke similar processes of attention and memory – i.e. it should sensitize the observer to information contradictory to assumed hypotheses, and make them more deeply processed and more easily retrieved from episodic and semantic memory (Darley & Fazio, 1980; Jussim, 1986; Roese & Sherman, 2007). Similarly, in the case of attribution processes, violating the intra- and interpersonal expectancies should prompt one to attribute surprising results of medical or educational treatments to the influence of uncontrolled factors that are external, respectively, to a patient or a student – e.g. to (un)lucky coincidence (Levesque & Lowe, 1992; Roese & Sherman, 2007).

In relation to emotional processes, disconfirmation of positive intra- and interpersonal expectancies is usually a source of negative affect – e.g. a surprise, anxiety, or disappointment – and unexpected failure – e.g. of an applied medical procedure that is widely considered to be effective or of additional educational activities directed at allegedly gifted students – and should evoke a much stronger negative affect in a patient or teacher than an expected failure. In the case of placebo, Hahn (1985, 1997) distinguishes the placebo side effect as a negative outcome of positive expectations. In contrast, falsification of negative intra- and interpersonal expectancies – e.g. concerning the failure of medical procedures applied in the treatment of a specific disease or negative math test results of students belonging to stigmatized groups – is a source of positive affect – e.g. surprise, joy, and happiness of patients or teachers. And in this case an unexpected success should evoke a stronger positive affect than the expected success does (Jussim, 1986; Olson *et al.*, 1996). In case of nocebo, Hahn (1985, 1997) distinguishes the nocebo side effect as a positive outcome of negative expectations.

On the other hand, intra- and interpersonal expectancies can play regulatory functions in relation to emotions (Roese & Sherman, 2007). By manipulating the assessment of the probability of a positive or negative event as well as the assessment of its significance, individuals can reduce the negative affect – e.g. a smoker can judge that developing lung cancer is a very important change in life, but rather unlikely in his or her life, and a student can judge that failing a test is highly probable, but not significant from the point of view of his or her priorities in life. And, in the other direction, a negative affect associated with falsification of positive intra- and interpersonal expectancies motivates people to process available information more deeply and carefully, and consequently they make more accurate judgments about their physical and social environment, whereas a positive affect motivates people to process available information more automatically and superficially

(Fredrickson & Branigan, 2005; Gasper, 2004; Gasper & Clore, 2002; Olson *et al.*, 1996; Roese & Scherman, 2007; Stangor & McMillan, 1992).

Finally, the cognitive and affective processes which specificity is determined by the level of expectancy confirmation, influence a person's behavioral responses to oneself and to his or her interaction partners. For example, positive expectancies and the accompanying optimism regarding the efficacy of applied therapies or strategies for teaching allegedly gifted students can mobilize patients or teachers to engage more in the activity, and that, in return, increases the probability of success – i.e. health improvement or a good score in a school achievement test.

Formal characteristics

It seems that intrapersonal and interpersonal expectancy effects have similar formal characteristics. In both cases, the process is initiated by the creation of inaccurate intra- or interpersonal expectancies – e.g. concerning the effectiveness of a medicine – or personal qualities of an interaction partner, under the influence of false information from various sources – e.g. a physician, mass media, one's own cognitive schemas, a parent, other teachers, or social stereotypes (Jussim, 2012).

These expectancies are then communicated through various verbal and non-verbal behaviors to interaction partners – e.g. physicians or students – that their efforts are (or are not) effective, which in return can influence the level of their engagement in the treatment/learning process. Finally, as a result of systematic mediation of various expectancies, objects begin to behave or achieve results consistent with the initially inaccurate expectations – e.g. oncological patients start smoking again, people fighting obesity experience the yo-yo effect, and students begin to show achievements below (or above) their objective abilities (Friedman, 1993; Rubie-Davies, 2015).

One can also imagine a situation where negative/positive interpersonal expectancies – e.g. about the effectiveness of a therapy or a sales process – are communicated to patients/employees, which influences their self-expectations – e.g., their perceived self-efficacy, and consequently the level of their engagement in the activity and the achieved results of the applied medical or selling procedures (Darley & Fazio, 1980; Madoux, in this volume; Medoff & Colloca, in this volume; Weinstein, 2002).

Intrapersonal and interpersonal expectancies: a round trip ticket

Assuming that at the root of the effects of both types of expectancies there are similar or identical cognitive, affective, and behavioral processes and mechanisms, it is a cognitively and theoretically intriguing idea to attempt to use: (1) the models of intrapersonal expectancy effects (the placebo and nocebo effects) to interpret the operation and outcomes of interpersonal expectations, and (2) the models of self-fulfilling prophecy (the Galatea and Golem effects) to interpret the operation and outcome of intrapersonal expectancies.

From intrapersonal expectancies to interpersonal expectancies

Considering the former possibility, it seems particularly interesting to try to analyze the process of creating a self-fulfilling prophecy within the model of formation of intrapersonal expectancies. Kirsch (1985, 1997) suggested that, among others, classical conditioning, verbal persuasion, and modeling may be the means by which response expectancies are acquired and changed. Miller and Colloca (2010), on the basis of Peirce's theory of signs (Peirce, 1940), suggested a learning model of the formation of the placebo effect in which placebo effects result from expectancies acquired by decoding information from psychosocial context. From Peirce's (1940) theory, they incorporated three forms of signs which belong to that psychosocial context and convey to an interpreter information about objects – i.e. (1) "indices" that are dynamically linked to their objects, and to the senses or memory of interpreter; (2) "symbols" referring to the object that it denotes because of a conventional rule that makes the symbol interpreted as referring to that object (e.g. language), and (3) "icons" which signify their objects because of a likeness between the icon and the object (e.g. picture). According to Miller and Colloca's (2010) model (see also Colloca & Miller, 2011), placebo effects are produced by expectancies which are based on the decoding and interpreting of indices (e.g. conditioned stimuli), symbols (e.g. verbal suggestions), and icons (e.g. observation of a model).

In summary, there are different ways of acquiring and changing expectancies, including classical conditioning, verbal suggestions, and observational learning (modeling). From this point of view, the above mentioned ways of acquiring and changing expectancies do not directly induce placebo effects, but they do it indirectly by acquiring and changing expectancies. In other words, the placebo effects induced by classical conditioning, verbal suggestions, and observational learning (modeling) are mediated by expectancies.

False interpersonal expectancies induced in the first stage of the process of self-fulfilling prophecy can be interpreted as a conditional response of an experimenter, teacher, physician, therapist, etc., caused, fixed, and generalized in the course of interaction with an object – e.g. an experimental animal, student, patient, client, etc. One can imagine a situation in which an initially neutral object, as a result of perceived similarities of external appearance, place of residence, social status, surname, etc., with objects evoking low vs. high expectations, begins to evoke similar expectancies in the observer – e.g. concerning the speed of learning on how to navigate a maze, solving math problems, or a recovery process (Rosenthal, 1969, 2003).

One can also assume that along with the increase in the frequency of an observer's contact with objects, the induction of expectancies characteristic for them will become more automatic, and expectancies created that way will be generalized to an ever wider range of objects that are similar to some extent – e.g. due to their gender, ethnic, and racial descent, social and economic status, etc. – to the initial stimulus object (Cooper, 1979, 1985; Jussim, 2012; Rist, 1970; Taylor, 1993).

Expectancy effects **167**

In this view, the process of automatization and generalization of expectancies can be identified with transformation of episodic expectations (e.g. I predict that Chris, who has always been good at mathematics, will get a good grade in the next math test), into more abstract semantic expectancies (Chris is a boy; boys are good at math and sciences, therefore Chris should get a good grade in the next test in that subject; Roese & Sherman, 2007).

Apart from expectations, initially neutral and now conditional objects can evoke in observers behaviors by which false predictions are signaled to the objects, and that can be associated with the second stage of the process of self-fulfilling prophecy – i.e. mediation of interpersonal expectancies. For example, in a consulting room, a physician or therapist can more often maintain eye contact, smile, or listen patiently to the comments by a patient/client (DiMatteo, 1993; Friedman, 1993; Harris, 1993) who is associated with other patients/clients evoking similar responses.

Recent studies have shown that both placebo (Colloca & Benedetti, 2009; Hunter *et al.*, 2014) and nocebo effects (Świder & Bąbel, 2013; Vögtle *et al.*, 2013) can be induced by social observational learning. Medoff and Colloca (this volume) noticed that "this suggests that observing beneficial treatment in another person elicits placebo effects." On the other hand, Benedetti (2013) states that observation of unsuccessful treatment may have a negative effect on patients in clinical settings.

A similar mechanism of social learning can also influence the size of interpersonal expectancy effects. For example, in a school or hospital, observers – i.e. teachers and physicians – can observe how their workmates respond to students and patients, and on that basis they can learn proper – in a specific context – emotional responses to selected objects – e.g. satisfaction in contact with the students who are favored by other teachers, or with patients who comply with physicians' recommendations. It is easy to predict that this kind of emotional response – positive vs. negative – may pave the way for friendly vs. hostile behaviors of observers toward objects, thus strengthening the process of communication of interpersonal expectations, and consequently their behavioral confirmation.

Placebo analgesia and noceba hyperalgesia found in studies on placebo effects induced by social observational learning (Colloca & Bendetti, 2009; Hunter *et al.*, 2014; Świder & Bąbel, 2013) correlated with dispositional empathy in those who were observing a model. In other words, people who had higher ability to experience empathy gained more during the process of social learning in both placebo and nocebo effects. The results of meta-analyses by Cooper and Hazelrigg (1988) suggest that similar regularities also occur in studies on interpersonal expectancy effects. It has been found that among significant personal moderators of the phenomenon of self-fulfilling prophecy, there is a high ability of objects to decode the incoming information, a trait that is important for accurate interpretation of other people's mental states.

Finally, analyzing the importance of verbal instructions in the creation of the placebo/nocebo effect, Medoff and Colloca (this volume) note: "If a patient is verbally told that they will experience pain reduction, they will recall a previous

168 Przemysław Bąbel and Sławomir Trusz

experience of analgesia and will experience similar pain relief." Similarly, within the process of self-fulfilling prophecy in a classroom or an experimental psychologist's laboratory, an observer – i.e. a teacher/researcher – can create various and false expectancies about students/tested objects (e.g. rats), when they learn from other teachers or the principal experimenter that a part of students/animals will achieve remarkable results in learning during the next several days, weeks, or months of working with them. In a series of spectacular experiments, Robert Rosenthal proved that the indicated mechanism can significantly influence the expectations and behavior of researchers in a lab (the so-called experimenter expectancy effect – see Rosenthal, 1969; Rosenthal & Rubin, 1978) and teachers in a classroom (the Pygmalion effect – see Babad *et al.*, 1982; Rosenthal & Jacobson, 1968).

Putting interpersonal expectancy effects into the frames of the model by Colloca and Miller (2011) seems to be a very interesting proposition that allows to describe and explain phenomena which so far have been insufficiently interpreted – e.g. automatism in creation of false interpersonal expectations and communication about them to one's interaction partners. It also seems that it would be equally interesting to add operant (instrumental) conditioning to the methods producing placebo effects suggested by the authors – i.e. classical conditioning, observational learning (modeling), and verbal suggestions. Although this goes beyond the model by Colloca and Miller (2011), such "two-factor theory" allows to explain coherently the specific nature of the process of self-fulfilling prophecy at all its stages, starting with the induction of false interpersonal expectancies (classical conditioning, vicarious classical conditioning, i.e. modeling, and verbal suggestions), their communication (classical and operant conditioning, particularly negative and positive reinforcements, as well as punishments described within Rosenthal's theory of four mediating factors (Harris, 1993; Harris & Rosenthal, 1985; Rosenthal, 1974), Cooper's model (1979, 1985), and Bellamy's behavioral model of the Pygmalion effect (1975)), and confirmations (instrumental conditioning, especially the behavior of objects – e.g. students, patients – presented as a consequence of the positive vs. negative climate, feedback, input, and output generated by observers, e.g. teachers or physicians).

From intrapersonal expectancies to interpersonal expectancies

Considering the second suggested possibility of integrating intra- and interpersonal perspectives on expectancy effects, it seems particularly interesting to attempt to analyze the placebo and nocebo effects within Rosenthal's theory of four mediating factors in the formation of interpersonal expectancy effects (DiMatteo, 1993; Harris, 1993; Rosenthal, 1974), namely: (1) climate, (2) feedback, (3) input, and (4) output. Each of them is related to a specific class of behavior. Climate includes an observer's action that creates a cold or warm emotional atmosphere – e.g. a physician could smile at his/her patient, nod his/her head, reduce the physical distance, etc. Feedback is related to praise and criticism, reinforcement, and punishment directed at objects – e.g. a therapist could praise his/her client's good homework solution, or a physician could criticize their patient when he/she doesn't

Expectancy effects **169**

follow their recommendations, etc. Input includes behaviors related to the amount of and/or complexity of medical/therapeutic procedures – e.g. a therapist proposes a more complex and deeper interpretation of a patient's problem and a physician proposes more complex physiotherapy, etc. The last factor – output – is related to observer behavior that facilitates or inhibits an object's behavior which proves their competences – e.g. a physician waits for his/her patient's answer for a longer time, and provides additional hints and suggestions about medical procedures when patient asks about them, etc.

The results of many studies show that expectancies and – in effect – the behaviors of a physician or a therapist may influence not only the effectiveness of the placebo effects but also the effectiveness of an active (non-placebo) treatment (for reviews, see Crow et al., 1999; Di Blasi et al., 2001). The results of the research (DiMatteo, 1993; Friedman, 1993; Harris, 1993; Roter & Hall, 2006) which examined the influence of the climate in a physician's/therapist's consulting room, feedback, as well as a physician's/therapist's input and efficiency on the pace of their patients' recovery allow the assumption that physicians' behaviors, traditionally associated with the process of communicating diverse interpersonal expectations, can have a significant influence on various parameters of the placebo and nocebo effects. For example, Kaptchuk and colleagues (2008) found that placebo acupuncture together with a patient–practitioner relationship augmented by warmth, attention, and confidence provided much more robust treatment effects than placebo acupuncture alone. Moreover, a review of the results of studies on the effectiveness of five medical and surgical treatments, once considered to be efficacious by their proponents but no longer considered effective based on later controlled trials, showed that in the case of 70 percent of them, excellent or good results were reported by their proponents (Roberts et al., 1993). The authors concluded that the power of nonspecific effects may account for as much as two-thirds of successful treatment outcomes when both the healer and the patient believe in the efficacy of the treatment.

In summary, not only do intrapersonal expectancies of patients or research participants have an effect on the placebo effects, but also the interpersonal expectancies of a physician or researcher are crucial factors in the genesis of both placebo and nocebo effects. Harris (1993) stresses that "one important component of placebo effects is the patients' own self-expectancies about the course of their illness and the treatment; the second important component is the communication of the health professionals' expectations" (p. 367).

Diverse physicians' behaviors may have a positive vs. negative influence on patients' self-expectations – e.g. concerning the effectiveness of a particular type of therapy – which, in turn, may modify patients' readiness to undertake actions that are important from the point of view of the state of their health. For example, patients with high self-expectations can lead a more active lifestyle, avoid stimulants, and have a healthier diet. Moreover, as Friedman (1993) suggests: "They may also be more likely to cooperate with their medical regimens, such as taking medications properly and returning for medical follow-up" (p. 187), as compared to patients with low self-expectations.

170 Przemysław Bąbel and Sławomir Trusz

One of the most important psychological variables determining the results of medical treatment is patient adherence (compliance) to the treatment. The level of adherence (compliance) correlates positively with the degree to which medical treatment is consistent with the patient's expectations and his/her needs are met in contact with a friendly vs. indifferent/cold physician. Patients/clients who do not follow physicians'/therapists' recommendations may lose confidence in themselves and even the power of their bodies to heal, resulting in a higher probability that they will realize the negative scenario of the nocebo effect (DiMatteo, 1993; see also Czajkowski & Chesney, 1990; Horwitz & Horwitz, 1993).

Patients with positive expectations (attitudes) in relation to medical treatment are in a far more favorable situation. For example, the research results show that among patients who strictly adhered to recommendations in medical treatment for hypertension, blood pressure improvement was greater than among those who did not act this way. Similar results were obtained in a group of patients treated for diabetes and coronary disease (DiMatteo, 1993). Moreover, it turns out that the positive effects of treatment associated with stricter adherence to physicians' recommendations are found regardless of whether patients receive actual medical procedures or placebo (Czajkowski & Chesney, 1990; Horwitz & Horwitz, 1993).

DiMatteo (1993) explains these results as follows: "Patients who adhered to treatment recommendations may have had more positive expectations for their own health outcomes, and these expectations may have served as a self-fulfilling prophecy. On the other hand, the act of adhering may have generated new habits and cognitive patterns that brought about improvement and even more self-confidence, resulting in the enactment of still more health-related behaviors" (p. 299). In total, both factors – i.e. self-expectations of patients and their pro-health patterns of behavior and thinking – correlated with the supportive actions of physicians, increasing the probability of realizing the positive scenario of the placebo effect.

Describing the determinants of matching patients to medical treatment, and thus their susceptibility to placebo/nocebo effect, DiMatteo (1993) lists behaviors by which physicians communicate to patients various expectations concerning their health or prognosis. These behaviors include:

1   Avoiding vs. excessive use of medical jargon in conversations with patients; such jargon can evoke their embarrassment and affect whether they understand the information provided properly, and even their conviction that they are incompetent, more stupid, and worse as a person than the physician.
2   Attentive vs. inattentive listening to patients, which, together with a physician's empathic engagement in the relationship with patients, signals respect for them, and is one of the most important nonspecific factors of most therapies (Butler & Strupp, 1986; Chatoor & Kurpnick, 2001).
3   Educating vs. not educating patients, including informing them on appropriate ways of taking medication, prevention, and pro-health behaviors, etc. DiMatteo (1993) notes:

Expectancy effects **171**

> [B]ecause many physicians expect their patients to need prolonged expectations or to be unable to understand medical treatment altogether, they avoid providing any. Physicians tend, however, to underestimate how much information their patients can understand, as well as how much information they desire to have.
>
> (p. 304)

Lack of relevant information from a physician can induce patient behaviors that are dangerous to their health or life – e.g. a patient may take medicine not in accordance with their schedule or abstain from their taking, and that can raise the probability that a negative effect of intrapersonal expectancies will occur in them. Generally, information provided to the patients seems to be very powerful, as it can not only enhance the effects of an active agent (Benedetti *et al.*, 2003; Dworkin *et al.*, 1984; Kirsch & Rosadino, 1993; Kleijnen & de Craen, 1994), but also attenuate, or even change the direction of the effects of an active intervention (Dworkin *et al.*, 1983; Flaten *et al.*, 1999; Kleijnen & de Craen, 1994).

4   Promoting activity vs. passivity of patients in the physician's consulting room, through verbal behaviors – e.g. open vs. closed questions – and non-verbal behaviors – e.g. a smile, eye contact, posture, etc. – encouraging vs. discouraging patients to comment on their ailments, their possible causes, their level of understanding of medical instructions, etc. The feeling of being an active agent vs. passive object of medical treatment that is elicited by physicians' behaviors can influence patients' self-expectations concerning the effectiveness of medical procedures and their pro-health behaviors (Rodin & Langer, 1980), and that, in return, can raise their susceptibility to the placebo vs. nocebo effects.

5   Extending vs. shortening the duration of a patient's visit in the consulting room, which naturally influences the possibility of communicating to them high vs. low expectations concerning the effects of recommended medical procedures. Longer time of interaction, and thus a greater number of a physician's behaviors indicating his/her interest in the problems of the patient – e.g. a smile, nodding, and body orientation, can reduce the level of anxiety in patients and encourage them to provide more information, which is important from the point of view of treated ailments. On the other hand, an obvious shortening of the duration of a visit can signal a lack of interest in the patient's matters, and evoke his/her negative attitude toward the recommended medical procedures, which consequently can reduce the size of the positive effects of intrapersonal expectancies.

Harris (1993) made a comprehensive list of the ways in which health professionals and psychotherapists communicate differential expectancies about their patients and clients in medical settings, psychotherapy, and institutional care – e.g nursing homes. Considering the first of the indicated contexts, the author lists the following mediators:

172 Przemysław Bąbel and Sławomir Trusz

1 nonverbal warmth;
2 tone of voice;
3 eye contact;
4 verbal and nonverbal confidence;
5 body orientation;
6 treatment regimen prescribed;
7 physical format of placebo − e.g. pills vs. injections, size of pill, use of complicated equipment.

Within the second context, the author indicates the following factors:

1 selective questions about client history;
2 nature of interpretations offered;
3 nonverbal warmth;
4 tone of voice;
5 eye contact;
6 smiles, facial expressions;
7 nods;
8 touch;
9 interpersonal distance.

Finally, with respect to institutional care, Harris lists the following mediators:

1 nonverbal warmth;
2 nonverbal condescension;
3 eye contact;
4 touch;
5 baby talk − e.g. higher pitch, greater variability in pitch, limited vocabulary, repetition, and clarifying devices;
6 control over activities;
7 restrictions on timing of activities − e.g., sleeping, eating;
8 type of entertainment provided − e.g. TV;
9 performing basic bodily and hygienic functions − e.g., eating, grooming.

It is worth stressing that out of 25 proposed mediators, as many as 17 (i.e. 68 percent) can be associated with the factor of climate, according to the taxonomy of mediating factors in the formation of interpersonal expectancy effects proposed by Rosenthal (1974) and Harris and Rosenthal (1985). The effect size calculated in meta-analyses for the climate (affect) in the relationship between the class of behavioral indicators of observers' expectancies was $r = 0.23$, whereas between observers' behaviors that communicate expectations and the achievements of objects, it was $r = 0.36$. According to the measure of BESD proposed by Rosenthal et al. (2000), the indicated values mean an increase in the number of observers' behaviors relevant to the climate in relations with objects from around 23 percent (for low-expectancy individuals) to around 73 percent (for high-expectancy individuals), and an increase of objects' achievements from around 14 percent (for low-expectancy individuals) to around 86 percent (for high-expectancy individuals).

Considering the specific nature of institutional care settings, the indicated communicating behaviors, as suggested by Harris, can be associated with two classes of medical staff activities. The first concerns nonverbal behaviors serving to infantilize the target – e.g. baby talk – whereas the second refers to behaviors stemming from care providers' efforts to exert control over the patients' actions – e.g. restrictions on timing of activities. The consequence of both can be self-induced dependence among residents, increasing their susceptibility to adverse effects of intrapersonal expectancies.

It seems, then, that the relationship between inter- and intrapersonal expectancies may be as follows: interpersonal expectancies of a physician may have an effect on their behaviors and – as a result – on a patient's intrapersonal expectancies, which may influence their health both directly (the effect on intrapersonal expectancies on a patient's nonvolitional responses) and indirectly (the effect of intrapersonal expectancies on a patient's volitional behaviors). The behaviors of a physician induced or at least mediated by their interpersonal expectancies include both verbal and nonverbal as well as both volitional and nonvolitional or intentional and unintentional behaviors. From Rosenthal's four-factor theory perspective (DiMatteo, 1993; Harris, 1993; Rosenthal, 1974), they may be seen as elements that work together to form a physician's disposition toward their patient(s), belonging to one of the classes of behaviors: climate, feedback, input, output. According to Miller and Colloca's (2010) model (see also Colloca & Miller, 2011), a physician's behaviors would belong to the psychosocial context. They might be seen mainly as "symbols"; however, it is also possible to see some of the physician's behaviors as "indices" and "icons."

The question still remains, what is the mechanism of the effects of physicians' behaviors on patients' intrapersonal expectancies? Classic studies showed that anxiety may be the mechanism of analgesic and hyperalgesic placebo effects (Evans, 1974; McGlashan et al., 1969). According to reconstruction of the anxiety theory, analgesic placebo reduces anxiety and hyperalgesic nocebo increases anxiety (Bąbel, 2005). However, it is not clear if anxiety is a distinct mechanism from expectancy and classical conditioning, or mediating mechanism between expectancy/classical conditioning and placebo effects. The latter is supported by the results of a few studies on analgesic and hyperalgesic placebo effects that revealed the correlations between anxiety and expectancy (Bąbel, 2008; de Jong et al., 1996; Vase et al., 2005). Kirsch (1997) has suggested that changes in anxiety may be a mediating mechanism between expectancy and placebo effects. It is possible, then, that the behaviors of physicians may have an effect, not only on patients' intrapersonal expectancies but also on their level of anxiety, or that anxiety may be a mediating mechanism between physician behavior and a patient's intrapersonal expectancies.

The editors of the volume realize that the presented list of elements/areas that integrate intrapersonal and interpersonal perspectives on expectancy effects is not complete. Moreover, it concerns two very specific outcomes of intrapersonal expectancies (the placebo and nocebo effects) and interpersonal expectancies (the Golem and Galatea effects in the context of a classroom). It is rather a starting point, an invitation to discuss these cognitively fascinating and practically important issues.

In our view, when planning future studies, it is worth answering the following questions:

1 Can intrapersonal expectancy effects be the source for interpersonal expectancy effects, and vice versa?
2 What are their mutual relations – i.e. how and to what extent do intra- and interpersonal perspectives on expectancies penetrate each other at various stages of their formation?
3 To what extent is it worth analyzing intra- and interpersonal perspectives on expectancies, taking into account the double-track nature of expectancy processes – i.e. their automatic vs. conscious/deliberative evoking, communication, and confirmation – see e.g. Bargh, 1999; Chen & Bargh 1997).
4 What is the mechanism of the effects of intrapersonal expectancies on interpersonal expectancies, and vice versa?

Note

1 Preparation of this chapter was supported by the National Science Centre in Poland under grant number 2014/14/E/HS6/00415 awarded to the first author and under grant number 2012/05/D/HS6/03350 awarded to the second author.

References

Babad, E. (2009). *The Social Psychology of the Classroom*. New York: Routledge.

Babad, E., Inbar, J. & Rosenthal, R. (1982). Pygmalion, Galatea, and the Golem: Investigations of biased and unbiased teachers. *Journal of Educational Psychology, 74*, 459–474.

Bąbel, P. (2005). [Anxiety as a mechanism of the anaglesic and hyperalgesic placebo action] Lęk jako mechanizm analgetycznego i hiperalgetycznego działania placebo. [*Pain*] *Ból, 6*, 6–10.

Bąbel, P. (2008). [Psychological mechanisms of the negative placebo action. An empirical analysis] Psychologiczne mechanizmy negatywnego działania placebo. Analiza empiryczna. [*Psychological Studies*] *Studia Psychologiczne, 46*, 13–24.

Bargh, J.A. (1999). The cognitive monster: The case against the controllability of automatic stereotype effects. In S. Chaiken and Y. Trope (eds), *Dual-Process Theories in Social Psychology* (361–382), New York: Guilford.

Bellamy, G.T. (1975). The Pygmalion effect: What teacher behaviors mediate it? *Psychology in the Schools, 12*, 454–461.

Benedetti, F. (2013). Responding to nocebos through observation: Social contagion of negative emotions. *Pain, 154*, 1165.

Benedetti, F., Maggi, G., Lopiano, L., Lanotte, M., Rainero, I., Vighetti, S. & Pollo, A. (2003). Open versus *hidden* medical treatments: The patient's knowledge about a therapy affects the therapy outcome. *Prevention & Treatment, 6*, Article 1a.

Blanck, P. D. (ed.). (1993). *Interpersonal Expectations: Theory, Research and Applications*. New York: Cambridge University Press.

Butler, S. F. & Strupp, H. H. (1986). Specific and nonspecific factors in psychotherapy: A problematic paradigm for psychotherapy research. *Psychotherapy: Theory, Research, Practice, Training, 23*, 30–40.

Chatoor I. C. & Kurpnick, J. (2001). The role of non-specific factors in treatment outcome of psychotherapy studies. *European Child & Adolescent Psychiatry, 10*, S19–S25.

Chen, M. & Bargh, J. A. (1997). Nonconscious behavioral confirmation processes: The self-fulfilling consequences of automatic stereotype activation. *Journal of Experimental Social Psychology, 33*, 541–560.

Colloca, L. & Benedetti, F. (2009). Placebo analgesia induced by social observational learning. *Pain, 144*, 28–34.

Colloca, L. & Miller, F. G. (2011). How placebo responses are formed: A learning perspective. *Philosophical Transactions of the Royal Society of London. Series B, Biological Sciences, 366*, 1859–1869.

Cooper, H. (1979). Pygmalion grows up: A model for teacher expectation communication and performance influence. *Review of Educational Research, 49*, 389–410.

Cooper, H. (1985). Models of teacher expectation communication. In J. Dusek (ed.), *Teacher Expectancies* (135–158). Hillsdale, NJ: Erlbaum.

Cooper, H. & Good, T. (1983). *Pygmalion Grows Up: Studies in the Expectation Communication Process*. New York: Longman.

Cooper, H. & Hazelrigg, P. (1988). Personality moderators of interpersonal expectancy effects: An integrative research review. *Journal of Personality and Social Psychology, 55*, 937–949.

Crow, R., Gage, H., Hampson, S., Hart, J., Kimber, A. & Thomas, H. (1999). The role of expectancies in the placebo effect and their use in the delivery of health care: A systematic review. *Health Technology Assessment, 3*, 1–96.

Czajkowski, S. M. & Chesney, M. A. (1990). Adherence and the placebo effect. In S. A. Shumaker, E. B. Schron, J. K. Ockene, C. T. Parker, J. L. Probstfield & J. M. Wolle (eds), *Handbook of Health Behavior Change* (409–423). New York: Springer.

Darley, J. M. & Fazio, R. H. (1980). Expectancy confirmation processes arising in the social interaction sequence. *American Psychologist, 35*, 867–881.

de Jong, P. J., van Baast, R., Arntz, A. & Merckelbach H. (1996). The placebo effect in pain reduction: The influence of conditioning experiences and response expectancies. *International Journal of Behavioral Medicine, 3*, 14–29.

Di Blasi, Z., Harkness, E., Ernst, E., Georgiou, A. & Kleijnen, J. (2001). Influence of context effects on health outcomes: A systematic review. *Lancet, 357*, 757–762.

DiMatteo, M. R. (1993). Expectations in the physician-patient relationship: Implications for patient adherence to medical treatment recommendations. In P. D. Blanck (ed.), *Interpersonal Expectations: Theory, Research, and Applications* (296–315). New York: Cambridge University Press.

Dworkin, S. F., Chen, A. C., LeResche, L. & Clark, D. W. (1983). Cognitive reversal of expected nitrous oxide analgesia for acute pain. *Anesthesia and Analgesia, 62*, 1073–1077.

Dworkin, S. F., Chen, A. C., Schubert, M. M. & Clark, D. W. (1984). Cognitive modification of pain: Information in combination with N2O. *Pain, 19*, 339–351.

Evans, F. J. (1974). The placebo response in pain reduction. In J. J. Bonica (ed.), *Advances in Neurology, Vol. 4: International Symposium on Pain* (289–296). New York: Raven Press.

Flaten, M. A., Simonsen, T. & Olsen, H. (1999). Drug-related information generates placebo and nocebo responses that modify the drug response. *Psychosomatic Medicine, 61*, 250–255.

Fredrickson, B. L. & Branigan, C. (2005). Positive emotions broaden the scope of attention and thought-action repertoires. *Cognition & Emotion, 19*, 313–332.

Friedman, H.S. (1993). Interpersonal expectations and the maintenance of health. In P. D. Blanck (ed.), *Interpersonal Expectations: Theory, Research, and Applications* (179–193). New York: Cambridge University Press.

Gasper, K. (2004). Do you see what I see? Affect and visual information processing. *Cognition & Emotion, 18,* 405–421.

Gasper, K. & Clore, G. L. (2002). Attending to the big picture: Mood and global versus local processing of visual information. *Psychological Science, 13,* 34–40.

Hahn, R. A. (1985). A sociocultural model of illness and healing. In L. White, B. Tursky & G. E. Schwartz (eds), *Placebo: Theory, Research and Mechanisms* (167–195). New York: The Guilford Press.

Hahn, R. A. (1997). The nocebo phenomenon: Scope and foundations. In A. Harrington (ed.), *The Placebo Effect: An Interdisciplinary Exploration* (56–76). Cambridge: Harvard University Press.

Harris, M. (1993). Issues in studying the mediation of expectancy effects: A taxonomy of expectancy situations. In P. D. Blanck (ed.), *Interpersonal Expectations: Theory, Research, and Applications* (350–378). New York: Cambridge University Press.

Harris, M. J. & Rosenthal, R. (1985). Mediation of interpersonal expectancy effects: 31 metaanalyses. *Psychological Bulletin, 97,* 363–386.

Hilton J. L. & Darley, J. M. (1985). Constructing other persons: Limit on the effect. *Journal of Experimental Social Psychology, 21,* 1–18.

Hilton J. L. & Darley, J. M. (1991). The effects of interaction goals on person perception. *Advances in Experimental Social Psychology, 24,* 235–267.

Horwitz, R. I. & Horwitz, S. M. (1993). Adherence to treatment and health outcomes. *Archives of Internal Medicine, 153,* 1863–1868.

Hunter, T., Siess, F. & Colloca, L. (2014). Socially induced placebo analgesia: A comparison of a pre-recorded versus live face-to-face observation. *European Journal of Pain, 18,* 914–922.

Jussim, L. (1986). Self-fulfilling prophecies: A theoretical and integrative review. *Psychological Review, 93,* 429–445.

Jussim, L. (2012). *Social Perception and Social Reality: Why Accuracy Dominates Bias and Self-fulfilling Prophecy.* New York: Oxford University Press.

Jussim, L., Eccles, J. & Madon, S. J. (1996). Social perception, social stereotypes, and teacher expectations: Accuracy and the quest for the powerful self-fulfilling prophecy. *Advances in Experimental Social Psychology, 29,* 281–388.

Kaptchuk, T. J., Kelley, J. M., Conboy, L. A., Davis, R. B., Kerr, C. E., Jacobson, E. E. & . . . Lembo, A. J. (2008). Components of placebo effect: Randomised controlled trial in patients with irritable bowel syndrome. *BMJ: British Medical Journal, 336,* 999–1003.

Kirsch, I. (1985). Response expectancy as a determinant of experience and behavior. *American Psychologist, 40,* 1189–1202.

Kirsch, I. (1997). Specifying nonspecifics: Psychological mechanisms of placebo effects. In A. Harrington (ed.), *The Placebo Effect: An Interdisciplinary Exploration* (166–186). Cambridge: Harvard University Press.

Kirsch, I. & Rosadino, M. J. (1993). Do double-blind studies with informed consent yield externally valid results? An empirical test. *Psychopharmacology, 110,* 437–442.

Kleijnen, J. & Craen, A. J. N. de (1994). Placebo effect in double-blind clinical trials: A review of interactions with medications. *Lancet, 344,* 1347–1349.

Levesque, M. J. & Lowe, C. A. 1992. The importance of attributions and expectancies in understanding academic behaviour. In F. J. Medway & T. P. Cafferty (eds), *School Psychology: A Social Psychological Perspective* (47–81). Hillsdale, NJ: Lawrence Erlbaum Associates.

McGlashan, T. H., Evans, F. J. & Orne, M. T. (1969). The nature of hypnotic analgesia and placebo response to experimental pain. *Psychosomatic Medicine, 31,* 227–246.

Miller, F. G. & Colloca, L. (2010). Semiotics and the placebo. *Perspectives in Biology and Medicine*, *53*, 509–516.

Neuberg, S. L. (1994). Expectancy-confirmation processes in stereotype-tinged social encounters: The moderating role of social goals. In M. P. Zanna & J. M. Olson (eds), *The Psychology of Prejudice: The Ontario Symposium* (Vol. 7, 103–130). Hillsdale, NJ: Erlbaum.

Olson, J. M., Roese, N. J. & Zanna, M. P. (1996). Expectancies. In E. T. Higgins & A. W. Kruglanski (eds), *Social Psychology: Handbook of Basic Principles* (211–238). New York: The Guilford Press.

Peirce, C. (1940). Logic as semiotic: The theory of signs. In J. Buchler (ed.), *Philosophical Writings of Peirce* (98–119). New York: Dover.

Rist, R. C. (1970). Student social class and teacher expectations: The self-fulfilling prophecy in ghetto education. *Harvard Educational Review*, *40*, 411–451.

Roberts, A. H., Kewman, D. G., Mercier, L. & Hovell, M. F. (1993). The power of nonspecific effects in healing: Implications for psychosocial and biological treatments. *Clinical Psychology Review*, *13*, 375–391.

Rodin, J. & Langer, E. (1980). Aging labels: The decline of control and the fall of self-esteem. *Journal of Social Issues*, *36*, 12–29.

Roese, N. J. & Sherman, J. W. (2007). Expectancy. In A. W. & E. T. Higgins (eds), *Social Psychology: Handbook of Basic Principles* (2nd edn) (91–115). New York and London: Guilford Press.

Rosenthal, R. (1969). Interpersonal expectations: Effects of the experimenter's hypothesis. In R. Rosenthal & R. L. Rosnow (eds), *Artifact in Behavioral Research* (181–277). New York: Academic Press.

Rosenthal, R. (1974). *On the Social Psychology of the Self-fulfilling Prophecy: Further Evidence for Pygmalion Effects and their Mediating Mechanisms*. New York: MSS Modular Publications.

Rosenthal, R. (1981). Pavlov's mice, Pfungst's horse, and Pygmalion's PONS: Some models for the study of interpersonal expectancy effects. In T. A. Sebeok & R. Rosenthal (eds), *The Clever Hans Phenomenon: Communication with Horses, Whales, Apes, and People*. Annals of the New York Academy of Sciences (Vol. 364, 182–198). New York: New York Academy of Sciences.

Rosenthal, R. (2003). Covert communication in laboratories, classrooms, and the truly real world. *Current Directions in Psychological Science*, *12*, 151–154.

Rosenthal, R. & Jacobson, L. (1968). *Pygmalion in the Classroom: Teacher Expectation and Pupils' Intellectual Development*. New York: Irvington.

Rosenthal, R. & Rubin, D. B. (1978). Interpersonal expectancy effects: The first 345 studies. *Behavioral and Brain Sciences*, *3*, 377–386.

Rosenthal, R., Rosnow, R. L. & Rubin, D. B. (2000). *Contrasts and Effect Sizes in Behavioral Research: A Correlational Approach*. Cambridge: Cambridge University Press.

Roter, D. & Hall, J. A. (2006). *Doctors Talking with Patients/Patients Talking with Doctors: Improving Communication in Medical Visits*. Westport, CT: Praeger.

Rubie-Davies, C. (2015). *Becoming a High Expectation Teacher: Raising the Bar*. London and New York: Routledge.

Snyder, M., Tanke, E. D. & Berscheid, E. (1977). Social perception and interpersonal behavior: On the self-fulfilling nature of social stereotypes. *Journal of Personality and Social Psychology*, *35*, 656–666.

Stangor, C. & McMillan, D. (1992). Memory for expectancy-congruent and expectancy-incongruent information: A review of the social and social developmental literatures. *Psychological Bulletin*, *111*, 42–61.

Sutherland, A. & Goldschmid, M. L. (1974). Negative teacher expectation and IQ change in children with superior intellectual potential. *Child Development*, *45*, 852–856.

178 Przemysław Bąbel and Sławomir Trusz

Świder, K. & Bąbel, P. (2013). The effect of the sex of a model on nocebo hyperalgesia induced by social observational learning. *Pain, 154,* 1312–1317.

Taylor, M. C. (1993). Expectancies and the perpetuation of racial inequity. In P. D. Blanck (ed.), *Interpersonal Expectations: Theory, Research, and Applications* (88–124). New York: Cambridge University Press.

Vase, L., Robinson, M. E., Verne, G. N. & Price D. D. (2005). Increased placebo analgesia over time in irritable bowel syndrome (IBS) patients is associated with desire and expectations but not endogenous opioid mechanisms. *Pain, 115,* 338–347.

Vogtle, E., Barke, A. & Kroner-Herwig, B. (2013). Nocebo hyperalgesia induced by social observational learning. *Pain, 154,* 1427–1433.

Weinstein, R. S. (2002). *Reaching Higher: The Power of Expectations in Schooling.* Cambridge, MA, London: Harvard University Press.

Word, C. O., Zanna, M. P. & Cooper, J. (1974). The nonverbal mediation of self-fulfilling prophecies in interracial interaction. *Journal of Experimental Social Psychology,* 10, 109–120.

AUTHOR INDEX

Notes: spelling follows US scheme; italics denote figures.

Abramson, L. Y. 4
Ajzen, I. 27
Allport, G. W. 113
Alvidrez, J. 118, 137
Anderson, T. H. 112, 119, 141, 142, 143

Babad, E. 7, 10, 14, 118, 125–131, 146, 147, 150, 152, 163, 164, 168
Bąbel, P. 1–15, 79, 80, 162–174
Backenstrass, M. 53, 55, 56, 57
Baker, T. B. 63, 64
Baldwin, A. S. 91
Baltman, J. 10, 11–12, 23, 47–50
Bandura, A. 4, 41–42, 43, 44, 45, 46, 62
Barber, T. 125
Bargh, J. A. 113, 174
Barker, D. J. 37
Bassi, M. 45
Batzle, C. S. 146
Baumeister, R. F. 118
Beck, A. T. 26
Beecher, H. K. 28–30
Benedetti, F. 31, 76, 77, 78, *78*, 79, 81, 82, 167, 171
Benet-Martinez, V. 56
Ben-Porath, D. D. 55
Benson, H. 1, 6
Betz, N. E. 45
Biesanz, J. C. 104, 107
Blanck, P. D. 13, 163

Blatchford, P. 152
Bohlmann, N. L. 136
Bolles, R. C. 2–3
Bootzin, R. R. 5
Bosson, J. K. 10, 13, 96–100
Bovbjerg, D. H. 70, 71
Bowers, K. 47
Braffman, W. 32
Braly, K. 110
Brandon, T. H. 10, 12, 23, 62–66
Branigan, C. 165
Brashares, H. J. 53
Brattesani, K. A. 136
Brewer, W. F. 3
Brophy, J. 7, 87, 127, 131, 135, 145–146, 147
Brown, S. A. 63
Burgess, C. A. 49
Burke, P. J. 97
Burns, D. D. 52
Butler, S. F. 170

Cantril, H. 110, 112, 114–115
Cast, A. D. 97
Catanzaro, S. J. 10, 12, 23, 52–58
Cepeda-Benito, A. 63
Chabris, C. F. 48
Chambless, D. L. 26
Chartrand, T. L. 113
Chatoor, I. C. 170
Chen, M. 174

180 Author index

Chesney, M. A. 170
Claire, T. 111
Clark, M. S. 114
Clark-Polner, E. 114
Cloer, T. 146
Cloitre, M. 55, 57
Clore, G. L. 165
Coleman, L. M. 118
Colloca, L. 10, 13, 23, 76–82, 78, 165, 166, 167–168, 173
Cooper, H. M. 146, 162, 166, 167, 168
Cooper, L. M. 49
Copeland, A. L. 63, 64, 65, 90, 91, 92
Courbasson, C. 55, 57
Craen, A. J. N. de 171
Creasey, G. 55, 56
Crow, R. 169
Czajkowski, S. M. 170

Dalton, S. R. 146
Darkes, J. 65
Darley, J. M. 7, 8, 9, 91, 102, 110, 111, 162, 164, 165
Davidson, R. J. 57
Davis, R. N. 54
Davison, G. 26
de Boer, H. 10, 14, 157–160
DeHart, T. L. 54, 56
de Jong, P. J. 173
De La Ronde, C. 97
Dennett, D. C. 24
Di Blasi, Z. 169
Diener, E. 130
DiMatteo, M. R. 162, 167, 168, 169, 170–171, 173
Ditre, J. W. 65
Doerfler, L. A. 52
Doering, B. K. 76
Dolan, P. 130
Driessen, G. 158
Durlach, P. J. 80
Dusek, J. 8, 13
Dweck, C. 15
Dworkin, S. F. 171
Dywan, J. 47

Eccles, J. S. 117, 118
Eden, D. 13, 122, 131
Elashoff, J. D. 112, 125
Eli, I. 32
Ely, R. J. 97, 98, 103, 117
Engert, V. 81
Erdelyi, M. H. 47, 48
Evans, F. J. 5, 173
Everston, C. 130–131

Fazio, R. H. 7, 8, 9, 102, 110, 111, 162, 164, 165
Ferrarelli, F. 57
Ferrer, A. R. 63
Fiorio, M. 81, 82
Fishbein, M. 27
Fisher, S. 29
Fiske, S. T. 108
Flaten, M. A. 171
Frank, J. D. 4
Franko, D. L. 52
Fredrickson, B. L. 165
Friedman, H. S. 165, 167, 169

Gaitan-Sierra, C. 36
Galef, J. B. 80
Gaschke, Y. N. 52
Gasper, K. 165
Geraghty, A. D. W. 36
Gilbert, D. T. 111
Gilboa-Schechtman, E. 56
Gill, M. J. 91
Godfrey, K. M. 37
Goetz, C. G. 30
Goffman, E. 118
Goldman, M. S. 65
Goldschmid, M. L. 118, 164
Goldstein, A. J. 26
Gómez, . 98
Good, T. L. 7, 87, 135, 145, 146, 162
Gosselin, J. T. 41, 42, 43, 44, 45, 46
Gøtzsche, P. C. 29–30
Gracely, R. H. 82
Green, J. P. 50
Greenwood, G. 53
Gregory, A. 138
Gross, J. J. 57

Hahn, R. A. 5–6, 163–164
Hall, J. A. 169
Hammond, D. C. 32
Harber, K. D. 7, 127
Harris, M. J. 7, 8, 9, 30, 104, 117, 146, 152, 162, 167, 168, 169, 171–173
Harrison, R. F. 30
Hastorf, A. H. 110, 112, 114–115
Hatchell, H. 146
Hattie, J. 7, 152
Haugen, J. A. 90, 91
Hazelrigg, P. 167
Hemenover, S. H. 53–54, 56
Hendricks, P. S. 10, 12, 23, 62–66
Hilton, J. L. 91, 162
Horwitz, R. I. 170
Horwitz, S. M. 170

Author index **181**

Hróbjartsson, A. 29–30, 80
Huang, F. 138
Humphries, L. 141
Hunter, T. 78, 79, 167
Hyland, M. E. 10, 11, 23, 35–39

Ickes, W. 104

Jacobson, L. 7, 13, 96, 111, 112, 117, 119, 125, 134–135, 137, 145, 151, 163, 168
Jensen, K. B. 81
Jensen, M. P. 32
Jiminez, S. S. 57
John, O. P. 57
Joiner, T. E., Jr. 57
Jones, E. E. 111, 113
Joseph, G. 8
Judice, T. N. 104
Juliano, L. M. 64, 66
Jussim, L. 7, 8, 9, 10, 14, 15, 87–88, 90, 92, 102, 106, 110–115, 117, 118, 119, 120, 121, 122, 127, 146, 162, 163, 164, 165, 166

Kahneman, D. 130
Kaptchuk, T. J. 30, 31, 169
Kassel, J. D. 54, 55
Katz, D. 110
Kenardy, J. 28
Kenrick, D. T. 107
Khan, A. 30
Kirsch, I. 3, 5, 10–11, 15, 23–32, 35, 38, 48, 49, 53, 69, 70, 76, 166, 171, 173
Klatzky, R. L. 47
Kleijnen, J. 171
Klein, O. 8, 90, 91, 119, 120, 121
Kleinhauz, M. 32
Klinger, R. 76
Klopfer, B. 1
Kogan, N. 125
Kuklinski, M. R. 136, 147
Kurpnick, J. 170
Kuyper, H. 158

Ladd, A. 55, 56
Lader, M. 26
Langer, E. 171
Lanzetta, J. T. 80
Laurent, J. 55
Levesque, M. J. 164
Levitt, J. T. 55
Lewin, K. 128
Lewis, J. 45
Lewis-Esquirre, J. M. 63
Lewith, G. T. 35

Li, Q. 146
Löckenhoff, C. E. 43
Lowe, C. A. 164
Lynn, S. J. 10, 11–12, 47–50
Lyvers, M. 55

McCarthy, C. J. 55
McCrae, R. R. 43
McGlashan, T. H. 173
McKown, C. 136, 137, 147, 148
McMillan, D. 165
McNally, R. J. 26, 27
McNulty, S. E. 97
Maddux, J. E. 10, 11, 23, 41–46
Madon, S. 7, 10, 14, 92, 94, 112, 117–122, 164
Maier, S. F. 4
Marlatt, G. A. 64
Marsh, H. W. 153
Marshall, H. H. 136
Master, A. 15
Mathews, A. 26
Mauch, T. G. 53, 54, 56
Mayer, J. D. 52
Mazzoni, G. 81
Mearns, J. 10, 12, 23, 52–58
Medoff, Z. M. 10, 13, 23, 76–82, 165, 167–168
Meece, J. R. 45
Melzack, R. 37
Memon, A. 50
Merton, R. J. 6–8, 87, 110, 117, 120, 134
Michniewicz, K. S. 99
Middlestadt, S. E. 135
Miller, D. T. 8, 90, 113
Miller, F. G. 13, 77, 166, 168, 173
Miller, G. E. 37
Milling, L. S. 32
Mischel, W. 3
Montgomery, G. H. 10, 12, 23, 27, 30, 31, 69–73
Mrnak-Meyer, J. 54
Mustian, K. M. 70
Myers, M. G. 63

Neuberg, S. L. 9, 10, 13–14, 92, 102–108, 162
Neuschatz, J. 50
Niles, B. L. 57

Oakes, J. 153
Olson, J. M. 5, 8, 9–10, 15, 162, 164, 165
Orbach, I. 54
Orr, S. P. 80

182 Author index

Page, S. 146
Pajares, F. 45
Park, C. L. 57
Patihis, L. 48
Patterson, D. R. 32
Peirce, C. 166
Pelham, B. W. 97
Pellegrini, A. D. 152
Perkins, K. A. 64
Peterson, E. R. 149
Petty, R. E. 53
Pfeiffer, N. 53, 56
Polzer, J. T. 98
Pratto, F. 99
Price, D. D. 30, 70

Rash, C. J. 63
Read, S. J. 97
Reiss, S. 5, 26, 27, 52
Rescorla, R. A. 3
Richards, C. S. 52
Rief, W. 76
Rippere, V. 52
Rist, R. C. 111, 112, 119, 166
Roberts, A. H. 169
Robinson, J. P. 146
Rodin, J. 171
Roese, N. J. 9, 15, 162, 164, 165, 167
Roome, A. C. 53
Rosadino, M. J. 171
Roscoe, J. A. 70
Rosenthal, R. 7–8, 13, 87, 96, 104, 111,
    112, 117, 118, 119, 125, 128, 129, 131,
    134, 137, 143, 145–146, 151, 152, 162,
    163, 166, 168–169, 172, 173
Rosnow, R. L. 7
Ross, L. D. 110, 111, 114
Ross, M. 5
Roter, D. 169
Rotter, J. B. 3, 5, 26, 27, 52, 62
Rubie-Davies, C. M. 7, 10, 13, 14, 131,
    137, 138, 145–154, 163, 165
Rubin, D. B. 7, 117, 118, 125, 168
Ruck, M. D. 146
Rusting, C. L. 54, 56

Salovey, P. 52
Sapirstein, G. 29–30
Schaller, M. 107
Schneider, D. J. 114
Schneider, P. F. 30
Schnur, J. 10, 12, 23, 69–73
Schoenberger, N. E. 27, 28
Schunk, D. H. 45
Scoboria, A. 50

Seligman, M. E. 4, 129
Shaw, G. B. 2, 128, 142
Sherman, J. W. 9, 15, 162, 164, 167
Silva, C. E. 49
Silver, M. 125
Simmons, V. N. 65
Simons, D. J. 48
Skinner, B. F. 2
Smith, A. E. 118, 119
Smith, D. M. 91, 106
Smith, S. M. 48, 53
Snow, R. E. 112, 125, 145
Snyder, M. 8, 10, 13, 89–93, 96, 102, 103,
    104, 110, 111, 117, 119, 120, 121, 164
Sohl, S. J. 71, 72
Solomon, D. 146
Southworth, S. 27, 28
Spiegel, H. 6
Spitz, H. H. 7
Stangor, C. 165
Steele, C. M. 139
Stets, J. E. 97
Stevens, S. T. 7, 10, 14, 110–115
Stinnett, T. A. 146
Strupp, H. H. 170
Stukas, A. A. 90, 91, 119, 120, 121
Sucala, M. 10, 12, 69–73
Sugarman, M. A. 30
Sutherland, A. 118, 164
Swann, W. B. 90, 91, 92, 96, 97, 98, 99,
    103, 117
Swann, W. B., Jr. 10, 13, 96–100

Świder, K. 79, 80, 167
Swim, J. K. 102

Taylor, M. C. 166
Taylor, P. B. 147
Taylor, S. 28
Teasdale, J. D. 52
Tenenbaum, H. R. 146
Thomas, D. A. 98
Thomas, W. I. 6
Thompson, E. P. 103
Thorberg, F. A. 55
Timmermans, A. C. 157–160
Tolman, E. C. 2, 25–26
Tough, P. 56
Tresno, F. 54, 56
Trope, Y. 103
Trusz, S, 1–15, 88, 162–174
Turnbull, W. 8, 90, 113
Turner, E. H. 30
Turner, J. C. 98
Tversky, A. 130

Vandello, J. A. 99
van der Werf, M. P. C. 10, 14, 157–160
Vase, L. 30, 173
Virdin, L. M. 92
Vögtle, E. 79, 80, 167
Volkmann, J. R. 41, 43

Wagemaker, H. 148
Wagstaff, G. F. 48, 49–50
Wallach, M. 125
Wampold, B. E. 29
Watson, A. 31
Watson, J. B. 2, 25, 31
Webb, M. S. 65
Weinstein, C. 130–131
Weinstein, R. S. 10, 14, 111, 118,
    134–139, 146, 147, 148, 165

West, C. K. 10, 14, 112, 119, 141–144
Wetter, D. W. 64
Whalley, B. 36
Whitehouse, W. G. 48
Wickless, C. 32
Wiesenfeld, B. M. 100
Willard, J. 10, 14, 117–122
Wilson, S. 32
Wineburg, S. S. 7, 112
Wolpe, J. 25
Word, C. O. 103, 104, 111, 164
Worrell, F. C. 137

Yapko, M. D. 48–49
Young, J. 49

SUBJECT INDEX

Notes: spelling follows US scheme; italics denote figures.

addiction *see* alcohol use; drug
    dependency; smoking
adolescence: alcohol use 55, 118, 120–121;
    mood regulation in 56; smoking 62, 63,
    66
agoraphobia 28
alcohol use: in adolescence 55, 118,
    120–121; and mood regulation 54–55,
    57; and self-fulfilling prophecy 118,
    120–121
alternative medicine *see* complementary
    and alternative medicine (CAM);
    hypnosis
AN *see* anticipatory nausea
anger management 58
anticipatory nausea (AN), in chemotherapy
    patients 70–71, 72–73
anxiety 25–28, 43, 45, 52, 54, 64; placebo
    effects for 30, 69–70, 173; *see also*
    depression; emotional distress; stress
Anxiety Sensitivity Index 27–28
asthma 35

behavioral confirmation in social
    interaction 13–14, 89–93, 102–108,
    167; and identity negotiation 13,
    96–100
bias: accuracy 110–115; in teachers'
    expectations 14, 126, 136, 147,
    157–160; *see also* self-fulfilling prophecy
    (SFP)

body programming theory 37–39
bone density 30
borderline personality disorder 55
brain activity: and mood regulation 57; in
    patient-clinician interactions 81–82
breast cancer treatment, side-effects 70–73

CAM *see* complementary and alternative
    medicine
cancer treatment 12, 69–73
career/work, and self-efficacy 45
chemotherapy, side-effects 70–73
child development, and mood regulation
    56, 58; *see also* adolescence
children, awareness of differential behavior
    14, 134–139, 146
classical (Pavlovian) conditioning 2–3, 5,
    13, 25–26; and anxiety 173; and cancer
    treatment 70; and placebo effects 27,
    31–32, 76–77, 79, 80, 166, 168; and
    response expectancy 25–26, 27, 31–32,
    166
classroom environment *see* education
    systems; teacher expectancy
Classroom Management (CM), trends on
    129–131
climate, in interpersonal expectancy effects
    168–169, 172–173
CM *see* Classroom Management
complementary and alternative medicine
    (CAM) 35–39; meditation/mindfulness

186 Subject index

57; relaxation 25–26, 29, 71–72; *see also* hypnosis
conditioning *see* classical (Pavlovian) conditioning; operant (instrumental) conditioning
coping, and mood regulation 12, 53–56
cultural differences, and mood regulation 56

DBT *see* dialectical behavior therapy
depression: and mood regulation 52, 54, 56, 57; and placebo effects 29–30
dialectical behavior therapy (DBT) 55
distress *see* emotional distress; stress
drug dependency 54–55, 57
drug response *vs.* drug effect 29–30

eating disorders 43, 55, 57
education systems 45, 57–58, 139, 152–154; Netherlands (study) 14, 157–160; *see also* Pygmalion effect; teacher expectancy
efficacy expectation 4; *see also* self-efficacy
electronic cigarettes (e-cigarettes) 66
emotional distress 12, 53–55; and cancer treatment 12, 71–73
emotional intelligence 52
emotional self-regulation 44, 46
emotional states, and self-efficacy 42, 45
empathy, and placebo effects 79, 81, 167
endocrine placebo responses 77
erroneous beliefs 92, 102
expectancies 1–10, 87–88; intra- and interpersonal, integrative approach 15, 162–174; *see also* interpersonal expectancies; intrapersonal expectancies
experimenter expectancy effect 7, 8, 168

fatigue, in cancer treatment 71, 72–73
fear 5, 26, 27–28, 52
feedback, in interpersonal expectancy effects 168–169, 173
flower essence study 35–36
four-factor theory perspective (climate, feedback, input, output) 168–169, 172–173

Galatea (myth) 2, 128
Galatea effects 163, 165, 174
gender 80, 99, 146
goals/motivations, in confirmation processes 13–14, 102–108
Golem (myth) 2, 128
Golem effect 163–165, 174

Handbook of Classroom Management 130–131
homeopathy 35–36
hormones, endocrine placebo responses 77
hypnosis 5, 31–32; and cancer treatment 72; and memory recall 11–12, 47–50

IBS *see* irritable bowel syndrome
identity negotiation 13, 96–100
illness, and mood regulation 54
infertility 30
input, interpersonal expectancy effects 168–169
instrumental (operant) conditioning 2–3, 25, 168
interpersonal expectancies 6–10, 13–15, 88; and intrapersonal expectancies, integrative approach 15, 162–174; *see also* behavioral confirmation; identity negotiation; motivations/goals, in confirmation processes; Pygmalion effect; self-fulfilling prophecy; teacher expectancy
intrapersonal expectancies 5–6, 10–13, 23–24, 87–88; and interpersonal expectancies, integrative approach 15, 162–174; *see also* cancer treatment; hypnosis; motivational concordance; negative mood regulation expectancies (NMRE); placebo effect; response expectancy; self-efficacy; smoking
in vivo exposure therapy 28
irritable bowel syndrome (IBS) 30–32

laws (principles) of learning 2–3
learned helplessness 4
lifestyle 39

mass psychogenic illness 81
mediation of expectancy effects 8, 11, 13–14, 15, 23, 24; and cancer treatment 71, 72–73; and intra- and interpersonal effects, integration of 162, 165, 166, 167, 168, 171–173; and mood regulation 54, 55, 56, 57; and motivational concordance 37–39; and motivations/goals, in confirmation processes 102–103; and placebo effects 31, 76, 77; and response expectancies 25, 27; and smoking 64, 65; and teachers 135–137, 138, 147, 159, 171–173
meditation/mindfulness 57
memory recall, and hypnosis 11–12, 47–50
"meta-experience" of mood 52

Subject index **187**

mindfulness/meditation 57
moderation *see* mediation of expectancy
 effects
mood regulation *see* negative mood
 regulation expectancies (NMRE)
motivational concordance, therapeutic
 ritual 35–39
motivations/goals, in confirmation
 processes 13–14, 102–108
motor disorders 81–82
"Mr. Wright" (case) 1

nausea, in cancer treatment 70–71, 72–73
negative mood regulation expectancies
 (NMRE) 12, 52–58
negative mood regulation (NMR) scale 53,
 54, 56
Netherlands, teacher expectancy study 14,
 157–160
neuropsychology 57
NMR *see* negative mood regulation
 (NMR) scale
NMRE *see* negative mood regulation
 expectancies
nocebo effects 6, 13, 79–81, 163–164,
 167–170

observational learning/modeling 13, 42,
 44–45, 77, 79–81, 166–168
operant (instrumental) conditioning 2–3,
 25, 168
outcome/stimulus expectancy *see*
 stimulus/outcome expectancy
output, in interpersonal expectancy effects
 168–169

pain: in cancer treatment 71, 72–73; and
 placebo effects 29, 32, 76–80, *78*; and
 smoking 65
panic disorders 28, 52
parents: and mood regulation 56, 58; and
 self-fulfilling prophecy 118–122; and
 teacher expectancies 158–159
Parkinson's disease 30
patient-clinician interactions, and placebo
 effects 81–82
patients, adherence to treatment 170–173
Pavlovian conditioning *see* classical
 (Pavlovian) conditioning
personality 3, 11, 43
phobic anxiety 25–28
physical health, and self-efficacy 42–45
physician-patient interaction: adherence to
 treatment 170–173; and placebo effects
 81–82

placebo effect 5–6, 13, 27–29, 76–82, *78*,
 166–174; in cancer treatment 12,
 69–73; and complementary and
 alternative medicine (CAM) 35–39; and
 depression 29–30; and phobic anxiety
 26; *vs.* placebo response 29–30; and
 smoking 64, 65; and socially-induced
 analgesic responses 78–80, *78*; in
 therapeutic relationships 31–32, 81–82
'placebo psychotherapy' 38
placebo response 37–38; *vs.* placebo effect
 29–30
Positive Psychology, trends on 129–131
post-traumatic stress disorder (PTSD)
 57–58
Powerful Placebo, The 28–29
prevention programs 57–58
principles (laws) of learning 2–3
psychotherapy: and mood regulation 55,
 57–58; and self-efficacy 44–45
PTSD *see* post-traumatic stress disorder
Pygmalion (myth) 2, 128
Pygmalion (Shaw) (play) 2, 128, 142
Pygmalion effect 7–8, 145–146, 168;
 accuracy 111–115, 137–138; current
 trends on 14, 125–131; and high and
 low expectation teachers 14, 145–154
"Pygmalion managers" 131

radiotherapy 71–72
relaxation 25–26, 29, 71–72
repeated belief model 120
response expectancy 5, 10–11, 23–32, 166;
 and cancer treatment 12, 69–73;
 individual differences in 134–139
rituals, therapeutic 11, 36–38

schools *see* education systems; Pygmalion
 effect; teacher expectancy
self-determination theory 11, 36
self-efficacy 4, 11, 41–46, 62–63
self, expectancy about *see* intrapersonal
 expectancies
self-fulfilling prophecy (SFP) 6–9,
 166–167; accuracy 14, 106–108,
 110–115, 157–160; in education 14,
 125–131; and response expectancies 27;
 and social problems 14, 117–122; *see also*
 behavioral confirmation; Pygmalion
 effect
self-harm 56
self-organisational change 37
self-regulation 37, 44, 46
sexual arousal 25, 69–70
SFP *see* self-fulfilling prophecy

188 Subject index

signs theory 166
SLT *see* social learning theory
smoking 12, 62–66
social learning theory (SLT) 52, 62
social problems, and self-fulfilling prophecy 14, 117–122
spirituality 11, 35–38
stereotypes 92, 102, 112–115, 121
stimulus/outcome expectancy 2–5, 26–27; and smoking 62–63; and spirituality 11, 35–36
stress: and body programming theory 37–39; and mood regulation 53–56, 58; and self-efficacy 44; *see also* anxiety; emotional distress
students, awareness of differential treatment 14, 134–139, 146
substance dependency *see* alcohol use; drug dependency; smoking
suicidal thoughts/behavior 54–55
synergistic accumulation 120–121
systematic desensitization 25–27

teacher expectancy: high and low 8–9, 145–147; inaccuracies 157–160; individuality in 147–154; individual responses to 141–144; and self-fulfilling prophecy 118–122; trends on 14, 125–131; *see also* education systems; Pygmalion effect
Teacher Expectation Project (TEP) 149–152, 153
teachers' differential behavior (TDB) 126–128; children's awareness 14, 134–139, 146
Teacher Treatment Inventory (TTI) 135–136
TDB *see* teachers' differential behavior
TEP *see* Teacher Expectation Project
therapeutic ritual 11, 36–38
"tripartite pattern", in social perception 110–115
TTI *see* Teacher Treatment Inventory

verbal suggestion: and placebo effects 76, 77, 79–80, 166, 168; and self-efficacy 42, 45
Voodoo death (case) 1

work, and self-efficacy 45
workplace management 131

young adults *see* adolescence